About the Author

Naseeb Shaheen is a native of Chicago, Illinois. He received his B.A. from the American University of Beirut, and his M.A. and Ph.D. degrees from the University of California, Los Angeles. He is now Professor of English at Memphis State University and has published numerous works on Shakespeare, Spenser, and Milton. As a result of his research into Shakespeare's biblical references, he owns a large collection of early English Bibles, which includes more than forty-five editions of the Geneva Bible, besides numerous editions of other pre–King James Bibles.

Biblical References
in Shakespeare's Tragedies

Biblical References in Shakespeare's Tragedies

Naseeb Shaheen

DELAWARE

Newark: University of Delaware Press
London and Toronto: Associated University Presses

Associated University Presses
440 Forsgate Drive
Cranbury, NJ 08512

Associated University Presses
25 Sicilian Avenue
London WC1A 2QH, England

Associated University Presses
2133 Royal Windsor Drive
Unit 1
Mississauga, Ontario
Canada L5J 1K5

PR
2983
.S43
1987

The paper used in this publication meets the
requirements of the American National Standard for
Permanence of Paper for Printed Library Materials Z39.48–1984.

Library of Congress Cataloging-in-Publication Data

Shaheen, Naseeb, 1931–
  Biblical references in Shakespeare's tragedies.

  Bibliography: p.
  Includes index.
  1. Shakespeare, William, 1564–1616—Tragedies.
  2. Bible in literature.   3. Shakespeare, William,
  1564–1616—Sources.   I. Title.
  PR2983.S43   1987   822.3'3   85-40636
  ISBN 0-87413-293-2 (alk. paper)

Printed in the United States of America

Contents

Introduction

The present study of Shakespeare's biblical references differs from previous ones[1] in that it considers Shakespeare's references in the light of his literary sources. In preparing this volume, I have undertaken to read every source that Shakespeare is known to have read or consulted prior to writing each play, as well as those works that give evidence of having come to his mind as he wrote the play.

My original plan was simply to list the biblical references that are to be found in each play, since many valid references have been overlooked by previous scholars, and to annotate these references more fully than has been done. But as the work progressed, it soon became apparent that such a plan would be inadequate. For a study of Shakespeare's biblical references to be of real value, it would have to ascertain the origin of his references. My study should enable the reader to determine which references Shakespeare borrowed from his plot sources and which he himself added from his own memory as part of his own design for the play. Shakespeare's handling of his subject is often best understood when compared with his sources, and this is also true of his biblical references. Thus I have made every effort to discover which biblical references in his literary sources he accepted, which he rejected, and how he adapted the ones that he did borrow. This information is especially valuable when one considers the theological interpretations that are sometimes imposed on his plays.

A second factor that made a thorough check of Shakespeare's sources necessary was the need to determine if the many passages in Shakespeare that resemble Scripture but are not clear biblical references were actually taken from Scripture. Often the verbal similarity between Shakespeare and Scripture is negligible, while the spirit of Shakespeare's lines and the context in which they appear haunt us with the suspicion that they were inspired by a similar passage in Scripture. The best way to resolve the problem would be to check Shakespeare's sources. If the perplexing passage in Shakespeare also occurs in one of Shakespeare's sources as, for instance, in Plutarch, we can reasonably conclude that no biblical reference is involved; Plutarch was Shakespeare's source and the similarity to Scripture is accidental. If no parallel incident occurs in Shakespeare's sources, then the likelihood that Shakespeare may have borrowed that idea or passage from Scripture is increased.

A few illustrations follow. When the conspirators in *Julius Caesar* come to Caesar's home to accompany him to the Senate, Caesar greets them with the words, "Good friends, go in, and taste some wine with me" (2.2.126). Are there overtones of the Last Supper in this incident? Are we to understand this episode as Caesar's Last Supper before his betrayal? A check of Plutarch as well as all the other sources that Shakespeare used for *Julius Caesar* fails to reveal a parallel incident; the wine-tasting episode was added by Shakespeare. In Plutarch's "Life of Caesar," only Decius Brutus Albinus went to Caesar's house to bring him to the Senate, persuaded him to ignore the evil omens, and, without partaking of any food or drink, "he tooke Caesar by the hand, and brought him out of his house." In Plutarch's "Life of Brutus," none of the conspirators went to Caesar's house; instead they waited for him at Pompey's Porch. After a considerable delay Caesar arrived without anyone going after him.

Had Plutarch's account contained the wine-tasting episode, we could confidently conclude that no overtones of Scripture are involved, particularly since Plutarch was a pagan and knew nothing about the Last Supper. But inasmuch as no comparable sharing of wine occurs either in Plutarch or in any of the secondary sources Shakespeare used for *Julius Caesar*, the chances are increased that Shakespeare might have had the Last Supper in mind. The evidence is by no means conclusive. Shakespeare may not at all have conceived of this event as Caesar's Last Supper. The wine-tasting episode may only have been intended to dramatize Caesar's liberality, since Plutarch relates that even when Caesar was a young man, he won the friendship of all by his courtesy and generosity, for "he ever kept a good bourde, and fared well at his table." If that is the case, then Caesar's invitation to taste wine with him was not at all intended to parallel the Last Supper, but was Shakespeare's method of dramatizing Caesar's characteristic hospitality. Whatever the case may be, the evidence would not be complete without consulting Shakespeare's sources in order to determine which interpretation is the most likely one. *Julius Caesar* has more than its share of passages with equally perplexing echoes of Scripture, all of which have been carefully checked against the play's sources.

Consider also Othello's description of how he won Desdemona's heart:

> But still the house affairs would draw her thence,
> Which ever as she could with haste dispatch,
> She'd come again, and with a greedy ear
> Devour up my discourse.
>
> (1.3.147–50)

Did the inspiration for these lines come from Luke's well-known account of Jesus at the home of Mary and Martha, according to which Mary sat at Jesus' feet and heard his words while Martha "was combred about much seruing"? The answer would be no, if anything remotely similar could be found in one of Shakespeare's sources, chiefly the works of Cinthio and Bandello, or in the French and English translations of their works. But a search of these sources fails to uncover a parallel event. Shakespeare himself added this scene to what he found in his sources, which increases the likelihood that it was modeled on the account of Jesus at supper with Mary and Martha. In *Othello*, Desdemona would correspond to both Mary and Martha, being occupied with domestic duties and at the same time greedily listening to Othello's words. The circumstances of Othello's arrest provide another example of a tantalizing parallel with Scripture that needs to be checked against Shakespeare's sources.

A final example from *Timon of Athens*. When Timon invites his false friends to his second banquet, they all attempt to excuse themselves from coming, but he insists that they appear. As the First Lord explains,

> He hath sent me an earnest inviting, which many my near occasions did urge me to put off; but he hath conjur'd me beyond them, and I must needs appear.

The Second Lord responds,

> In like manner was I in debt to my importunate business, but he would not hear my excuse.
>
> (3.6.9–14)

Was Jesus' parable of the wedding invitation the model for this passage? In none of Shakespeare's nonbiblical sources is there a parallel scene. But in Jesus' parable at Matthew 22 and Luke 14, those bidden to the feast "with one mynde began to make excuse" with the words, "I pray thee, haue me excused" (Luke 14.18–19). The absence of a parallel in Shakespeare's sources strongly suggests that the inspiration for these lines was Jesus' parable. But in each case it is essential to check the sources.

I have consulted Shakespeare's sources not only for passages such as these over which there is considerable doubt, but for every reference listed in this volume. Even in instances where a reference to Scripture seems certain, if a similar passage also occurs in one or more of Shakespeare's sources, then that passage is pointed out with the words, "Closest parallel in Shakespeare's sources...." This comparison will enable the reader to judge for himself to what extent Shakespeare's biblical reference may have been influenced by a similar passage in his sources, or whether that passage, although not itself a reference, may have suggested the biblical reference that Shakespeare makes in his play.

Finally, checking Shakespeare's references against his sources makes it apparent that some passages in Shakespeare's plays that appear to be clear references to Scripture are not biblical references at all. The witches' prediction that Macbeth would not be harmed by any "man that's born of woman" seems to be a clear borrowing from Job 14.1 and the Burial Service quotation of Job, where we read that "man that is borne of a woman hath but a short time to liue, and is full of misery." The verbal similarities between *Macbeth* and Job appear sufficiently close to conclude that Shakespeare borrowed the phrase from either Job or the Prayer Book quotation of Job. However, Shakespeare's source for these words was not Scripture but the Macbeth story as he found it in Holinshed and as Holinshed, in turn, found it in his sources, principally the *Scotorum Historiae* of Hector Boethius. Holinshed three times repeats the words of a "certeine witch" that Macbeth would never be slain by "man borne of anie woman." This prediction had always been an essential feature of the Macbeth story from the very beginning; it appeared in the earliest accounts written almost two centuries before Shakespeare's time. Without it, the Macbeth narrative would be completely different. Holinshed's narrative, therefore, and not Scripture, was Shakespeare's primary source for the witches' words. Job was a book that Shakespeare knew especially well, and he was no doubt aware that the witches' words were similar to Job and the Burial Service quotation of Job. But no direct reference to Scripture on Shakespeare's part is involved.

Some have argued that the relationship between Macbeth and his wife was inspired by the account of King Ahab and Queen Jezebel in 1 Kings 21. Just as Jezebel encouraged Ahab to murder Naboth for his vineyard, so Lady Macbeth goaded her husband to murder Duncan.

Here, again, a check of Shakespeare's sources makes it apparent that these comparisons are unwarranted. Holinshed was Shakespeare's prime source for the story of Macbeth's being incited by his wife to murder the king. Shakespeare borrowed not only from that regicide account, but also from Holinshed's account of Donwald, whose wife urged him to slay King Duff. These examples and many more like them stress the need to compare Shakespeare's text with his sources constantly, a practice that has been much neglected.

Shakespeare's sources have been checked time and again for each reference that appears in this volume. Whenever Shakespeare's lines resemble both Scripture and one of his sources, all three passages (Shakespeare, Scripture, and the source) are quoted for the reader's consideration. If no quotation from a source appears after a reference, it should be understood that there is no similar passage in any of Shakespeare's sources and that the reference is Shakespeare's own.

I have made every effort to find not only all of Shakespeare's biblical references, but also his references to the *Book of Common Prayer* and the *Book of Homilies*. My aim, however, has not been to present the longest list of references. Many marginal items that have been suggested by previous authorities have been excluded, since they are not *bona fide* references. On the other hand, many references that have been overlooked by previous scholars are included for the first time.

Unless indicated otherwise, quotations are made from the Geneva Bible of 1582, *Short-Title Catalogue* 2133. Whenever other versions are referred to, the following editions have been used:

Bishops' Bible	1572	*STC* 2107
Great Bible	1553	*STC* 2091
Coverdale Bible	1553	*STC* 2090
Matthew Bible	1549	*STC* 2077
Taverner Bible	1539	*STC* 2067
Tyndale's New Testament	1535	*STC* 2830
Rheims New Testament	1582	*STC* 2884
Douay Old Testament, 2 vols.	1609–10	*STC* 2207

Quotations from the Psalms appear from the Prayer Book Psalter, the version of the Psalms that was read or sung daily in the morning and evening services of the Anglican Church, the version of the Psalms that Shakespeare heard most often. The Psalter was actually Coverdale's version of the Psalms as it appeared in the Great Bible. That version was adopted by the Prayer Books of 1549, 1552, and 1559 and became the Psalter used in all the services of the English Church. I have used the edition of the Psalter that appeared in the Second Folio of the Bishops' Bible of 1572, printed side by side with the Bishops' translation of the Psalms.

Sternhold and Hopkins' highly popular metrical version of the Psalms is quoted from the 1583 edition published by John Day (*STC* 2466). Tomson's New Testament is according to the edition of 1583 (*STC* 2885), and the Junius Revelation follows the edition of 1600 (*STC* 2991).

Quotations from the *Book of Common Prayer* are from the 1605 edition, *STC* 16329a. The text for the *Book of Homilies* is that of 1623 (*STC* 13659), a Jacobean reprint of the Elizabethan Homilies, but I have also consulted *The Seconde Tome of Homelyes*, 1563 (*STC* 13663).

Except for Tyndale's New Testament and the Taverner Bible, which I have been unable to acquire, my research into Shakespeare's use of Scripture has been done in original editions of all these Bibles. Thus in attempting to determine which Bible Shakespeare used, I have not had to rely on the readings of reprints, including hexapla and octapla editions of the Bible, which are not always reliable. Although exceptionally rare, Tyndale's New Testament has been published in facsimile, and the Taverner Bible is available on microfilm. Whenever it seemed necessary, I checked the text of the Geneva Bible, the most popular version of the day, in ten or more editions published between 1560 and 1607. In a few instances I have checked almost every edition of the Geneva Bible ever published at the library of the British and Foreign Bible Society in England.

The text of Shakespeare's plays is that of *The Riverside Shakespeare*, edited by G. Blakemore Evans, 1974. Unless indicated otherwise, I have reproduced passages from Shakespeare exactly as they appear in *The Riverside Shakespeare*, but have often added an initial capital letter and end punctuation, even though such punctuation does not occur in the text. Shakespeare's sources are most frequently quoted from Geoffrey Bullough's *Narrative and Dramatic Sources of Shakespeare*, eight volumes, 1957–75.

NOTE

1. The most important study of Shakespeare's use of the Bible is Richmond Noble's *Shakespeare's Biblical Knowledge and Use of the Book of Common Prayer*, published in 1935. Secondary works include studies by Thomas Carter (1905), William Burgess (1903), and Charles Wordsworth (1880). Works of lesser importance are listed in the bibliography.

Biblical References
in Shakespeare's Tragedies

1
The English Bible in Shakespeare's Day

John Wycliffe

The history of the English Bible properly begins with the Oxford theologian John Wycliffe (1320?–84), who caused a great stir at Oxford when he began to question civil and ecclesiastical authority. By 1378 he held the position that Scripture was his prime authority, and his teachings attracted many followers. Between 1380 and 1400, Wycliffe and his followers produced two versions of the Bible, not from the original Hebrew and Greek, but from the Latin Vulgate. This was the first complete Bible to be translated into English that Shakespeare could have consulted; only extracts of Scripture had appeared in English prior to Wycliffe's time.

Wycliffe and his followers were strongly condemned by the authorities in 1381. The Wycliffe Bible was banned in 1407, but it spread in spite of the prohibition. Nearly two hundred manuscript copies of the Wycliffe Bible or portions of it are extant today. Some are large, carefully written volumes with elaborately decorated initials and fine bindings. Others are small volumes for everyday use, with little or no decoration, that contain only the New Testament, a single Gospel, or an individual book. Most of these copies were produced between 1420 and 1450, after the prohibition. The British Library possesses a magnificent copy of the earlier Wycliffe version that once belonged to Thomas of Woodstock, Duke of Gloucester, who was executed by order of Richard II in 1397.

The outstanding characteristic of the Wycliffe Bible is its highly Latinate diction. The Latin order of words is often retained and Latin constructions are imitated in English. So literal was the first translation that no sooner was it completed than a revision was undertaken into more idiomatic English. In spite of its shortcomings, the Wycliffe Bible continued to be circulated widely until it was superseded by printed Tudor versions of the sixteenth century.

It is unlikely that Shakespeare possessed a copy of the Wycliffe Bible or that it had any influence on him, for it was not printed until 1731, when the New Testament of the revised version was first published. The New Testament of the earlier version was first printed in 1848, and the complete Wycliffe

Bible, in 1850. Its chief importance is historical, as it is the first complete vernacular translation of the Bible in England.

The invention of printing opened up a completely new chapter of Bible history. Once English Bibles began to be printed, a variety of translations became readily available to Shakespeare.

William Tyndale

In 1526 William Tyndale (1494?–1536) defied the prohibition of the Church in Britain against Bible translation and printed his New Testament in English. His was the first new English translation since Wycliffe's, which by that time had become difficult to read. Tyndale translated not from the Latin Vulgate, but from the third edition of Erasmus's Greek text (1522). He also consulted the Vulgate, Erasmus's Latin version, and Luther's German New Testament of 1522. Tyndale was forced to publish his version on the Continent, first at Cologne and finally at Worms, where an octavo edition of three thousand copies was printed. English merchants smuggled these into England by the hundreds, often hidden in bales of merchandise, and Tyndale's New Testament was on sale in England by March 1526 for anywhere from two to four shillings a copy.

Tyndale was unable to finish translating the entire Bible. In 1530 he published his translation of the Pentateuch and in 1531, his translation of Jonah. His final revision of the New Testament, the 1535 "G. H." edition (published by Godfried van der Haghen), became the definitive Tyndale New Testament. Then he was arrested and imprisoned by the authorities, and burned at the stake in 1536.

It would be difficult to emphasize sufficiently the debt that the English Bible owes to Tyndale. The debt is not because he was the first to translate from the original Hebrew and Greek, but because of his matchless style that has influenced the English language so profoundly. His was a clear and direct English prose, free from needless ornament. In narrative he had no peer. Moreover, he was innovative and either coined or was among the first to use many words and phrases that are still current today, such as *passover*, *the Lord's anointed*, *beautiful*, and *die the death*. He did not always translate literally. In Luke 4.5, where the Greek and Latin texts say that the devil showed Jesus all the kingdoms of the world "in an instant of time," Tyndale followed Luther's German text, *Augenblick*, and has "in the twincklynge of an eye." Whatever shortcomings might be pointed out in Tyndale's translation, they are minor compared with its virtues. The fact remains that all of the later sixteenth-century English Bibles (with the exception of the Rheims New Testament with its highly Latinate diction) were but improvements on Tyndale's basic style. One-third of the text of the King James New Testament is worded exactly as Tyndale left it. In the remaining two-thirds, the underlying sentence structure follows the pattern that Tyndale laid down. The same is true of Tyndale's translation of the Old Testament.

Miles Coverdale

The work of translating the Bible that Tyndale left unfinished was completed by Miles Coverdale (1488–1568), an acquaintance of Tyndale whose name stands second in importance only to Tyndale's in the history of the English Bible. Coverdale's Bible was the first complete Bible to be printed in English; it is the *editio princeps* of the printed English Bible. In 1529, on Tyndale's invitation, Coverdale had spent eight months at Hamburg helping Tyndale with his translation of the Pentateuch. In 1534 he was employed by Jacob van Meteren, a Lutheran merchant at Antwerp, to translate the complete Bible into English. It appeared in Cologne and was dated 4 October 1535. Coverdale dedicated it to the king, Holbein designed the title page, and Cromwell supported its distribution. Even the queen, Anne Boleyn, had a copy in her chamber. Tyndale had not yet been executed when it appeared.

The Coverdale Bible was not, as is often supposed, a mere completion of Tyndale's work. Coverdale relied heavily on Tyndale in the portions of the Bible that Tyndale had already translated, yet his version was a new translation. He did not translate from the original Hebrew and Greek, but consulted a total of five Latin, German, and English versions. He was one of the most eloquent preachers of his day and his version reflects the eloquence of his sermons. He had an ear for rhythm and balanced utterance, so that in numerous instances where he differs from Tyndale, his readings were adopted by the translators of the Authorized Version of 1611. His style is not so vigorous or terse as Tyndale's, but it is smoother and more melodious.

Coverdale is at his best in his translation of the Psalms, and the version of the Psalms that he prepared for a later translation, the Great Bible, had a profound influence on Shakespeare. The Psalter of the Anglican Church, the version of the Psalms that was read daily during Morning and Evening Prayer, was based on Coverdale's version of the Psalms that appeared in the Great Bible. Shakespeare refers to the Psalms more frequently than to any other book of the Bible except Matthew. Whenever it is possible to trace Shakespeare's references to the Psalms to a particular version, it is almost always the Psalter.

Coverdale separated the Apocrypha from the rest of the Old Testament. The Apocrypha consists of those books that are to be found in the Septuagint and the Vulgate, but not in the Hebrew text of the Old Testament. In Wycliffe's Bible, the books of the Apocrypha are interspersed throughout the Old Testament as they are in the Latin Vulgate. The Council of Trent (1545–63) declared most of these books to be canonical. But because they are

not part of the Hebrew text, Coverdale followed the lead of European translations and separated them from the Old Testament placing them between
the Old and New Testaments. In time, the Apocrypha was dropped
altogether from Protestant versions of the Bible. The Apocrypha, however,
was well known to Shakespeare, for it appeared in all complete English
Bibles published during his lifetime. Shakespeare refers more often to the
Apocryphal book of Ecclesiasticus alone than he does to all of the Minor
Prophets combined. When the Authorized Version of 1611 appeared, it included the Apocrypha.

Thomas Matthew

While Coverdale worked on his translation, another version was being
prepared. Printed in Antwerp and published in England, the new version
was called "Matthew's Bible," since its compiler, John Rogers (1500?–55),
adopted the pseudonym "Thomas Matthew," lest he meet Tyndale's fate. In
1534 Rogers had gone to Antwerp as chaplain to the English merchants.
There he met Tyndale, under whose influence he abandoned the Roman
Catholic faith. Before Tyndale was executed, Rogers obtained from him the
portion of the Bible from Joshua to Second Chronicles that Tyndale had
translated but was unable to publish. These Rogers printed for the first time
along with Tyndale's 1530 (not 1534) edition of the Pentateuch, Coverdale's
translation of the rest of the Old Testament and the Apocrypha, and Tyndale's 1535 "G. H." edition of the New Testament. Thus Rogers's work
involved no translation, only compilation, and was two-thirds the work of
Tyndale and one-third that of Coverdale. Yet, whereas Tyndale's translation
under his own name had been banned in England, Matthew's Bible, which
was basically Tyndale's, was granted a royal license when it appeared in 1537
in an edition of fifteen hundred copies. Its title page bore the words: "Set
forth with the Kinges most gracyous lycence." Matthew's Bible was the
basis for all later authorized versions in England. Thus it came about that
Tyndale's work greatly influenced subsequent versions of the Bible.

Matthew's Bible contained some two thousand notes. A few of these were
by Rogers himself, some by Coverdale, many by Tyndale, some by Luther,
and many by such scholars as Erasmus, Olivetan, and Bucer. These notes are
sufficiently controversial to make us wonder why Henry allowed them. It is
also surprising that Matthew's Bible should have been the first to be granted
royal license, particularly since it was primarily the work of Tyndale. It
appears from the injunctions prepared by Cromwell in 1536 but never
issued, that Henry intended to order that the Coverdale Bible be placed in
every church. Anne Boleyn had persuaded him to do so. Although open
to persuasion, the king was cautious. But when it became known that
Matthew's Bible was being prepared, the king gave it his approval. The fact

that Coverdale's Bible was not translated from the original languages may have kept it from being the first to be given official recognition.

Rogers later became the first of the Marian martyrs. On the accession of Queen Mary, Rogers preached a sermon at Paul's Cross commending the "true doctrine taught in King Edward's days," and warning his hearers against the dangers of popery, idolatry, and superstition. Ten days later (16 August 1553) he found himself under house arrest. He was later imprisoned and examined about his religious convictions, which he ably defended. A commission appointed by Cardinal Pole sentenced him to death for denying the Christian character of the Church of Rome and the "real presence" of Christ's body in the sacrament.

Richard Taverner

Before we come to the well-known Great Bible of 1539, one other version must be mentioned, Taverner's Bible, also published in 1539. The Taverner Bible was a revision of Matthew's Bible made at the request of the printers. It was the first English Bible to be printed entirely in England. Richard Taverner (1505?–75) was a lawyer known to be an outstanding Greek scholar. He knew no Hebrew and thus used the Vulgate to revise the Old Testament portion of Matthew's Bible. A prominent feature of his version is its terse, vigorous style, even more Anglo-Saxon than Tyndale's. At times he substituted an Anglo-Saxon word for a Latinate one, such as *spokesman* for *advocate*; occasionally he coined a word, such as *mercystock* for *that obtaineth grace*. Elsewhere, however, he is excessively literal. Although some of the phrases he coined were adopted by later versions, his influence on later versions was small. It was unfortunate that his Bible had to compete with the Great Bible, which had royal sanction and thus eclipsed Taverner's Bible. During the reign of Edward VI, a revised edition of Taverner's Bible appeared in five installments (1549–51) so that poor people "whiche ar not able to bie the hole, may bie a part."[1]

The Great Bible

The Tyndale-Coverdale-Matthew-Taverner period of Bible translation culminated in the Great Bible and ended a second period of English Bible development. Wycliffe's pioneering work had been the first step; the Great Bible, based mainly on the labors of Tyndale and of those who followed him, was the second step; and a further development was not to begin until 1560, when the Geneva Bible appeared.

Coverdale played the principal part in the production of the Great Bible. In 1538, Cromwell commissioned him to prepare another English Bible. There were only two complete English Bibles in circulation at that time,

Coverdale's and Matthew's. The former could not satisfy the scholars because it was not translated from the original languages, while the latter had notes that offended many.[2] Thus Coverdale revised Matthew's Bible, rather than his own version, using the Vulgate as well as Munster's Hebrew-Latin Bible of 1535 for the Old Testament and Erasmus's Greek text for the New. The Apocrypha was left almost as it had been in Matthew's Bible. The new revision lacked Tyndale's vitality, but it made many minor improvements.

The Great Bible, so called because of its large size, was the first authorized version of the English Bible, and a copy was ordered to be placed in every church. Previous Bibles had only been given royal license, that is, they were allowed to circulate. The title page of the Great Bible shows Henry enthroned, handing the Word of God to Cranmer and Cromwell for distribution to the clergy and laity, amid cries of "God saue the King." The first edition of the Great Bible appeared in April of 1539, and by December of 1541 seven editions had been published. An impressive preface by Cranmer appeared in the second and all five subsequent editions, and thus the Great Bible is often called "Cranmer's Bible," although Cranmer had nothing to do with the translating work. The second edition of April 1540 became the standard text bearing the words, "This is the Byble apoynted to the vse of the churches."

In preparing the first edition of the Great Bible, Coverdale was pressed for time; he was unable to revise Matthew's Bible thoroughly. Thus the second edition contained many significant improvements over the first. To some extent changes occurred in all sixteenth-century Bibles. No edition of any one version was identical with the previous edition. Often there were variations between the different editions, since with each edition the type was completely reset, and particularly because the quires of one edition were often bound in the same volume with quires of a later edition. In theory, when a Bible was reprinted, the reprint was supposed to be word perfect with the original, with variations only in the spellings. This was generally true of most Bibles, since great care was taken in reprinting them. But word variations also occurred through error or other factors. The greatest variations occurred when a volume appeared in a mixed state, with the quires of one edition bound in with the quires of a later edition. If, as in the case of the Great Bible, a later edition was substantially revised, then quires of the first unrevised edition that were left over might be bound in with quires of the revised edition, and there would be variations between copies of the same edition. These facts should be kept in mind when dealing with the problem of which version Shakespeare used, for the problem involves not only the version, but also the particular edition of that version.

The Great Bible was both enthusiastically welcomed and looked on with suspicion. Episcopal dissatisfaction came to a head in 1542 when Convocation voted for still another revision; they wanted the Great Bible to be corrected by the Vulgate. Henry decided to refer the matter to the universities, but in the end nothing was done.

The novelty of making an English Bible freely available to the people led to a variety of interpretations and many disorders, and Henry's government reversed its position and took steps to restrict circulation of the Bible. An act of 1543 prohibited the use of the Tyndale or any other annotated Bible in English, and forbade unlicensed persons to read or expound the Bible to others in any church or open assembly. In 1546 the prohibition was extended to include Coverdale's New Testament. Soon the Great Bible alone remained unforbidden and a great destruction of earlier Bibles and Testaments took place. Henry did not oppose an English Bible, but he wanted uniformity of worship and doctrine.

Considering the reaction against and destruction of Bibles in the latter part of Henry's reign, the chances that Shakespeare possessed a Bible published prior to 1547, with the possible exception of the Great Bible, are slight. Sir Thomas More and Bishop Tunstall succeeded in destroying most of the Tyndale Bibles that had been smuggled into England earlier, and by 1547 most English Bibles, except for the seven editions of the Great Bible, had been destroyed.

With the accession of Edward VI in 1547, many editions of the Bible followed each other in rapid succession. Not only were complete Bibles and New Testaments printed, but also prose and metrical versions of the Psalms, portions of the Bible ascribed to Solomon, and other select books of the Bible appeared. The second edition of the *Short-Title Catalogue* provides the most complete survey of Bibles, New Testaments, and other portions of Scripture published during that time. It lists many new editions that have come to light and corrects the classifications of others.[3] The Bibles of the period can be summarized in table 1, which covers the years 1542–46, when for a second time the Bible was suppressed under Henry, 1547–53, when Bible reading and publication were encouraged under Edward VI, and 1553–58, when the Bible was suppressed under Mary. Only English Bibles published or issued in England are accounted for, although a few were printed on the Continent. Editions of the paraphrases of Erasmus upon the New Testament containing the Great Bible text of the New Testament are included, but liturgical Epistles and Gospels as well as "psalms for daily meditation" are omitted.

Table 1

	1542–46	1547–53	1553–58
Complete Bibles	0	11	0
New Testaments	2	29	0
Metrical versions of the Psalms by Sternhold and Hopkins	0	13	1
All other metrical and prose versions of the Psalms	1	18	0
All other portions of the Bible	3	16	0
Totals	6	87	1

Of the eleven editions of the complete Bible that were published during the reign of Edward VI, two were Coverdale Bibles, two were Matthew Bibles, five were Great Bibles, one was E. Becke's revision of Matthew's Bible, and one was Becke's revision of Taverner's Old Testament bound with a Tyndale New Testament. Of the twenty-nine editions of the New Testament published during the same period, ten were Tyndale New Testaments, two were Coverdale New Testaments, and five were Great Bible New Testaments. Three were Tyndale New Testaments printed with Erasmus's Latin translation of the New Testament, four were Tyndale New Testaments revised by R. Jugge, and five were Great Bible New Testaments that were published with the paraphrases of Erasmus upon the New Testament. The first two Books of Common Prayer, which provided for extensive Bible reading in the churches, also appeared during Edward's reign.

When Mary came to the throne in 1553, public use of the Bible was banned and Bible burnings were held in which hundreds of Bibles in the vernacular were publicly destroyed. Although no act of Parliament or of the queen was issued against the Bible, the policy of the queen towards the English Bible and Bible translators was clear. The old laws against heresy were revived in 1555, and a stern persecution of Protestants began. Rogers, who had published the Matthew's Bible, was burned at the stake, as were Bishops Cranmer, Hugh Latimer, and Nicholas Ridley; Coverdale barely escaped to the Continent. Nearly three hundred persons were burned at the stake during the last three years of Mary's reign.

The Geneva Bible

Indirectly, however, Mary was responsible for what would become the most popular and scholarly sixteenth-century translation of the English Bible, produced by the Marian exiles at Geneva. The principal translators were William Whittingham, Anthony Gilby, and Thomas Sampson; Coverdale may also have helped. Whittingham was the principal (perhaps sole) translator of a new version of the New Testament in 1557. Calvin supported him in his work and wrote the introductory epistle. Geneva was humming with

Bible scholarship. Calvin and Beza were both there, and, to everyone's advantage, French and Italian versions of the Bible were being prepared at the same time as the Geneva Bible.

Whittingham's New Testament was thoroughly revised, and in 1560 appeared as the New Testament of the popular Geneva Bible. The reasons for the popularity of the Geneva Bible were obvious. For the first time an English Bible was printed in Roman type. Although the first edition was a large quarto, most editions were published as compact, handy-sized quarto volumes. The Geneva Bible was obviously meant to be quoted, for it followed the Whittingham New Testament practice of dividing the text into both chapters and verses, rather than just chapters, and each verse was made a separate paragraph. The Geneva translators had the advantage of consulting important texts not available to previous translators. In an attempt to be faithful to the original languages, it printed in italics additional English words required by English idiom, a practice that the Authorized Version of 1611 followed. Those books of the Old Testament that Tyndale had not been able to translate prior to his execution were now for the first time carefully brought into line with the original Hebrew. In addition to its greater accuracy, the Geneva Bible originated a number of striking words and phrases that have become part of the language, such as "smote them hippe and thigh," and "through a glasse darkely."[4]

The marginal comments in the Geneva Bible made it all the more popular, for there was great demand by the public for explanatory notes. Many of them are scholarly and illuminating, but many others are quite tendentious. Some stress predestination or justification by faith alone, while others attack Rome. More helpful were notes that gave variant translations of an original Hebrew or Greek word in the margin, variant readings that "seme agreable to the mynde of the holy Gost and propre for our langage."[5]

Several misconceptions surround the Geneva Bible: (1) it was the Bible of the Puritans; (2) because of its obvious advantages, it became the most popular version of the Bible as soon as it appeared; (3) it was generally published in italic or Roman letter.

On the first point, one should note that although Puritans may have preferred the Geneva Bible over the authorized translations, so did many Anglicans. Not a few of these were bishops and archbishops. Even after the Authorized Version of 1611 was published, many bishops continued to use the Geneva Bible. Lancelot Andrews, not only a bishop but also one of the translators of the 1611 Authorized Version, almost always preached from the Geneva Bible and rarely from either the Bishops' Bible or the version he helped translate. Of the more than fifty sermons Bishop Hall preached between 1611 and 1630, he used the Geneva Bible in twenty-seven and the Bishops' in only five. Bishops Laud and Carleton as well as Dean Williams all used the Geneva Bible as late as 1624. In Shakespeare's day, Babington (Bishop of Worcester), George Abbot (afterwards Archbishop of Canterbury), John King (afterwards Bishop of London), Richard Hooker, and Archbishop Whitgift all used the Geneva Bible.

Second, while it is true that the Geneva Bible was the most popular Bible throughout most of Shakespeare's lifetime, it did not become so until 1576, when the first complete Geneva Bible was published in England. In 1560, Queen Elizabeth gave John Bodley an exclusive patent to publish the Geneva Bible for seven years, but the patent decreed that the Geneva Bibles he published be in an edition approved by the bishops of Canterbury and London. Archbishop Parker discouraged publication of the Geneva, since the return of Marian exiles eager for a more thorough reform of the English Church concerned him, and he wanted an edition without the bitter notes of the Geneva. In 1564, well before the license expired, both Parker and Grindal recommended the renewal of Bodley's license for another twelve years. But no Geneva Bibles were printed until Parker died in 1575 and a Geneva New Testament was published by Christopher Barker. The first complete Geneva Bible to be published in England appeared the following year.

Because of Parker's policy towards the Geneva Bible, it got off to a slow start. Between 1560 and 1575, eighteen editions of the complete English Bible were published. Eight of these were Great Bibles, seven were Bishops', but only three were Genevas, published in Geneva in 1560, 1562, and 1570. During the same period six editions of the Bishops' New Testament and six Tyndale New Testaments appeared, but only two of the Geneva were published, one of these being the Geneva New Testament that was published in London for the first time in 1575.

Once the printing of the Geneva commenced in England, however, it outsold all other versions. Of the twenty-seven editions of the complete Bible published in the decade from 1576 to 1585, twenty were Geneva Bibles, while only seven were Bishops' Bibles. No other version of the complete Bible was published during that time. From 1576, when the Geneva Bible first began to be printed in England, until 1611, when Shakespeare's dramatic career was almost over and the King James Bible appeared, ninety-two editions of the complete Bible were published in England. Eighty-one of these were Geneva Bibles, and eleven were Bishops' Bibles. These statistics illustrate the relative availability of the various versions of the Bible during most of Shakespeare's lifetime.

Finally, although the first seven editions of the Geneva Bible appeared in Roman letter, almost as many editions of the Geneva were published in black letter. The first black letter edition appeared in 1578 in a huge folio edition, but black letter editions of the Geneva Bible appeared regularly thereafter. Between 1560 and 1616, when the last complete Geneva Bible was published in England, a total of ninety editions of the complete Geneva Bible appeared. Forty-four of these were in Roman and forty-six in black letter. More than half of these complete Geneva Bibles appeared in black letter.[6]

The Geneva Bible is often called "The Breeches Bible," since Genesis 3.7 says that Adam and Eve sewed fig leaves together and made themselves "breeches," whereas other contemporary versions have "aprons." But "Breeches Bible" is hardly an appropriate name, especially since the Geneva Bible was not the only version to use "breeches" at that passage. Both Wycliffe and Caxton's *Golden Legend* (in which Caxton incorporates large portions of Scripture) used the term "breeches" at Genesis 3.7. Yet many people are hardly aware that the "Breeches Bible" is actually the Geneva; an inappropriate nickname has become more popular than the correct designation.

The last Geneva Bibles to be published in England appeared in 1616. In spite of its popularity, shortly after the Authorized Version appeared, King James would not allow the Geneva Bible to be published in England, since he took exception to its notes. But after production ceased in England, many editions of the Geneva Bible continued to be published on the Continent and exported to England, often bearing the imprint of an English publisher. The last edition of the Geneva Bible was published in 1644 in Amsterdam, eighty-four years after the translation first appeared.

The Bishops' Bible

When Elizabeth ascended the throne in 1558, the Great Bible was allowed to retain its place as the official version of the English Church. The Injunctions of 1559 required that the whole Bible of the largest volume should appear in every parish church. People were exhorted to read the Bible as long as they did not contend over what they read. But the circulation of the Geneva Bible made the defects of the Great Bible apparent. In 1561, therefore, Archbishop Parker took steps to bring out a new version. He divided the Bible into several parts, and sent each part to a bishop or some other learned person for revision. The revisers then returned their revisions to the Archbishop, who published the new version. Since most of the revisers were bishops, the version became known as the Bishops' Bible.

The revisers were instructed to follow the Great Bible and not to deviate from it except where it clearly varied from the Hebrew and Greek originals, in the light of which the Great Bible was to be corrected. They were "to make no bitter notis vppon any text, or yet to set downe any determinacion in places of controversie."[7] Unedifying passages were to be marked so that they might be avoided in public readings; offensive words were to be altered. The printer was to print the New Testament on thicker paper "bicause yt shalbe most occupied."[8]

The Bishops' Bible appeared in 1568 in a magnificent folio volume. More than 140 woodcuts appeared throughout the volume. Over half of these appeared in six books: Genesis (17), Exodus (13), Judges (10), 1 Samuel (9), 1 Kings (10), and Revelation (20). Elizabeth's portrait appeared on the title page, Leicester's preceded Joshua, and Burghley's appeared alongside the first Psalm. Archbishop Parker was responsible for preparing Genesis, Exodus, Matthew, Mark, and 2 Corinthians to Hebrews, inclusive. He hoped that the contributors would exercise greater care in their work if their initials were printed after the books that they had revised, but this was not done consistently. The Bishops' Bible displaced the Great Bible as the official Bible of the English Church. Although the Bishops' Bible was not the result of royal decree, in 1571 Convocation decreed that it was the version to be read in the churches.

The principal defect of the new version was the difference in quality in its various parts, since the revisers did not consult each other to ensure uniformity. The New Testament, for example, was considerably better than the Old since the Greek scholarship of the revisers was superior to their Hebrew scholarship. Moreover, the superior New Testament was carefully revised in 1572 under the direction of Giles Lawrence, an outstanding professor of Greek at Oxford, while the revisions in the Old Testament were minor. That 1572 edition of the Bishops' Bible with the revised New Testament became the standard text. A special feature of this Second Folio edition of 1572 appears in the Psalms: the Prayer Book Psalter was published in black letter along with the Bishops' version of the Psalms in Roman type, the two versions appearing in parallel columns. The Bishops' version of the Psalms appeared alone in the 1568, 1569, and 1585 editions. Both versions of the Psalms appeared in the 1572 edition. In all other editions of the Bishops' Bible, the Prayer Book Psalms were substituted for the Bishops' version of the Psalms.

Were it not for the Geneva Bible, the Bishops' would have been the best English Bible to appear in the sixteenth century. But the scholarship of the Geneva Bible was superior to that of the Bishops'. The Geneva Bible, with an eye to the original languages, was a much more careful and thorough revision of earlier versions than was the Bishops'. There was a strong demand by the public for explanatory marginal notes, and the Geneva had far more notes than the Bishops'. Moreover, the Bishops' Bible was primarily designed for use in the churches. The average person could hardly afford to buy a heavy, expensive folio edition, yet the last handy quarto edition of the complete Bishops' Bible was that of 1584. The Bishops' New Testament continued to be published in handy octavo editions until 1617, making it more accessible to the public, but that was not sufficient to enable it to compete with the Geneva.

Tomson's New Testament

An important version of the New Testament appeared in 1576, when Laurence Tomson published his revision of the Geneva New Testament. Tomson was a fellow of Magdalen College, Oxford, and a member of Parliament. The importance of Tomson's New Testament lay not in the text, which differed little from the Geneva, but in the notes that accompanied the text. The distinguishing feature of the text is that Tomson followed Beza in emphasizing the Greek definite article. Thus we have, "I am that good shepherd: that good shepherd giueth his life for his sheepe," at John 10.11, and "Syr, we would see that Iesus," at John 12.21. At Revelation 20.10 Tomson has "that beast and that false prophet," rather than "the beast and the false prophet." Occasionally the results of emphasizing the Greek article are extreme, as at 1 John 5.12:

He that hath that Sonne, hath that life: and he that hath not that Sonne of God, hath not that life.

Except for this peculiarity, Tomson's New Testament is much like the Geneva's.

The notes in Tomson's text, however, created a great demand for his New Testament. Most of these notes were taken from Beza. In 1565, Theodore Beza, Calvin's successor at Geneva, published a critical Greek text of the New Testament, with a Latin translation of that text and extensive annotations. Tomson discarded the Geneva notes completely and inserted Beza's. Some of these notes are quite learned, but others are sectarian and narrow. The religious climate of the times can be seen in the success of Tomson's New Testament, with its strongly Calvinistic notes that stress predestination and a presbyterian form of church government. Tomson's soon became the most popular New Testament of the day. So much so, that it often replaced the Geneva New Testament. Starting in 1587, the Tomson New Testament began to be bound with the Geneva Old Testament and Apocrypha to form a Geneva-Tomson Bible. Most quarto Geneva Bibles printed in Roman type after 1587 contained the Tomson New Testament; black letter quartos and most folio editions contained the standard Geneva New Testament.

Between 1576, when Tomson's New Testament first appeared, and 1612, when Shakespeare's dramatic career ended, thirty-six editions of Tomson's New Testament and fifteen Bishops' New Testaments were published, but only one Geneva New Testament appeared. The Geneva New Testament was seldom published apart from the Old Testament. During the same period of time, however, the number of Geneva Bibles published with the original Geneva New Testament outnumbered Geneva Bibles published with Tomson's New Testament three to one.

Shakespeare appears to have had either a copy of Tomson's New Testament or else a Geneva-Tomson version of the Bible. Several of Shakespeare's plays appear to reflect information contained in Tomson's notes, which made his New Testament so popular.

Franciscus Junius

In 1592 Richard Field published a volume entitled *Apocalypsis. A briefe and learned commentarie vpon the Reuelation of Saint Iohn the Apostle and Euangelist, applied vnto the historie of the Catholike and Christian Church. Written in Latine by M. Francis Iunius, Doctor of Diuinitie ... And translated into English.* Although the translator is not named, he is believed to have been Thomas Barbar. The work consisted of a new translation of the book of Revelation and of the commentary on it by Franciscus Junius (Francois du Jon, 1545–1602), a Huguenot professor of divinity at the University of Heidelberg whose works were highly regarded by Protestants. Almost every verse in the book of Revelation is accompanied by Junius's extended comments on it, so that the Junius Revelation contains more comments than text.

Tomson's New Testament, like Beza's, contained few notes on Revelation. In fact, Tomson's edition of Revelation contained far fewer notes than did the original 1560 Geneva text. The desire for more extensive notes on Revelation in a Geneva Bible was remedied when the Junius notes on Revelation were substituted for Tomson's in Geneva Bibles with a Tomson New Testament. The first Geneva-Tomson-Junius Bible appeared in 1602 (*STC* 2902).[9] In these editions, the Junius text of Revelation was generally not used; instead Junius's notes were substituted for Tomson's in Tomson's text of Revelation. This "Junius" Revelation appears in most folio Geneva Bibles published after 1602 and in most of the Roman letter quartos. Even before 1602, however, the Junius Revelation was often inserted in Geneva Bibles at the end of either the original Geneva New Testament or Tomson's New Testament, so that these copies contained two versions of the book of Revelation, one following the other. In these instances, what was inserted consisted of both Junius's text of Revelation and his notes on the text.

The notes on Revelation in the 1560 edition of the Geneva Bible exhibited the usual Protestant prejudice against Rome, as the translators were Protestants who fled to Geneva from Catholic Mary out of fear for their lives. Those antipapal notes, however, were mild when compared with Junius's notes on Revelation. Today these notes seem violently anti-Rome, but they were part of the religious controversies of the day in which both sides bitterly attacked each other.

Shakespeare was acquainted with the book of Revelation. Although only three chapters of Revelation were appointed to be read during Morning and Evening Prayer in the Anglican Church (chapter 19 on 1 November, All

Saints' Day, and chapters 1 and 22 on 27 December, the Feast of Saint John), Shakespeare refers to Revelation in several of his plays. His use of Revelation in *Antony and Cleopatra* is outstanding. But no trace of Junius's notes on Revelation is evident in the plays.

The Rheims New Testament

Just as the Protestant Marian exiles produced the Geneva Bible, so also the Catholic Elizabethan exiles sought to bring out a vernacular translation of their own. Of the several schools and seminaries that were founded on the Continent by Catholic exiles for the training of English priests, that at Douay in northern France, founded by Dr. Willian Allen in 1568, proved to be the most important. To meet the Protestant challenge, Dr. Allen insisted that priests must be able to quote Scripture as well as their adversaries in the vernacular. Moreover, if no Catholic translation were available, the danger existed that the faithful would read the translations of heretics. Accordingly, in 1568 Dr. Allen obtained authority from the Pope to undertake an English translation of the Bible, and in 1578 Gregory Martin, a member of Allen's college, began the translating work. He translated two chapters a day, first the Old Testament and then the New. The New Testament was published first in 1582 in Rheims, where the college was located from 1578–93 because of disagreements with the authorities at Douay. The Old Testament was published in two volumes in 1609–10, after the college had returned to Douay.

The new version was based on the Latin Vulgate and not on the original Hebrew and Greek. The translators sensed this was a shortcoming that would bring much criticism, and they devoted many pages of their preface to justifying their use of the Latin. They declared that the Council of Trent had decreed the Latin Vulgate to be the only "authentical" Latin text, which was to be refused by none. They further argued that the Vulgate represented a Greek text that was more ancient and accurate than any available at the time, but overlooked the fact that down through the centuries the Vulgate had become considerably more corrupt than the Greek texts.

The Rheims was a scholarly and conscientious work, published carefully in an attractive format. But it was so pedantic and literal that many passages were altogether unintelligible. Its highly Latinate diction, especially in the Epistles, often resulted in passages that could be understood only by those proficient in Latin. The Old Testament is at its worst in the Psalms, which were a translation of a translation of a translation, since the Latin edition of the Psalms that Martin translated was not Jerome's version from the Hebrew, but the Gallican Psalter, a version of the Psalms that Jerome made from the Greek Septuagint. A few of the many words of Latin origin employed by the Rheims New Testament are *supererogate* for *spend more, prefinition of worlds* for *eternal purpose, exinanited* for *made himself of no reputation, depositum* for *that which is committed, neophyte* for *novice,* and *prescience* for *foreknowledge.* Even the Lord's Prayer has "Giue vs to day our supersubstantial bread." And at Hebrews 13.16 the Rheims has "Beneficence and communication do not forget: for with such hostes God is promerited." Unfamiliar Latinisms were used in the text "for feare of missing, or restraining the sense of the holy Ghost to our phantasie." The translators did not wish to be like the heretics who used "presumptuous boldnes and libertie in translating."[10]

Stranger still was the translators' habit of carrying over into English many Latin and Greek terms without translating them. They expected the English reader to get used to these Latin and Greek terms that they transliterated rather than translated. But such words as *Pasche, Corbona, Parasceue,* and *Azymes* are as strange sounding today as they were in 1582.

The preface of the Rheims was strongly combative and tendentious. The translators invited criticism of their work, attacked all previous English versions (although they borrowed many readings from those versions, particularly from the Geneva), and seemed more intent on circulating their doctrinal and controversial ideas than they were on producing a Catholic English translation of the Bible. In fact, the preface says that the translation was in itself neither desirable nor necessary, but was undertaken "vpon special consideration of the present time," and on account of the circulation of the heretics' many false translations. The notes in the Rheims took every opportunity to attack its opponents, point out how dishonest Protestant translations were, and support Catholic teaching.

Nonetheless, the Rheims New Testament influenced the Authorized Version of 1611. After Tyndale, the Authorized Version owes most to the Geneva Bible, and, after the Geneva, to the Rheims. The translators of the Authorized Version borrowed a number of words of Latin origin from the Rheims.

Although the readings of the Rheims New Testament are taken into consideration throughout this volume, it is most unlikely that Shakespeare possessed a copy or that he was acquainted with its readings. Arguments by a few Catholic scholars that Shakespeare was an adherent of the Old Faith and was acquainted with the Rheims are too far-fetched and contrived to be taken seriously. Whenever a biblical reference in Shakespeare appears to be closest to both the Rheims and the Geneva versions and least like the authorized versions of the day, it is not because Shakespeare possessed a copy of the Rheims as a few scholars claim, but because the translators of the Rheims frequently borrowed Geneva readings in their translation, although at the same time they attacked all Protestant translations. Possession of a Rheims New Testament in Elizabeth's day was suspect. Priests found with copies of it were imprisoned; those who circulated it were often tortured.

A few passages in Shakespeare's plays match the Rheims and no other English translation. But these few passages hardly prove that Shakespeare was acquainted with the Rheims, that he possessed a copy of it, or that he was a secret adherent of the Church of Rome. The strongest example that has been advanced for Shakespeare's use of the Rheims is the phrase at *Coriolanus*, 3.1.70, "the cockle of rebellion." But as can be seen from the discussion of this passage in the references on *Coriolanus*, we can be reasonably certain that the word "cockle," which is indeed peculiar to the Rheims New Testament at Matthew 13.24–25, comes from North's translation of Plutarch.

The Rheims New Testament was known in Shakespeare's day primarily by means of Fulke's refutation of the Rheims. In 1589, William Fulke published his *Confutation*, which printed the Rheims and Bishops' New Testaments in parallel columns with Fulke's refutation of the Rheims text and its annotations. Master of Pembroke College, Cambridge, Fulke made it his goal to leave no Catholic work of controversy unanswered. His *Confutation* proved fairly popular and was reprinted in 1601, 1617, and 1633. In this way the Rheims New Testament received wider circulation than it otherwise would have had.

Other Translations

The present study is not concerned with the Authorized Version of 1611. Shakespeare's dramatic career was almost over by then, although he may have written *The Tempest* and most of *Henry VIII* around 1611–13. Brief mention, however, ought to be made of three minor translations of various books of the Bible that appeared in Shakespeare's time.

Hugh Broughton (1549–1612), who is probably best known for being parodied by Ben Jonson in *The Alchemist*, was an eminent scholar, an eloquent preacher, and one of the best Hebraists of his day. But he was strongly disliked for his quarrelsome, arrogant disposition. As early as the 1560s he announced that he would publish his own version of the Bible based on a revision of the Geneva, which he considered to be the best English version. His comments about the Bishops' Bible were typical of his scornful nature. The errors in that version, he said, were as numerous as the cockles of the sea shore and the leaves of the forest, and Englishmen might as well read the Koran as the Bishops' Bible. As a result of his bad temper and intolerance of anyone who disagreed with him ("I will suffer no scholer in the world to crosse me in Ebrew and Greek, when I am sure I have the trueth"), he was not invited to take part in preparing the Authorized Version. When the new version appeared, he declared that he would rather be torn in pieces by wild horses than that the new version should be urged upon the churches. He wrote, "I require it to be burnt."[11]

Broughton never finished his revision of the Geneva. He was so involved in controversy both in England and on the Continent that he died before completing his long-promised project. But in 1596 he published his translation and comments on the book of Daniel, and between 1605 and 1610 his translations of Ecclesiastes, Lamentations, and Job appeared. He also wrote many treatises on how the Bible should be translated and on passages of Scripture that he denounced as having been improperly translated. Although he could have made an important contribution to Bible translation in the sixteenth century, his cantankerous personality kept him from completing work on more than a few books of the Bible.

About 1550, Sir John Cheke (1514–57), who had been a professor of Greek at Cambridge and tutor to Edward VI, began to translate the New Testament according to a completely original plan. Although he was one of the foremost classical scholars of his time, Cheke wanted a translation of the New Testament that would use words of pure English or Anglo-Saxon origin. To accomplish this he had no scruples against freely coining words in order to substitute a word of English origin for one derived from Latin or Greek. Thus, instead of *proselyte* he used *freshman*; *apostle* became *frosent*; *crucified* became *crossed*; for *centurian* he used *hundreder*; *resurrection* became *uprising*; and *captivity* became *outpeopling*. The only words of Latin origin that he used were those which he regarded as no longer foreign to the English language, such as *disclosed*, *delivered*, and *profitable*. His was to be a New Testament for the uneducated people of his day in nonlearned, non-Latin English.

Cheke's translation was in sharp contrast to the Latinate vocabulary of the Rheims New Testament that was to come thirty years later. He also attempted to pave the way for spelling reform by adopting rules of spelling that would represent the pronunciation of words as closely as possible. He rendered Jesus' words at Matthew 11.28–30 thus:

> Comm to me al that labor and be burdeind and I wil eas iou. Taak mi iook on iou and learn of me for I am mild and of a lowli hart. And ie schal find quietnes for yourselves. For mi iook is profitabil, and mi burden light.

Cheke translated only the Gospel of Matthew and part of the first chapter of Mark. Although his translation was not published until 1843, it was not unknown, and it attracted the interest of contemporary scholars if for no other reason than its originality in an age when most translations were simply improvements of previous versions. Many texts in his translation are startlingly refreshing and serve to restore the impact of passages long blunted by overfamiliarity with English Bibles in the Tyndale tradition.

Finally, the Bible translation of George Joye (d. 1553) deserves mention. In 1530 an English translation of the Psalms was published on the Continent, probably in Antwerp. This edition of the Psalms was the first portion of the Old Testament to be printed in English, and it influenced later English Primers. The person responsible for this 1530 Psalter was George Joye, who had fled to the Continent for refuge after having been accused of heresy against the Church. There he became associated with Tyndale but broke with him and undertook independent Bible translation. In 1534 Joye published under his own name another translation of the Psalms which varied considerably from the 1530 version.

Joye then published a translation of Isaiah in 1531, and Jeremiah in 1534; an edition of Proverbs and Ecclesiastes published in 1534–35 is most likely his. His version of Isaiah was the first English text of Isaiah to be printed. Although a Cambridge graduate and fellow, he was not the scholar Tyndale was, and probably translated it from the Latin. His translation of Isaiah came four years before Coverdale's, but Coverdale's is by far the superior work. Joye's translations are free rather than scholarly.

In 1534, Joye also published a New Testament. This was a pirated edition of Tyndale's 1526 New Testament, but Joye claimed that a corrected edition was needed. He put neither his name nor Tyndale's on this edition, but the changes he made in the text angered Tyndale, and a dispute broke out between them. If Joye was going to alter the text (for example, substituting "the life after this life" for "resurrection"), then Tyndale felt that Joye should put his own name on the editions he published, rather than attempt to pass them off as Tyndale's. The following year Joye corrected and reprinted his 1534 New Testament. Tyndale revised and published his New Testament in 1534 and again in 1535. When he did so, the pirated editions were exposed for what they were.

Joye is an interesting though minor figure in the history of the sixteenth-century English Bible. His English translations of the Bible were probably not part of a comprehensive plan to translate the entire Bible in a systematic manner. He was no great scholar, his style was not outstanding, and he had no great influence on later translators. He is important chiefly on account of his association with Tyndale and because his translations appeared so early in the history of the printed English Bible.

Which Version Shakespeare Used

Which of these versions did Shakespeare use? The vast majority of Shakespeare's biblical references cannot be traced to any one version, since the many Tudor Bibles are often too similar to be differentiated. But of the more than three hundred references that are listed in this volume (excluding thirty-two references to the Psalms, which will be discussed separately), there are twenty-three instances in which Shakespeare is closer to one version, or to several related versions, than to others.

Shakespeare referred to the Geneva Bible more than to any other version. It was the most popular version of the day, and it is only natural to assume that he owned a copy. There are fourteen passages in the eleven tragedies in which Shakespeare clearly refers to the Geneva Bible, or in which he is closer to that version than to others:

1. *Hamlet* 5.2.219–20: "There is special providence in the fall of a sparrow." The Geneva, Taverner, and Rheims have "fal on the ground" at Matt. 10.29. All other versions have "light on the ground." There is little likelihood that Shakespeare had the Taverner Bible in mind, for it was one of the least available versions of the day. And whenever the Rheims New Testament matches the Geneva, it is almost always because it borrowed the Geneva reading. Thus, Shakespeare's reference is most likely to the Geneva.

2. *Hamlet* 3.3.80: "'A took my father grossly, full of bread." Only the Geneva has "fulnes of bread" at Ezek. 16.49. All other versions have "fulnesse of meate."

3. *Julius Caesar* 4.3.86: "A friend should bear his friend's infirmities." Only the Geneva has "beare the infirmities" at Rom. 15.1. The other translations have "beare the fraylenesse," "beare the fraylite," or "susteine the infirmities."

4. *Othello* 2.3.296–97: "Give place to the devil." The Geneva was the first version to read "giue place to the deuil" at Eph. 4.27. Earlier versions had "geue place vnto the backebyter." The Bishops' followed the Geneva.

5. *Othello* 4.2.59–61: "The fountain from the which my current runs ... a cestern for foul toads." Only the Geneva has "fountaine" and "cisterne" at Prov. 5.15–18: "Drinke the water of thy cisterne.... Let thy fountaine be blessed." All other versions parallel the Bishops': "Drinke of the water of thine owne wel.... Let thy wel be blessed."

6. *Timon of Athens* 4.3.173: "Thou spok'st well of me." The Geneva has, "Wo be to you when all men speake well of you" at Luke 6.26. All other Bibles except the Rheims have, "Wo vnto you when menne shal praise you." The Rheims has, "Wo, when al men shal blesse you."

The other passages where Shakespeare's use of the Geneva is probable are: *Hamlet* 3.1.77–79; 5.1.229–30; *Coriolanus* 5.4.23–24; 5.4.49–50; *Othello* 5.2.348; *Julius Caesar* 5.2.5; *Lear* 3.4.102–103; and *Titus Andronicus* 4.2.98.

But the Geneva was not the only version to which Shakespeare referred. There are nine passages in the tragedies in which Shakespeare is *least* like the Geneva and closer to one or more of the other English Bibles. The outstanding examples of Shakespeare's references to a version other than the Geneva are:

1. *Hamlet* 1.2.244: "Though hell itself should gape." A clear reference to any English Bible except the Geneva. Whereas all other English versions read, "Therefore gapeth hel" at Isa. 5.14, the Geneva has, "Hell hath inlarged it selfe."
2. *Romeo and Juliet* 2.3.3: "Fleckled darkness like a drunkard reels." Shakespeare appears closest to the Great and Bishops' Bibles, the two authorized Tudor versions, at Isa. 24.20: "The earth shal reele to and fro like a drunkarde." The Geneva has, "The earth shal reele to and fro like a drunken man."
3. *Timon of Athens* 4.1.27: "That 'gainst the stream of virtue they may strive." All versions but the Geneva have, "Striue thou not agaynst the streame" at Ecclus. 4.28. Geneva: "Striue for the trueth vnto death."
4. *Titus Andronicus* 1.1.83: "These that I bring unto their latest home." All versions but the Geneva have, "Because man goeth to his long home" at Eccles. 12.6. The Geneva has: "Man goeth to the house of his age" (12.5, Geneva).

The five remaining examples of Shakespeare's reference to a version other than the Geneva are *Titus Andronicus* 4.2.41–43; *Timon of Athens* 5.1.215–16; *Troilus and Cressida* 1.3.31: *Romeo and Juliet* 3.1.97–98; *Coriolanus* 1.1.206.

These examples make it clear that although the Geneva may have been the Bible that Shakespeare knew best and to which he referred most often, the influence of other versions is also evident. In addition to the Geneva, Shakespeare may have owned another Bible, perhaps the Bishops'. Folio editions of the Bishops' Bible were heavy, cumbersome volumes primarily intended for use in the churches, but Shakespeare may have owned a quarto edition of the Bishops'; quarto editions continued to appear until 1584. We must also keep in mind that some of Shakespeare's biblical references may not have come from reading the Bible but from everyday conversation, biblical phrases having become common expressions in a religious, Bible-reading age. The reference at *Timon of Athens* 5.1.215 to Timon's "everlasting mansion" is typical of these. Jesus' words at John 14.2 (Tyndale, Matthew, Great, Rheims), "In my fathers house are many mansions," were probably too well known to presuppose that Shakespeare had necessarily read John chapter 14 in one of the versions that has "mansions" rather than "dwelling places" or "dwellynges."

The problem is less complex in the Psalms, since the Anglican Psalter so completely dominated the field. Shakespeare was well acquainted with the Psalter not only because it was read daily in church during Morning and Evening Prayer, but also because it is likely that at school he learned certain Psalms by heart. The Psalter was frequently bound with copies of the popular Geneva Bible, and was generally published not only with the Prayer Book, but also with various editions of Morning and Evening Prayer.[12] There is little likelihood that Shakespeare had the Bishops' Psalms in mind, for its version of the Psalms was published in the Bishops' Bible only four times, in 1568, 1569, 1572 (when it appeared in parallel columns with the Psalter), and 1585. In all other editions of the Bishops' Bible, the Psalter was printed rather than the Bishops' Psalms. Moreover, the Psalter and the Great Bible edition of the Psalms are almost identical, since the Great Bible Psalms became the Psalter. And the Matthew and Coverdale Psalms, which are identical (the Matthew Bible was a compilation of earlier translations), are generally so close to the Psalter that they cannot be differentiated from it. Thus, the two principal choices, when considering which version of the Psalms Shakespeare refers to, are the Psalter and the Geneva Psalms.

Shakespeare refers to the Psalms more frequently than to any other book of the Bible except Matthew, and whenever the references verbally resemble a particular version of the Psalms, it is almost always the Psalter rather than the Geneva:

1. *Julius Caesar* 4.1.50–51: "Some that smile have in their hearts, I fear, / Millions of mischiefs."
   Psalm 28.3, Psalter: "Whiche speake frendly to their neighbours, but imagine mischiefe in their hartes."
   Geneva: "Which speake friendly to their neighbours, when malice is in their heartes."
2. *Timon of Athens* 5.1.165–66: "Who, like a boar too savage, doth root up / His country's peace."
   Psalm 80.13, Psalter: "The wilde boare out of the wood dooth roote it vp." The Geneva has "hath destroyed it" rather than "dooth roote it vp."
3. *Timon of Athens* 5.3.3: "Timon is dead, who hath outstretch'd his span."
   Psalm 39.6, Psalter: "Thou hast made my dayes as it were a spanne long." The Geneva and even the Bishops' have "hand breadth" instead of "span."
   (Shakespeare refers to the same text from the Psalter at *Othello* 2.3.71–72.)
4. *Othello* 1.1.154: "I do hate him as I do hell-pains."
   Psalm 18.4 and 116.3, Psalter: "The paynes of hel."
   Psalm 18.4, Geneva: "The sorowes of death."
   Psalm 116.3, Geneva: "The griefes of the graue."
   (Shakespeare makes the same reference to the Psalter at *Troilus and*

Cressida 4.1.58.)

5. *Antony and Cleopatra* 5.1.15–16: "The round world / Should have shook."

Psalm 93.2, Psalter: "He hath made the rounde world so sure: that it can not be moued."

The Geneva omits "rounde": "The world also shall be established, that it cannot be mooued."

(Shakespeare refers to the same text from the Psalter at *Macbeth* 2.1.56.)

There are three instances in the tragedies, however, where the influence of the Geneva Psalms *may* be apparent. The phrase "th' estate o' th' world" at *Macbeth* 5.5.49 may be from the superscription of Psalm 127 in the Geneva, "the whole estate of the worlde." Antony's words, "You blocks, you stones," in *Julius Caesar* 1.1.35 may have been influenced by the Geneva note at Psalm 115.8: "As much without sense, as blocks and stones." *Titus Andronicus* 3.1.273, "Till all these mischiefs be return'd again," may have been borrowed from Psalm 7.16, Geneva: "His mischiefe shall returne vpon his owne head." The Psalter (7.17) has, "His trauaile shal come vpon his owne head." But in all three instances, we may only be dealing with common expressions.

Thus, no one version can be referred to as "Shakespeare's Bible." Shakespeare was best acquainted with both the Geneva Bible and the Psalter. But in a significant number of passages, Shakespeare's references are least like the Geneva, and closer to the other versions of the day, particularly the Bishops' and Great Bibles, the two official Tudor versions. And there is some evidence that he may have read the Geneva Psalms.

NOTES

1. Preface of Taverner's Pentateuch published in 1551 (*STC* 2087).

2. Royal Injunctions in November 1538 forbade the printing or importation of English Bibles with notes or prologues unless authorized by the king.

3. I am indebted to the Council of the Bibliographical Society (London) for sending me prepublication proofs of the entire section on Bibles in the forthcoming *Short-Title Catalogue*, second edition.

4. Although "cloude of witnesses" is sometimes given as a Geneva contribution to the language, the Geneva translators may have borrowed that expression from Wycliffe, who had "cloude of witnessis" at Hebrews 12.1.

5. Prefatory letter "To the Reader" in the 1560 Geneva Bible (*STC* 2093).

6. This count does not include seven (possibly eight) "1599" editions of the Geneva Bible that were published on the Continent during the first half of the seventeenth century, but which were spuriously set forth as having been printed in London in 1599. All seven editions were in Roman type. Nor does it include three editions published in Edinburgh in 1579, 1601, and 1610, all of which were in Roman type.

7. Alfred W. Pollard, ed., *Records of the English Bible* (1911; reprint, Folkestone: Wm.

Dawson & Sons, 1974), 297.

8. Ibid., 298.

9. The spuriously dated 1599 editions of the Geneva Bible were all Geneva-Tomson-Junius combinations, but these editions were all published after 1602.

10. Preface of the 1582 Rheims New Testament, sig. c.iii.ᵛ.

11. Frederick F. Bruce, *The English Bible* (New York: Oxford University Press, 1970), 107; Hugh Pope, *English Versions of the Bible* (1952; reprint, Westport, Conn.: Greenwood Press, 1972), 330.

12. "On 1 Apr. 1578 Barker and W. Seres signed an agreement that henceforth Barker would print psalters only with the Bible or BCP, and that Seres and his assigns might continue to print morning and evening prayer with their psalters." *RSTC* 2351.7.

2
Shakespeare and the Anglican Liturgy

The religious service that Shakespeare was accustomed to was instituted in the English Church when Queen Elizabeth ascended the throne in 1558. During the first year of her reign, the Act of Uniformity was passed, the 1552 Prayer Book of Edward VI, slightly revised, was again ordered to be used in the service, and church attendance was made mandatory. In 1563 Convocation summarized the doctrines of the Anglican Church in the Thirty-nine Articles.[1] To the first *Book of Homilies* of 1547, a second volume was added in 1563. These homilies were to be read in church every Sunday and holy day.

By the time Shakespeare's dramatic career began around 1589, the Anglican service had been in effect for some thirty years. Shakespeare's plays give abundant evidence that he was thoroughly acquainted with that service. He makes references to almost all of the services in the Prayer Book, frequently echoes the homilies, and whenever his many references to the Psalms can be identified with any one version, it is usually to the Psalter, the Great Bible version of the Psalms that was used in the English Church.

The services of the Anglican Church were based on the *Book of Common Prayer*, the most cherished monument of the English Church. It first appeared in 1549. Prior to that time, service books existed only in Latin and were only for the priests. The service differed from one diocese to another. There was no uniform or "common" prayer throughout England.

Archbishop Cranmer took the first step toward a uniform service in 1543, when he authorized a chapter of the Bible to be read *in English* at what was soon to become "Morning Prayer." He directed that on every Sunday and holy day throughout the year, after the *Te Deum* and *Magnificat*, the curate of every parish should openly read to the people one chapter of the New Testament in English without exposition, and when the New Testament was read over, to begin reading the Old. The next step came in 1544 with the introduction of a Litany in English. Archbishop Cranmer wrote the Litany, a masterpiece of English prose, a prayer of great beauty and power. The present-day Litany is essentially that of 1544. In 1547 the reading of the Epistle and Gospel in English began. These were read during the Mass, which was still conducted in Latin. In 1548 came the Order of Communion in English.

But Cranmer and the other reformers were not content with Latin services interspersed with bits of English. They were determined that all Anglican churches should conduct services entirely in English and that all services should be uniform throughout England. This determination led to the first *Book of Common Prayer*, which appeared 7 March 1549. All subsequent Prayer Books were but revisions of that first edition. It took the place of all other uses and forms of worship, and for the first time, the entire English-speaking church worshiped in the same way.

That Prayer Book, however, was not a complete break with the past. In fact, most of its contents were taken from pre-Reformation service books. Cranmer skillfully adapted, translated, and simplified the four chief service books used in the pre-Reformation Church: the Breviary, the Missal, the Manual, and the Pontifical. Cranmer modeled morning and evening prayer on the Breviary. Communion with the Collects, Epistles, and Gospels followed the Missal. The Manual was the guide for the baptism, matrimony, and the burial services, while confirmation and the ordinal followed the Pontifical. From the earlier services Cranmer took whatever he considered valuable and scriptural and discarded the rest. From the Eastern Church he took the Prayer of Saint Chrysostom. Finally, the Prayer Book contained a good deal of original material, as the collects for the first two Sundays in Advent and the collect for Quinquagesima. The result was a literary and religious gem that has been the glory of the English Church ever since, second only to the English Bible.

Notwithstanding the excellence of the 1549 Prayer Book, various interest groups wanted a revision. Catholics felt that too much of the old had been discarded, while Protestants felt that too much had been retained. The spirit of the day favored the reformers, and when the Second Prayer Book appeared in 1552, it was decidedly more Protestant than the first. The word "mass" was removed from the title of the Communion Service, the Prayer of Consecration underwent a major change, and the famous "Black Rubric" was added on account of the controversy over the practice of kneeling at Communion. The "Black Rubric" declared that the kneeling indicated no adoration of either the bread or the wine. Certain additions were also made. Instead of Morning and Evening Prayer beginning with the Lord's Prayer as in the 1549 Prayer Book, the introductory Sentences, Exhortation, General Confession, and Absolution were added at the beginning of each service. The Ten Commandments and their Kyries ("Lorde haue mercie vpon vs") were added at the beginning of the Communion Service, while mention of "the glorious and most blessed virgin Mary," and the sign of the cross, among other things, were removed from it.

The Second Prayer Book was in use for only eight months when Queen

Mary came to the throne and forbade its use. She reinstituted the old forms of worship, and attempted to re-establish the Roman Catholic religion. But when she died in 1558, there was a strong desire to return to the reformed principles of religion.

At Elizabeth's accession, the question of the Prayer Book again came up. Elizabeth's policy was one of compromise, a *via media* between her Catholic and Protestant subjects. As part of the Elizabethan religious settlement, it was decided to revise the Second Prayer Book so that it might be more compatible with both sides. The principal changes were that the "Ornaments Rubric" was altered to authorize the use of the old vestments, which the Second Book had forbidden; the "Black Rubric" was omitted; and the suffrage in the Litany which declared, "From the tyranny of the Bysshop of Rome and al hys detestable enormities ... Good lord, deliuer vs," was removed. The revision became the 1559 Prayer Book of Queen Elizabeth, the Prayer Book in use during most of Shakespeare's lifetime. The revisions that were made in the Fourth Prayer Book of 1604 under King James were so slight that the 1604 Book was basically the same as the 1559. The one notable addition consisted of special prayers of thanksgiving for rain, fair weather, plenty, and peace.

The Prayer Book is of particular interest to us with reference to Shakespeare, since it stresses a systematic reading of the Bible. The Order of Service provided for the reading of the entire Psalter once each month during Morning and Evening Prayer, the New Testament three times a year, and the Old Testament once a year. The only portions of Scripture excluded were "certaine Bookes and Chapters, which be least edifying, and might best be spared," and these included the genealogies, the Song of Solomon, and most of Leviticus, Ezekiel, and Revelation. On Sundays and holy days the Prayer Book provided for a homily to be read from the *Book of Homilies* or, if the church had a licensed preacher, a sermon could be delivered by that preacher in lieu of reading one of the appointed homilies.

Much has been made of Shakespeare's attendance at church as an important means by which he became acquainted with Scripture. But church attendance was compulsory only on Sundays and holy days. In order to hear the Bible read as frequently as outlined in the Prayer Book, a person would have to attend both Morning and Evening Service every day in the year. It is hardly likely that Shakespeare did so, since during the week, his company was staging plays at the same time that Evening Prayer (held in the afternoon) was in progress. His usual practice was probably to attend church when required, on Sundays and holy days. The Privy Council had prohibited the performances of plays on Sundays both in London and in the suburbs, and Henslowe's *Diary* indicates that the prohibition was strictly observed at the theaters under his control between 1592 and 1597. When James came to the throne, one of his first acts was to issue a proclamation against Sunday plays. Thus, Shakespeare was free to attend both Morning and Evening Prayer on Sundays.

The situation is less clear regarding holy days. The companies were also expected not to play during Lent and other holy days, but the regulations were not always observed. In 1592 Strange's men performed plays right through Lent, with the exception of Good Friday, and several companies were, at one time or another, cited by the authorities for playing during Lent.

If we assume that Shakespeare's company complied with the regulations against plays on Sundays and holy days, and that Shakespeare attended both Morning and Evening Prayer regularly on these occasions, it is important to know which passages of Scripture he heard when he went to church, particularly the "proper lessons" appointed for Sundays and holy days. Then we can determine to what extent church attendance influenced his use of Scripture.

Morning Prayer opened with a reading from the introductory Sentences, passages of Scripture imploring God's forgiveness of sins. Then followed the General Confession, which Shakespeare echoes several times in this plays ("wee haue left vndone those things which wee ought to haue done, and we haue done those things which wee ought not to haue done"),[2] the Absolution, the Lord's Prayer, and the reading of Psalm 95. Then came the daily reading of the Psalms, "in order, as they be appointed in a Table made for that purpose," so that the entire book of Psalms was read once each month. The two lessons followed, the first lesson from the Old Testament and the second from the New, "except there be proper Lessons assigned for that day." That stipulation is important. For whereas there was little interference with the schedule for reading New Testament second lessons both in Morning and Evening Prayer, there was considerable interference with the schedule for reading Old Testament first lessons. Instead of the usual first lesson for Sundays and holy days, a "proper lesson" was appointed to be read; that is, a chapter of the Old Testament deemed particularly appropriate for that day was substituted for the Old Testament lesson that would normally have been read according to the calendar of readings. For the New Testament, on the other hand, proper lessons were appointed for only a few Sundays and holy days throughout the year. Hence particular attention should be paid to the proper first lessons, since these were specially designated Old Testament passages that Shakespeare heard when he attended church on Sundays and holy days. Evening Prayer followed a similar order, with the majority of first lessons being proper lessons.

The books of Isaiah, Genesis, Proverbs, and the Apocryphal book of Ecclesiasticus figured most prominently in proper first lessons, and Shakespeare referred to a number of these lessons in his plays. But a careful check of the tables of proper lessons in the Prayer Book reveals that there were many other lessons which he repeatedly heard in church and did not refer to. Even more significant is the fact that he often makes more references to chapters from those books that were not proper first lessons than to those that were. It seems clear, therefore, that Shakespeare's acquaintance with Scripture did not come primarily from church attendance. Most of his references to Revelation are taken from chapters that were not appointed to be read in church at any time.

The Homilies

The largest section of the Prayer Book consists of the Communion Service and the varying Collects, Epistles, and Gospels that were used in that service throughout the year. Immediately after the Nicene Creed in the Communion Service, this rubric occurs: "After the Creede, if there be no Sermon, shall follow one of the Homilies already set foorth, or hereafter to be set forth by common authoritie."

The *Book of Homilies*, like the Prayer Book, was one of the most influential and widely circulated books throughout Shakespeare's lifetime. "The Homilies already set foorth" refers to the first *Book of Homilies*, which had appeared in July, 1547 during the reign of Edward VI. The rubric also anticipates the second *Book of Homilies*, under preparation, which appeared in 1563.

As early as the Convocation of 1542, it was suggested that homilies be prepared for reading in the churches. The first *Book of Homilies* came out in July, 1547 six months after the death of Henry VIII, and almost two years before the first Prayer Book appeared. As with the Prayer Book, Archbishop Cranmer was the moving force behind the *Book of Homilies*. It contained twelve homilies; three of them (the third, fourth, and fifth) were written by Cranmer himself. The first three homilies were entitled, "A Fruitefull Exhortacion to the Readyng of Holye Scripture," "Of the Misery of All Mankynde," and "Of the Saluacion of All Mankynde." Other homilies dealt with faith, good works, Christian love, obedience to rulers and magistrates, as well as exhortations against swearing and perjury, the fear of death, adultery, and strife. In later editions, these twelve homilies were each divided into either two or three parts to be delivered on successive Sundays, so that the twelve homilies became thirty-one.

Even before King Edward died in 1553, the twelve homilies in the first *Book of Homilies* were thought to be inadequate for the instruction of the people. When Elizabeth became queen, a new edition of the first *Book of Homilies*, somewhat revised, was published, and a second *Book of Homilies* was planned. It appeared in 1563 and consisted of twenty additional homilies, although the two Good Friday homilies made the number twenty-one. Most of these were probably written by such men as Bishops Jewell, Grindal, Parker, and Pilkington. The new homilies dealt with doctrine (idolatry, prayer, the sacraments, Easter, matrimony) or morality (gluttony, excess of apparel, idleness).

The third and last phase in the development of the *Book of Homilies* occurred in 1571 when the homily "Against Disobedience and Wilfull Rebellion" was added on account of the Northern Rebellion of November, 1569. Although the uprising was suppressed within three months, it caused great alarm throughout England. Almost immediately afterwards Pope Pius V excommunicated Elizabeth and absolved her subjects from allegiance to her. The following year, 1571, the Ridolfi Plot came to light, a plot to invade England, depose Elizabeth, put Mary Queen of Scots on the throne, and restore Catholicism as the religion of England. The queen and her council instructed the bishops to prepare a new homily against disobedience and rebellion, in addition to the homily "Obedience to Rulers and Magistrates" that had appeared in the First Book. The second longest homily, "Against Disobedience and Wilfull Rebellion," was originally divided into five parts, and later into six. To each part was appended a special prayer imploring God to soften the stony hearts of those who seek "to trouble the quiet of this Realme." At the end of the sixth part, the prayer "A Thanksgiving for the Suppression of the Last Rebellion" also appeared.

Shakespeare was almost six years old when the Northern Rebellion occurred. Later in life as he listened to the homily "Against Disobedience and Wilfull Rebellion," he may have remembered seeing troops hurrying northward along the two London roads that met at Stratford to suppress the rebellion. As an alderman, his father would have been active in enlisting men for the Crown in Stratford.

Along with the Bible and the *Book of Common Prayer*, the homilies were among the best-known writings in Shakespeare's day. By means of them the government sought to mold the thoughts and control the lives of its subjects. The first *Book of Homilies* was in constant use throughout the reign of Edward VI (1547–53), and its message was strongly Protestant. The preface of the first edition explains that it was issued in reaction to the "manifold enormities, whiche heretofore haue crepte into his graces Realme" by means of the ungodly doctrines of the Bishop of Rome and of his adherents. These resulted in the decay of the Christian religion and the seduction of innumerable souls. The first homily stresses that Scripture alone contains all that is necessary for salvation. The third homily on salvation by faith in Christ alone explains that no man can be justified by his own good works, since even pagans can perform good works. Only the antichrist would affirm "that a man might by his owne workes" purge his own sins. The homily "Against the Feare of Deathe" makes no mention of purgatory, although it deals at length with the joys of heaven and the torments of hell.

The second *Book of Homilies* continues in the same vein. As in the First Book, there are homilies that are strongly anti-Rome and others that stress acceptable Christian living. The longest of all homilies, "Against Perill of Idolatrie, and Superfluous Decking of Churches," strongly attacks Roman Catholic use and veneration of images. The homily "Of Prayer" stresses the folly of praying to saints and angels, and argues against "the grosse errour of Purgatory." There are also many homilies on Christian living, and others that explain the significance of the various holy days: Christmas, Good Friday, Easter, Whitsunday, and Rogation Week. The last homily, added in 1571 after the Northern Rebellion, is clearly political in its attempt to prevent further rebellions. The biblical examples it gives (especially David's refusal to raise his hand against King Saul, the Lord's anointed) were simply the vehicle used to advance the government's desire for complete obedience from its subjects.

How often did Shakespeare hear these homilies? That he was well acquainted with them there can be little doubt; references to the homilies are particularly noticeable in *Hamlet*. While it is often thought that like the average Elizabethan churchgoer, Shakespeare heard the homilies week after week and year after year, this is not necessarily so. The rubric in the Communion Service stipulates that "if there be no Sermon, shall follow one of the Homilies." Likewise the preface to the homilies orders that they be read plainly and distinctly every Sunday and holy day "except there be a Sermon ... and then for that cause onely, and for none other, the reading of the sayd *Homilie* to bee deferred vnto the next Sunday, or Holyday following."

The term *sermon* as distinguished from *homily* refers to sermons delivered by licensed preachers. The homilies were provided not only because many of the clergy were poor preachers and insufficiently educated, but also because the government wanted to regulate preaching in the churches at a time of widespread religious differences. The preface to the homilies says that they were intended to assure the "pure declaring of Gods word" and to expose "erroneous and poysoned doctrines, tending to superstition and idolatry." By requiring that the homilies be read and making sure that no private preaching took place, the government was able to prevent recusant preaching, whether Catholic, Puritan, or other.

Whenever the loyalty of an Anglican clergyman to the established Church was assured, however, the archbishop, bishop, or either of the universities were authorized to issue a license to that clergyman enabling him to preach sermons that he himself had written. Whenever such a sermon was preached on a Sunday or holy day, the homily that would normally have been read was "deferred vnto the next Sunday, or Holyday following."

How often were sermons rather than homilies heard in the churches? According to the *Canons Ecclesiastical* of 1604, a beneficed cleric who was not licensed to preach was required to "procure Sermons to bee preached in his Cure once in euery moneth at the least, by Preachers lawfully licensed, if his liuing in the iudgement of the Ordinary, will be able to beare it" (Canon

46). Moreover, a beneficed clergyman who was a licensed preacher was required to preach "one Sermon euery Sunday of the yeere" either in his own Cure, or in a nearby church that had no licensed preacher (Canon 45). These regulations were enacted at the beginning of James's reign in 1603 and published in 1604, but it is probable that they merely clarified and codified what had already been general practice.

It appears, therefore, that during the time Shakespeare was associated with the theater in London, most London churches had licensed preachers, and sermons may have been heard in the churches at least as often as the printed homilies. Rural churches were less likely to have had licensed preachers; there the homilies would be read "plainly and aptly (without glozing or adding)," as stipulated in Canon 49. But if a rural church could afford a licensed preacher and it was convenient for one to come, he would be invited to deliver a sermon in that church at least once a month. Thus Shakespeare was more apt to have heard the homilies read on a regular basis in Stratford than in London.

Yet even Stratford had a licensed preacher. In 1569, when Shakespeare was five years old, Henry Heycroft became vicar at Holy Trinity Church. Two years later, Heycroft was given a license to preach by the Bishop of Worcester. Heycroft continued as vicar in Stratford until 1584. This means that even in Stratford Shakespeare probably heard a sermon rather than a homily once or twice a month. Nonetheless, Shakespeare's familiarity with the Homilies is evident in the plays, although he may not have heard them from the pulpit as regularly as is often supposed.

Sermons

The influence of sermons on Shakespeare's plays is considerably more difficult to assess than that of either the Prayer Book or the Homilies. First of all, it is not certain which church Shakespeare attended, how often sermons were delivered there, or by whom. Second, while hundreds of sermons by outstanding preachers of Shakespeare's time were published and can be studied to see if Shakespeare borrowed from them, numerous others remained unpublished. Finally, in addition to the sermons delivered in the churches, many others were delivered on public occasions outside the church, as at Paul's Cross. We can only surmise how many of these Shakespeare heard or read.

Three days after the Earl of Essex was executed in 1601, Dr. William Barlow delivered a sermon at Paul's Cross that was subsequently printed. Essex was a popular figure, and the government knew that there was much discontent over his execution. Sir William Cecil gave Barlow detailed instructions about what would be appropriate to say on that occasion. On account of the relationship between Shakespeare's company and the Earl (some of Essex's followers had persuaded the Lord Chamberlaine's men to revive *Richard II*, with its famous deposition scene, at the Globe on February 7, 1601, the day prior to the rebellion, and paid the company forty shillings to do so), Shakespeare and his fellow actors may have been present at Barlow's sermon. But there are no clear echoes of Barlow's sermon in Shakespeare's plays, although Shakespeare may have had more reason to attend that sermon than others.

The sermons of Shakespeare's day fall into two general categories: (1) those delivered in church on Sundays and holy days as part of the service in place of a homily, and (2) those that were preached on special occasions to commemorate an important event, such as the execution of Essex.

The first type of sermon, the church sermon, was overshadowed by the homily in the early part of Elizabeth's reign. But toward the end of the century, the sermon became at least as important as the homily in the church service, especially in London. The reason for this change is obvious. Early in Elizabeth's reign, there was a great shortage not only of licensed preachers, but also of qualified clergymen in general. But as time went on, the shortage of priests was relieved, the number of licensed preachers increased, and sermons became more frequent.

Only two of the Marian bishops continued to serve in their posts after Elizabeth came to the throne. The rest had either died or were removed for not recognizing Elizabeth as the Supreme Governor of the Church of England, and a long time passed before new bishops were appointed to all the sees. As for the lower clergy, many fled from their posts when the religion of the realm changed, and others were deprived of their offices for refusing to conform. It has been estimated that no more than two hundred were relieved of their duties, and yet there was a great shortage of capable clergymen throughout England's thirteen thousand parishes. Replacements were difficult to make and the universities could not train enough priests to fill the vacancies. Thus the bishops were forced to fill the ranks of the clergy with whatever men were available, and they either put the remaining cures in the hands of lay readers or left them vacant altogether. So great was the need for qualified preachers that even bishops had to go about preaching like lower clergy. John Jewel, Bishop of Salisbury, went on tours throughout his diocese, preaching to each of his congregations one by one.

Under these circumstances, the Homilies were heard far more often than the occasional sermon. As an emergency measure for parishes without a clergyman, lay readers were appointed to read from the Prayer Book or the *Book of Homilies* without commenting or adding to what they read, and, whenever possible, licensed preachers would be sent out to satisfy the spiritual needs of the people. With such great demands being made on the licensed preachers, it is probable that in the early part of Elizabeth's reign homilies were the order of the day in the services even in London, with sermons being preached only occasionally, perhaps once a month.

By the time Shakespeare arrived in London toward the end of the 1580s, however, the number of licensed preachers had greatly increased, and the shortage of priests was less serious. Thus the number of sermons delivered in London churches on Sundays and holy days in the place of homilies probably exceeded the required minimum of one a month. Canon 46 of the 1604 *Canons Ecclesiastical* required one sermon "in euery moneth at the least," which indicates that if licensed preachers were available, sermons several times a month on Sundays and holy days were not only permissible but even desirable. Since sermons were given more frequently in the latter part of Shakespeare's career, Shakespeare may have heard sermons more often than homilies when he attended church.

Whether a single hearing of a sermon would make a strong enough impression on Shakespeare for him to use phrases or ideas from that sermon in his plays is a matter of debate. As reтentive as Shakespeare's mind may have been, it is unlikely that hearing a sermon would have the same influence on him as reading it. This is particularly true in light of the circumstances under which services were conducted at that time.

Church services were not the dignified, sober occasions they are today. Churches were commonly used as public meeting places where business could be transacted and views exchanged; these events also took place while services were being conducted. Even St. Paul's Cathedral was a great business center and public promenade. Disorders that bordered on the ridiculous took place within the church. People still had their ears nailed to posts and even cut off for brawling and fighting within the cathedral. The Injunctions of 1559 stipulated that "no man shall willingly let [prevent] or disturb the preacher in time of his sermon, or let or discourage any curate or minister to sing or say the divine service now set forth; nor mock or jest at the ministers of such service" (Injunction 36). Yet church attenders continued to do all these things and more.

Early in Elizabeth's reign, when objection to clerical vestments was strongest, a preacher appeared in the pulpit at St. Margaret's wearing a surplice. On seeing this, the "wyves threw stons at hym and pullyd hym forthe of ye pulpyt, rentyng his syrplice and scrattyng his face."[3] In Chester, when a preacher followed his bishop's advice and preached a Protestant sermon to an audience with Catholic sympathies, he was put in the stocks by his hearers and pelted with eggs by the women of the parish. Instances are recorded of services being disrupted by disaffected persons beginning to sing popular songs loudly in the midst of the service, and refusing to be quiet when told by the minister to be silent. People were known to bring their hawks and hounds into the church during the service. As late as 1602, the practice was instituted of shutting the doors of St. Paul's during the services to prevent distractions from taking place, and we have record of at least one objection to this practice on the ground that "the trafficke of newes [is] much decayed."[4]

Disruptions of the service were most likely to occur during the sermon. If the normal Elizabethan churchgoer seems disrespectful and unruly by our standards, he was especially inclined to be so while listening to a sermon which he found objectionable. While some were content to stuff wool into their ears so that they would not have to hear an unacceptable message, others were not content with such passive measures. Coughing, heckling, and jeering were common forms of protest for an unpopular sermon. And what is true of sermons within the church is even more evident in the second category of sermons, the public sermons, preached at Paul's Cross and elsewhere.

Shakespeare's was an age of sermons. No important occasion was considered properly observed unless a sermon was preached. This principle applied not only to religious functions but to civil and social occasions as well. Whether the occasion was fire, drought, or plague, the public baptizing of a converted infidel or the excommunication of a priest, the opening of Parliament or of a session of court, the anniversary of the queen's accession or a national crisis, the death of a prominent person or the execution of a notorious criminal, an important birth or a state wedding, each and all required a sermon. On these occasions a preacher would be notified sufficiently in advance so that he could prepare a sermon suitable for the occasion, the request being considered a great honor. People would flock to hear these sermons, and the size of the audience sometimes ran into the thousands, particularly at Paul's Cross, the most important of London's pulpits. If the listeners were inattentive and unruly during the church sermons, they were even more so at public sermons.

The desire of Elizabethans for amusement and sensation was not confined to the theater; it extended to the pulpit. The disorderliness of the audiences at the theaters is well known, but audiences at public sermons were little better. What occurred during sermons at Paul's Cross when people were exhibited for penance often bordered on farce. Paul's Cross had a platform on the same level as the pulpit on which the penitents stood to be jeered and railed at by members of the audience, who sought to outdo one another with sallies of scurrilous wit. The jibes made by onlookers when persons were displayed for such offenses as bigamy or accusing their clergyman of "wenching" can best be left to the imagination. While public penance before a jeering crowd was a good way to punish offenders, it is unlikely that the audience absorbed much of the sermon.

Under these circumstances, the probability that a single hearing of a sermon was sufficient to provide Shakespeare with phrases or ideas for his plays is considerably less than might at first appear. Whatever influences there are in the plays from the sermons are more likely the result of Shakespeare's having read the sermons than having heard them. There was no lack of published sermons available for purchase. In spite of the hostility or the carnival atmosphere that often accompanied sermons, Elizabethans were generally interested in religion and eager to discuss religious topics, and printers did a brisk business from the sale of printed sermons. The *Short-Title Catalogue* lists over twelve hundred sermons printed during Elizabeth's reign; during the decade from 1590–1600, some 140 editions of printed sermons appeared, not of single sermons, but of collections. The sermons of Henry Smith were especially popular, and between 1589, when his first sermon was printed, and 1610, no less than eighty-three editions of his sermons appeared. Even so secular a writer as Thomas Nashe praised Smith as a "siluer tongu'd" preacher, and Nashe attests to having read his sermons, in addition to hearing them. "I neuer saw abundant reading better mixt with delight," writes Nashe in *Pierce Penilesse*.[5] Although we are probably safer in concluding that any influence on Shakespeare's plays from the sermons of the day primarily came from Shakespeare's having read them, we must not discount the fact that the atmosphere in which other sermons, particularly church sermons, were preached was both serious and upbuilding, and Shakespeare could have borrowed ideas and phrases from those sermons.[6]

With so many unknowns, we would do well to exercise caution in making claims about the influence of sermons on Shakespeare's plays. Whenever a parallel between a Shakespeare play and a printed sermon of the day has been observed, it is pointed out in the list of references. But for the most part, parallels between Shakespeare's plays and the sermons are tenuous; many of the claimed parallels are not at all convincing.

The Primer

Although the Primer was not part of the Anglican liturgy of Shakespeare's day, something ought to be said about it, since it was a forerunner of the Prayer Book and contained many passages of Scripture. Over 180 editions of the Primer appeared between 1525 and 1560, when its usefulness as a devotional work was superseded by the Prayer Book. An abbreviated form of the Primer attached to the Catechism was one of the two main texts from which Shakespeare learned how to read.

The two principal types of schools in the sixteenth century were the petty schools and the grammar schools. At the age of four a child usually entered the petty school, where he learned to read and was instructed in the elements of religion. After learning the alphabet from a hornbook (a tablet inscribed with the alphabet and the Lord's Prayer in English), the child was ready to learn how to read. Just prior to Shakespeare's time, the two principal petty school texts were the *ABC with the Catechism* and the Primer. These were in English. The ABC book was a pamphlet with the texts of the Paternoster, Ave Maria, Creed, Ten Commandments, and a few graces to be said before and after meals. But since the Catechism was studied after the ABC, the two pamphlets came to be published together.

Next came the Primer. The Primer also contained the Paternoster, Creed, and Ten Commandments, but it contained much more. Early in the six-teenth century, before the Prayer Book of 1549 appeared, the Primer served as a religious handbook. In the Medieval church, certain prayers were assigned to be said at certain hours, and thus the Book of Hours developed. The Primer was a miniature Canonical Book of Hours intended for private devotions. It also included familiar passages from the New Testament and some forty to sixty Psalms.

As a result of the Church's prohibition since the days of Wycliffe against publishing any portion of the Bible in English, the Psalms and all other passages of Scripture were published in Latin only, although portions of the Primer that were not directly from the Bible often appeared in English. The English Primer of 1534 (*RSTC* 15986) was probably the first book to be printed *in England* that contained entire Psalms and other biblical passages in English. The break with Rome had just occurred, and both Cromwell and Cranmer favored allowing the people to read the Bible in English.

Editions of the Primer continued to appear, each edition differing from the others. Toward the end of his reign, Henry desired to standardize educa-tion in England, and that included an authorized edition of the Primer. It appeared on 29 May 1545 (*RSTC* 16034) as "The Primer, set foorth by the Kynges maiestie and his Clergie,... and none other to be vsed." It contained the usual preliminary features, thirty-six Psalms, and ended with a seventy-page collection of miscellaneous prayers. The authorized version, it became known as the King's Primer. In 1545 and 1546 this authorized Primer went through thirteen editions. Every schoolmaster was ordered to use it im-mediately after the ABC in teaching the young.

Primers continued to be published in the reigns of Edward, Mary, and Elizabeth. But once the Prayer Book appeared in 1549, the Primer's useful-ness declined. The Prayer Book outlined a new form of Morning and Even-ing Prayer which replaced the Primer's Book of Hours. And when the English Bible became the most popular book of the day, the Prayer Book was often bound in the same volume with the Bible. England became a Bible-reading nation rather than a nation that recited certain prayers at certain hours. Primers were used in the petty schools in Elizabeth's day to teach the young how to read, but they were completely revised Primers with-out the Canonical Hours. Whereas the earlier Primers had been devotional manuals, by Shakespeare's time they were primarily English readers.

When Shakespeare attended Stratford's petty school between the ages of about four and seven, he learned his alphabet from a hornbook (the elementary schoolmaster in *Love's Labor's Lost*, 5.1.46 "teaches boys the horn-book"), and reading from *The ABC with the Catechism* and a Primer. When in *The Two Gentlemen of Verona* Shakespeare wrote that a lover sighs "like a schoolboy that had lost his A B C" (2.1.22–23), he probably refers to the *ABC with the Catechism*. The ABC book is also mentioned in *King John*, 1.1.196. The Primer Shakespeare used was most likely *The Primer and Cathechisme*, an adaptation of the older Primer joined to the ABC with the catechism. Several types of Primers that must be carefully distinguished were current early in Elizabeth's reign. Shakespeare's petty school Primer was one of the editions published by William Seres and "set forth by the Quenes maiesty to be taught vnto children."[7]

At about seven years of age Shakespeare went to grammar school, where for the next seven years (ca. 1571–78) his main concern was to learn Latin grammar. But daily prayer and religious instruction was a prominent feature of the grammar school curriculum, and either Calvin's or Nowell's *Catechism* was regularly taught and recited. Nowell's longer *Catechism* (*RSTC* 18708), a volume of some eighty leaves that rehearsed all the basic doctrines of Christianity and of the Anglican Church, was one of the best-known books of Shakespeare's day. But other than the Ten Commandments and similar set passages, it contained few direct quotations from Scripture. The most extensive passages of Scripture that the students encountered in all of this religious instruction may have been the Seven Penitential Psalms (Psalms 6, 32, 38, 51, 102, 130, and 143) that appeared in the Primer.

Was the English Bible also a part of Shakespeare's grammar school curriculum? Probably not. The Canons of 1604, adopted when King James came to the throne, simply repeated Elizabeth's Injunctions of 1559 and ordered that schoolmasters should train their students in "such sentences of holy Scripture, as shall bee most expedient to induce them to all godlinesse" (Canon 79). These "sentences of holy Scripture" were probably passages from the Bible that were dictated by the schoolmaster to the students, who copied them down and memorized them. Canon 79 specified Lily's Latin grammar as a required text ("the Grammer set forth by King Henry the eight, and continued in the times of King Edward the sixt, and Queene Elizabeth of noble memory, and none other"), but neither the Bible nor the New Testament was so designated. In some schools, the schoolmaster was allowed to use the New Testament as an optional text if he chose to do so, but this option was not the general practice. All that was required was that the students be trained in certain "sentences of holy Scripture," and this hardly suggests a systematic reading of the Bible or even of any one book of the Bible.

NOTES

1. The *Forty-two* articles of 1553 were actually reduced to thirty-eight in 1563, and finally reached the familiar number of thirty-nine in 1571.

2. *Julius Caesar* 4.2.8–9; *Othello* 3.3.204; *Antony and Cleopatra* 3.1.14; *Coriolanus* 4.7.24–25.

3. Alan Fager Herr, *The Elizabethan Sermon* (1940; reprint, New York: Octagon Books, 1969), 34.

4. Ibid., 32.

5. Thomas Nashe, *Pierce Penilesse his Supplication to the Diuell* (1592; reprint, Menston, England: Scolar Press, 1969), 17–17ᵛ.

6. The diary of John Manningham of the Middle Temple, which runs from January 1602 to April 1603, contains summaries of more than forty sermons, including sermons preached at Paul's Cross by such eminent clerics as Lancelot Andrewes, John King, and George Abbot. Some of these summaries are of considerable length. Manningham was not particularly religious, and he disliked Puritans, but his sermon summaries make it clear that the atmosphere at many sermons, including public sermons at Paul's Cross, was sober and edifying. But there is no evidence that Shakespeare made it a point to attend a wide variety of sermons throughout London as Manningham did.

7. Little more than pamphlets, very few of these petty school primers have survived. But compare *RSTC* 16090–93, 20377.3, 20377.5.

3
Criteria for a Valid Reference

The following events in Shakespeare's plays that have been put forward by various authorities as being based on Scripture, or at least having been inspired by Scripture, demonstrate the need for establishing guidelines as to what should be included in any list of biblical references and echoes in Shakespeare's plays. Most of these parallels have been suggested by well-known Shakespeare scholars.

1. When Brutus's boy falls asleep, it is reminiscent of the apostles in Gethsemane, to whom Jesus said, "What? coulde ye not watch with me one houre?"
2. The crowing of the cock in *Hamlet* echoes the crowing of the cock in the New Testament at the time of Christ's betrayal.
3. Lady Macbeth's sleepwalking parallels John 12.35: "He that walketh in the dark, knoweth not whither he goeth." So also Lady Macbeth, a wanderer in darkness, does not know whither she goes.
4. Macbeth's cut-off head recalls King Saul's (1 Samuel 31.9).
5. Cleopatra's death with her two attendants parallels the Crucifixion.
6. The child imagery that is so noticeable in *Macbeth* often recalls the Christ child and the Slaughter of the Innocents. Macbeth resembles Herod in that he can kill other children, but not the particular child (Malcolm), or children (Donalbain, Fleance) that represent good.
7. Romeo's words, "Thus with a kiss I die," make his death analogous to Christ's.
8. When the clown in *Antony and Cleopatra* says that the devils can mar five out of every ten women (5.2.276–77), Shakespeare may be adapting Jesus' parable of the virgins who failed to keep oil in their lamps.
9. After Antony falls on his sword and is lifted up limp into Cleopatra's arms, he becomes an ironic Christ.
10. Revelation 11.2 and 13.5 mention forty-two months during which Jerusalem would be trampled underfoot and the satanic beast would be given power to blaspheme. There are also forty-two scenes in *Antony and Cleopatra*. Although the Folio lacks act and scene divisions, editors assign forty-two scenes to the play on the basis of forty-two clearings of

the stage. Shakespeare's audience would not have been numbering the scenes as they unrolled, yet it is conceivable that Shakespeare planned to have forty-two scenes in the play in accord with the biblical number associated with a period of evil glory.

It should be apparent that examples such as these are too tenuous and far-fetched to be accepted as valid and convincing biblical parallels. Even if no claim is made that biblical references are involved, but only echoes and reminiscences of Scripture, yet even these ought to be chosen with more discrimination. In most of these examples the differences far outweigh the similarities and the supposed parallels are inconsistent with both Scripture and Shakespeare's context.

Cleopatra's death with two of her attendants, for example, comes from Plutarch, not from the New Testament. Shakespeare simply follows Plutarch when he has Charmian and Iras die alongside Cleopatra. The disparity between the life and death of Christ and of Cleopatra is too great to be ignored. Cleopatra's two attendants hardly correspond to the two thieves who were crucified with Jesus, one of whom berated him. So far-fetched is the comparison and at the same time so close is Shakespeare to Plutarch (who knew nothing about the Crucifixion) that it is unlikely that the Crucifixion entered Shakespeare's mind, much less that he based this scene on the Gospels. The most that these examples have to recommend them is not their validity, but the critics' ingenuity and cleverness in thinking them up. To include such slender parallels in any list of Shakespeare's biblical references and analogies would only undermine the credibility of the entire work.

What, then, constitutes a valid biblical reference? There are many passages in Shakespeare which we can be certain were drawn from Scripture. When Claudius says that his crime has "the primal eldest curse upon't" (3.3.37), we can be reasonably certain that this is a reference to Cain's murder of Abel, and that Hamlet's words, "there is special providence in the fall of a sparrow" (5.2.219–20), refer to Jesus' words at Matthew 10.29. In the latter example, we not only have a clear reference to Scripture, but are also able to determine which version of the Bible Shakespeare most likely had in mind. The majority of Tudor versions (Tyndale, Coverdale, Matthew, Great, Bishops') say that a sparrow cannot "light on the ground" without God's knowledge. Only the Geneva and Taverner have "fal on the ground"; the Rheims follows the Geneva. Shakespeare probably had the Geneva Bible in mind.

Equally certain would be the reference in *Troilus and Cressida*, that pleasure and revenge "have ears more deaf than adders to the voice" of any true decision (2.2.172). The reference is to Psalm 58.4–5: "Like the deafe Adder

that stoppeth her eares. Whiche refuseth to heare the voyce of the charmer."
A clear reference to Judas occurs in *Timon of Athens*: "Who can call him /
His friend that dips in the same dish?" (3.2.65–66). Jesus identified Judas as
his betrayer with the words, "Hee that dippeth his hand with me in the dish,
he shall betray me" (Matt. 26.23). In addition to passages such as these, there
are the many instances where Shakespeare refers to a Bible character or place
by name, such as Herod, Jephthah, Pilate, Golgotha, and Bashan. Examples
of this type are easy to deal with and leave little doubt as to their origin.

A second category involves passages in which the biblical references are
probable but not altogether certain. The examples in this category consist
mainly of striking words and phrases that seem to be borrowed from Scripture, or else contain figures or ideas that are peculiarly biblical. Hamlet's
words to his mother that Claudius was "like a mildewed ear, / Blasting his
wholesome brother" (3.4.64–65), seem to be a clear reference to Pharaoh's
dream wherein he saw "seuen thinne eares, and blasted with the east winde"
(Gen. 41.6; Shakespeare makes an explicit reference to the same dream in *1
Henry IV*). Othello's statement that Desdemona "turn'd to folly, and she
was a whore" (5.2.132) likewise appears to be a clear reference to Deuter-
onomy 22.21: "For she hath wrought follie in Israel, by playing the whore."
In fact, passages of this nature are so close to Scripture that some might
prefer to place them among the certain rather than the probable references.

When in *Romeo and Juliet* Friar Lawrence describes night's retreat as
"fleckled darkness like a drunkard reels" (2.3.3), or when Hamlet says of the
ghost, "I'll speak to it though hell itself should gape" (1.2.244), we have
passages that seem to be clear verbal echoes of Isaiah 24.20 (Great, Bishops')
"The earth shal reele to and fro like a drunkarde," and of Isaiah 5.14
(according to all versions of the day except the Geneva), "Therefore gapeth
hel." It is possible, of course, that Scripture was not Shakespeare's source
for these expressions, but that he borrowed these memorable phrases and
images from another source. But in the absence of evidence that these expressions occur in any other source, and in view of readily apparent biblical
parallels, the conclusion that these passages were drawn from Scripture
seems sound.

Other passages which contain probable but not altogether certain references would be Macduff's description in *Macbeth* of Malcolm's saintly
mother who "died every day she liv'd" (4.3.111), and Troilus's words to
Cressida that his fears concerning her among the gallant Greek warriors are
prompted by "a kind of godly jealousy" (4.4.80). These seem to allude to
Paul's words, "I dye dayly" (1 Cor. 15.31), and again to Paul's words to the
church at Corinth: "I am ielous ouer you, with godlie ielousie" (2 Cor.
11.2). The description of Coriolanus's fame, "I have seen the dumb men
throng to see him, and / The blind to hear him speak" (2.1.262–63), is

another probable reference. In this example the borrowing from Scripture is not so much verbal as it is the borrowing of an idea, yet Shakespeare's lines are strongly reminiscent of the crowds that thronged about Jesus to be healed, many of whom were blind and dumb. In the play, the crowds welcome Coriolanus home from victory in the field, while in the Gospels they flock to Jesus to be healed; yet the overtones of Scripture are apparent. Since no equivalent passage occurs in Plutarch, Shakespeare's primary source for the play, it appears likely that the passage was inspired by Scripture. Not all of these examples have an equally strong claim to Scripture, but they appear to be sufficiently recognizable and valid to be considered as probable references.

A final example of a probable reference can be found in Antony's words, "Kingdoms are clay" (*Antony and Cleopatra*, 1.1.35). The reference is to Nebuchadnezzar's dream of a great image that had a head of gold and feet that were "part of yron, and part of clay." Daniel interpreted the image as representing a series of kingdoms, and the feet of iron and clay as being a "kingdome ... partly strong, and partly broken" (Daniel 2.33, 42). The book of Daniel, with its vivid dreams and cryptic symbols, was well known in Shakespeare's day and was the subject of much speculation. The Geneva Bible has copious notes on its text, and it was the first book that the Hebraist Hugh Broughton chose to translate into English in 1596.

A third category consists of those passages in Shakespeare where a biblical reference or echo is possible, but where we are dangerously close to having nothing more than a parallel idea, a resemblance rather than a reference. In some of these instances Shakespeare may have echoed Scripture without being aware of it, since the thought had become his own, or he may have completely rephrased a biblical thought or fused it with passages from other sources. Should these passages be included in our list of biblical references? To exclude them, when a good possibility exists that their origin is scriptural, would be to withhold evidence that should be examined when considering Shakespeare's biblical references. It would be better to list these passages about which there is a measure of doubt and let the reader be the final judge.

Consider, for example, Menenius's advice to Coriolanus: "O me, the gods! ... You must desire them / To think upon you" (2.3.54–56). These words seem to echo Jonah 1.6, "Call vpon thy God, if so be that God will thinke vpon us." Was the text of Jonah in Shakespeare's mind as he penned *Coriolanus*? Had he recently read Jonah? We cannot tell. But the phraseology is so close that an item like this should be presented for the reader's consideration.

Just as uncertain is the possible reference at *Othello*, 3.3.117, where Iago says, "My lord, you know I love you." Does Iago's statement echo Peter's threefold reply to Jesus at John 21.15–17, "Yea Lord, thou knowest that I loue thee"? It could, but at the same time, this was a very common expression in Shakespeare's day. Here again, there is no way to tell whether Peter's words crossed Shakespeare's mind as he wrote this line, but the similarity is close enough to warrant including this passage and letting the reader decide for himself whether Shakespeare's line was patterned on Peter's words.

A more troublesome passage occurs in *Timon*: "When the day serves, before black-corner'd night, / Find what thou want'st by free and offer'd light" (5.1.44–45). Are these lines based on Jesus' well-known words at John 9.4, "I must worke the workes of him that sent me, while it is day: the night commeth when no man can worke"? Or is the resemblance accidental? Both passages share the words "day" and "night," and the thought in both passages is the same. Although Shakespeare may have had Jesus' words in mind and reworked them to achieve the required rhyme and meter, only an analogy rather than a reference may be involved. I am inclined to think that more than an analogy is involved, that there are conscious overtones of Jesus' words, particularly since John 9.4 was used in the Commination Service in the Prayer Book, and the margin gives "Iohn 9" as the source. The passage reads, "Therefore brethren, take wee heed betime ... for the night commeth, when none can worke." But since the resemblance is tenuous, I have included this passage with the more doubtful references set in small type and enclosed in brackets, with the observation that John 9.4 occurs in the Commination Service.

Lear's words over dead Cordelia provide a somewhat different example. His moan, "Thou'lt come no more" (5.3.308), parallels Job 7.9–10: "Hee that goeth downe to the graue, shall come vp no more. He shall returne no more." At first glance this example seems to have little merit as a biblical reference, since the thought is common and Lear's expression of grief is normal for the occasion. But this passage has in its favor the fact that Job was a book that Shakespeare knew especially well, and that, in *The Merry Wives of Windsor* (5.1.22–23), he makes a more certain reference to Job's words just three stanzas earlier (7.6), in which he compares man's life to the swiftness of a weaver's shuttle. Thus the chances that Shakespeare was echoing Job 7.9–10 in *King Lear* become more likely. At times, secondary considerations of this nature help us determine whether a passage is best classified as a probable, possible, or doubtful reference.

Only because of Shakespeare's close acquaintance with the book of Job are Brutus's words at *Julius Caesar* 5.5.41–42 included as a possible reference: "My bones would rest, / That have but labor'd to attain this hour." When cursing the day of his birth and longing for death, Job said of the grave, "There they that laboured valiantly, are at rest" (Job 3.17). Although these sentiments are common and the verbal similarity depends on just two words, I have included this passage from *Julius Caesar* as a possible reference because of Shakespeare's frequent reference to Job and since Brutus's words are closer to Scripture than to Plutarch. In Plutarch, Brutus says, "I will looke no more for hope ... but will rid me of this miserable world."

Finally, we might consider examples of passages that I have chosen not to include as possible references and the rationale for omitting them. When, in his funeral oration, Antony says of Caesar, "And none so poor to do him reverence" (3.2.120), these words do not seem to be an echo of Mark 15.19, "bowed the knees, and did him reuerence." "Do him reverence" was a common expression in Shakespeare's day corresponding to the modern expression "show him respect." The phrase was too widely used to warrant the conclusion that Shakespeare had the Gospel account in mind when he used that phrase. Thus this passage is cited only in brackets.

Macbeth contains another common expression that closely resembles not Scripture but the Dedicatory Epistle of the Authorized Version of 1611. In Macbeth's soliloquy,

> Thou sure and firm-set earth,
> Hear not my steps, which way they walk, for fear
> The very stones prate of my whereabout,
>
> (2.1.56–58)

the expression "which way they walk" is almost identical to words that the translators of the King James Bible used when dedicating that version to the king. They said that on the death of Queen Elizabeth, many enemies hoped that "some thicke and palpable cloudes of darkenesse would so haue ouershadowed this Land, that men should haue beene in doubt which way they were to walke."

Most people would probably agree that the resemblance is accidental and that both Shakespeare and the translators were using a common expression. It is hardly likely that the translators borrowed that phrase from Shakespeare's play. Rather, the statement that men were in doubt "which way they were to walke" parallels the modern expressions "they didn't know which way to go," or "they didn't know what to do," expressions so common that they cannot be validly attributed to any particular source.

In the final analysis, the decision whether a passage is a reference to Scripture or has valid overtones of Scripture is a subjective one, based on the reader's personal judgment. If several readers conclude independently that a certain passage refers to Scripture, it may be that Shakespeare also had Scripture in mind when he wrote that passage. I have sought the opinions of others on passages about which I have had doubts, and their reactions were taken into consideration. The opinions over the same passage ranged from skepticism to assurance, with the more religiously inclined tending to detect biblical echoes in almost every line. Macbeth's words, "A little water clears us of this deed" (2.2.64) may remind most people of Pilate's washing his hands to absolve himself of the death of Jesus, but there is no assurance that Shakespeare had Pilate's act in mind. Washing with water has always been a symbol of cleansing from sin or guilt.

King Lear 3.1.5–6 provides another example of a deceptive similarity between Shakespeare and Scripture that may not be a valid echo of Scripture: "Bids the wind blow the earth into the sea, / Or swell the curled waters 'bove the main."

In Psalm 46.2–3, the psalmist expresses his confidence in God, "though the earth be moued: and though the hylles be caryed into the middest of the sea. Though the waters thereof rage and swel."

At first glance the passage from *Lear* appears to be sufficiently close to the Psalm to conclude that Shakespeare had the Psalm in mind. But from the Renaissance point of view, Lear's fulminations were the usual description of the results of "chaos come again," when the established order and degree are not observed. Many writers elaborated on this theme, including Shakespeare in *Troilus and Cressida*. Moreover, the context of trust in God in the Psalm is considerably different from the spirit of *Lear*. Thus the passage in *Lear* is best an analogy to the Psalm rather than a reference.

In the list of biblical references for each of Shakespeare's plays, the following system has been employed to indicate whether a reference is certain, probable, or possible. Whenever a passage in Shakespeare is a certain or a highly probable biblical reference, the Bible text on which it is based is quoted without comment. For passages that are either probable or possible references, the Scripture excerpt is preceded by "Compare...." Thus when Macduff tells Malcolm that his saintly mother "died every day she liv'd," the probability that Shakespeare borrowed this expression from 1 Corinthians is indicated by "Compare 1 Cor. 15.31...." For passages in which the possibility that Shakespeare echoed Scripture is remote, or in which only a resemblance or a parallel idea may be involved, the biblical text is also preceded by "Compare...," but for these entries the comment is also made that most likely an analogy rather than a reference is involved. Finally, there are those instances where simply a common idea or phrase occurs in both Shakespeare and Scripture. These items appear only in small type enclosed in brackets, where they are cited rather than quoted. Some of these bracketed items involve passages that initially seemed to be conscious references to Scripture on Shakespeare's part, passages that would normally appear as valid or possible references. But a check of Shakespeare's sources indicated that his inspiration for the phrase or idea was not Scripture but secular sources, such as Holinshed, Cinthio, Bandello, or Plutarch. In these instances the secular source is also pointed out in the bracketed entry.

I have made every effort to find all the biblical and liturgical references in

Shakespeare's plays. I have also read all the significant scholarship, not only on Shakespeare's use of Scripture, but also on religious themes found in Shakespeare's plays. Whenever a biblical parallel suggested by the scholarship does not appear in this volume, it generally indicates that I have rejected that parallel as being invalid.

Scholars with varying degrees of religious commitment are generally the ones who find an excess of biblical analogies and meanings in Shakespeare's every word, and who try to justify their conclusions by tenuous and contrived arguments. But we must be careful not to read into Shakespeare something that is not there, nor to discover our own religious meanings in Shakespeare rather than Shakespeare's meanings. These critics could have eliminated many of the misleading similarities they have pointed out between Shakespeare and Scripture had they simply checked Shakespeare's secular sources to ascertain if the material actually came from those sources rather than from Scripture. Other faulty parallels could have been eliminated simply by weighing the similarities against the differences. If the differences far outweigh the similarities, and Shakespeare's context does not lend itself to such a comparison, then the comparison is clearly without merit and contrived.

Although I have sought the opinions of others regarding the validity of some of the biblical references, particularly the less certain ones, in the final analysis the responsibility for the choice of passages that appears in this volume is mine. And although the decision on the validity of any reference is necessarily subjective, it has been tempered, I hope, by a thorough knowledge of Shakespeare, Shakespeare's sources, Scripture, and the Anglican liturgy.

4
Biblical and Liturgical References in Shakespeare's Tragedies

Titus Andronicus

Titus Andronicus was one of the most popular plays in Shakespeare's day. Not only did three Quarto editions appear prior to the First Folio (1594, 1600, 1611), but as late as 1614 Ben Jonson, in the Induction to *Bartholomew Fair*, complained about the continued popularity of *Titus* and *The Spanish Tragedy*, about those who "will sweare, *Ieronimo*, or *Andronicus* are the best plays." Like *The Spanish Tragedy*, *Titus Andronicus* is a Senecan-type revenge play suited to the English popular theater, employing many sensational theatrical devices. Much has been written about the authorship and date of the play, but most authorities are now convinced that the play is entirely Shakespeare's and that it can best be dated ca. 1590–93.

Shakespeare's main source for the play has been lost, making it more difficult in *Titus* than in any of Shakespeare's tragedies to determine which biblical references he borrowed from his main source and which he himself added to the play. But it appears likely that the anonymous mid-eighteenth-century chapbook, *The History of Titus Andronicus*, was derived from and was substantially the same as Shakespeare's original source. The chapbook account of Titus contains one clear reference to Scripture (the Apocryphal account of Susanna and the Elders) and two other expressions which may have been borrowed from Scripture, but Shakespeare used none of these in his play.

Secondary sources for *Titus* include Ovid, Seneca, and Plutarch. Shakespeare knew Ovid's parallel tale of Philomela (*Metamorphoses* 6) which he refers to four times in *Titus*, and the way he handles his theme reflects Ovid's urbane, detached style. Several of Seneca's plays, especially *Thyestes*, influenced Shakespeare, and the Latin at 2.1.135 and 4.1.81–82 is taken from Seneca's *Hippolytus*. He also took several names and ideas from Plutarch's *Lives*. But Shakespeare did not borrow any biblical references from these works or from the Elizabethan translations of these works. In a few instances in the play (3.1.230; 5.2.183; 5.3.197–99) Shakespeare's lines resemble both Scripture and one of his nonbiblical sources. But the resemblance to Scripture in these passages seems to be accidental; Shakespeare was probably following his source, which contained an expression or a situation that was parallel to Scripture.

Finally, there are several tantalizing parallels between *Titus* and *The Spanish Tragedy*: Titus's feigned madness, his laughter (3.1.263–65), his digging in the earth (4.3.11–14), and the frequent use of Latin in both plays. The 1592 edition of *The Spanish Tragedy* contains seven probable and three possible references to Scripture, but none of these were borrowed by Shakespeare. Thus it appears safe to conclude that most of the biblical references which Shakespeare makes in *Titus* originated with him as he wrote the play and were not borrowed from his sources. Judging from Shakespeare's usual practice, even if the main source for *Titus* contained many biblical references, he probably borrowed few, if any, of them.

Almost half of the biblical references in *Titus* are to Job, the Psalms, Ecclesiastes, and Lamentations. No references occur in Act 2 of the play.

In the list that follows, page numbers cited for Seneca and the anonymous chapbook that are preceded by the number 6, as in (6.68), refer to volume 6 of Bullough.

1.1.55:   Commit my cause in balance to be weigh'd.

Compare Job 31.6: "Let God weigh me in the iust balance."
Compare Job 6.2: "Oh that my griefe were well weighed, and my miseries were laied together in the balance."
Compare Daniel 5.27: "Thou art wayed in the balance."
Shakespeare was probably using a common expression rather than making a reference to Scripture. The expression occurs frequently in English literature. Chaucer used it in "The Monk's Tale" (2586).

1.1.83:   These that I bring unto their latest home.

Compare Eccles. 12.6, Bishops': "Because man goeth to his long home."
Eccles. 12.5, Geneva: "For man goeth to the house of his age."
The Coverdale, Matthew, Taverner, and Great Bibles agree with the Bishops'. Thus if Shakespeare had Ecclesiastes in mind in this passage, his reference would be to any version of his day except the Geneva.

1.1.117–18:   Wilt thou draw near the nature of the gods?
              Draw near them then in being merciful.

A common thought. But compare the following prayer in the Litany: "O God, whose nature and propertie is euer to haue mercie...."
Compare also the Communion Service: "Thou art the same Lord, whose property is alwayes to haue mercy."
See also Ps. 145.8; 103.8; Ex. 34.6–7; Micah 7.18; Num. 14.18; etc.

Cicero expressed a similar thought: "Homines enim ad deos nulla re propius accedunt quam salutem hominibus dando." (In no way do men come nearer to the gods than by giving prosperity—or doing good—to men.) *Pro Ligario*, 12.38.

1.1.150–56:   In peace and honor rest you here, my sons,
                      ... repose you here in rest,
                      Secure from wordly chances and mishaps!
                      Here lurks no treason, here no envy swells,
                      · · · · · · · · · · · · · ·
                      No noise, but silence and eternal sleep.
                      In peace and honor rest you here, my sons!

Compare the words "rest," "chances," "envy," and "silence" with the parallel words in the following passages, all of which pertain to death, and all of which are taken from the Psalms and the "wisdom literature" of the Bible, books that Shakespeare knew particularly well:

Job 3.17–18: "There they that laboured valiantly, are at rest. The prisoners rest together, and heare not the voyce of the oppressour."
Eccles. 9.6: "Their loue, and their hatred, and their enuie is now perished."
Eccles. 9.11: "I sawe vnder the sunne that ... time and chance commeth to them all."
Ps. 115.17: "The dead praise not thee ... neyther al they that goe downe into the scilence."

1.1.331–32:   She will a handmaid be to his desires,
                      A loving nurse, a mother to his youth.

Compare 1 Sam. 25.41: "Let thine handmaid be a seruant to wash the feete of the seruants of my lord."
The similarity is not so much in language ("handmaid" was the usual term for a female servant) as it is in context. In each instance a woman accepts the marriage proposal of a ruler and seeks to express her unworthiness for such a favor by saying that she is more fit to be his servant than his wife. Since Tamora's response occurs in none of Shakespeare's known sources, it is likely that he borrowed it from Scripture.

[1.1.426: Acts 17.31.]

[2.4.15: Jer. 51.39, 57.]

3.1.16, 22:   O earth, ...

. . . . .

So thou refuse to drink my dear sons' blood.

Compare Gen. 4.11: "The earth, which hath opened her mouth to receiue thy brothers blood."
Compare Heb. 6.7: "The earth whiche drinketh in the raine."

3.1.206:   Here I lift this one hand up to heaven.

Compare Lam. 2.19: "Lift vp thine hands towarde him for the life of thy yong children."
Titus allowed his hand to be cut off in order to gain the lives of his sons, but the resemblance is probably accidental.
Compare Dan. 12.7: "When he helde vp his right hande, and his left hand vnto heauen."
Compare also *Titus* 3.2.42: "Thou shalt not sigh, nor hold thy stumps to heaven."

3.1.216:   Is not my sorrow deep, having no bottom?

Compare Lam. 1.12: "See, if there be any sorowe like vnto my sorowe."
Compare Lam. 1.18: "I pray you, all people, and behold my sorowe."

[3.1.225: Job 7.12.]

[3.1.228–29: Lam. 2.18–19; 3.48–49, 54.]

3.1.230:   For why my bowels cannot hide her woes.

Compare Lam. 1.20: "Howe I am troubled: my bowels swel."
Compare Lam. 2.11: "Mine eies do faile with teares: my bowels swell."
But compare Seneca's *Thyestes*, one of Shakespeare's sources for *Titus*, in which the Chorus says, "the tremblyng bowells shake" to hear of what happened to Thyestes's sons; and, after having dined on his sons, Thyestes asks, "What tumulte tumbleth so my gutts, and dothe my bowells gnawe?" (6.68, 70)

[3.1.237–38: Lam. 1.21; 2.17.]

3.1.242:   Be my heart an ever-burning hell!

Derived ultimately from the Bible's descriptions of hell.
Rev. 20.10: "A lake of fire and brimstone, ... shalbe tormented ... for euermore."
See also Matt. 25.41.

3.1.244:   To weep with them that weep.

Rom. 12.15: "Weepe with them that weepe."

3.1.263–65:   *Marc.* ... Now is a time to storm, why art thou still?
              Tit. Ha, ha, ha!
              Marc. Why dost thou laugh? It fits not with this hour.

Compare Eccles. 3.1, 4: "To all thinges there is an appoynted time.... A time to weepe, and a time to laugh."
Perhaps an analogy rather than a reference. But Marcus's words that this is a time to rage and not to laugh suggest a reference to Ecclesiastes. Titus's laughter in this passage has been compared to that of Hieronimo in *The Spanish Tragedy* 3.11.30–31.

3.1.273–74:   Till all these mischiefs be return'd again,
              Even in their throats that hath committed them.

Compare Ps. 7.16, Geneva: "His mischiefe shall returne vpon his owne head."
Psalter (Ps. 7.17): "His trauaile shal come vpon his owne head."
If Shakespeare had the Psalm in mind, then in this passage he reflects the Geneva version of the Psalms rather than the Psalter commonly used in the Church, the version of the Psalms that his plays generally reflect.
Shakespeare may have substituted the word "throats" for "heads," since that word occurs several times in his sources. It occurs three times in the chapbook, which was probably based on the same lost source that Shakespeare used (6.42–43), once in the ballad that was published with the chapbook (6.48), twice in Ovid's story of Philomela (6.54, 57), and in Seneca's revenge tragedy, *Thyestes* (6.66). In each instance the context is that of a throat being slit, or of Lavinia offering her throat to her ravishers rather than losing her honor (6.42, 54).

[3.2.23: Ecclus. 30.24.]

3.2.37–38:   She says, she drinks no other drink but tears,
             Brew'd with her sorrow.

Compare Ps. 80.5: "Thou feedest them with the bread of teares: and geuest them plenteousnesse of teares to drinke."

4.1.96–97:   But if you hunt these bear-whelps, then beware,
             The dam will wake.

2 Sam. 17.8: "Are chafed in minde as a beare robbed of her whelpes."
Hosea 13.8: "I will meete them, as a beare that is robbed of her whelpes."
Prov. 17.12: "It is better for a man to meete a beare robbed of her whelpes, then a foole in his follie."

4.1.128–29: But yet so just that he will not revenge.
             Revenge the heavens for old Andronicus!

Compare Rom. 12.19: "Auenge not your selues, ... for it is written, Vengeance is mine: I wil repay, saith the Lord."
A common Elizabethan theme, often repeated in the homilies.

4.2.32–33:   And now, young lords, was't not a happy star
             Led us to Rome ...?

With clear overtones of the star that led the Magi to Jesus. Matt. 2.2, 9.

4.2.41–43:   *Dem.* I would we had a thousand Roman dames
             At such a bay, by turn to serve our lust.
             Chi. A charitable wish, and full of love.

Probably a play on "loue" and "charitie" at Romans 13.9–10. If so, this would be according to the Bishops' Bible: "For this: Thou shalt not commit adulterie, thou shalt not kyl, ... thou shalt not lust ... is in fewe woordes comprehended in this sayeing: Namely, Thou shalt loue thy neyghbour as thy selfe.   [10]Charitie woorketh no yl to his neighbour, therefore the fulfyllyng of the lawe is charitie."
Though all versions have "Loue thy neighbour as thy selfe" in verse 9, only the Bishops' has "charitie" in the following verse. The other versions (Tyndale, Coverdale, Matthew, Taverner, Great, Geneva, Rheims) have "loue" rather than "charitie" in verse 10: "Loue doeth not euill to his

neighbour: therfore is loue the fulfilling of the Law" (Geneva); "Loue hurteth not hys neighbour. Therefore is loue the fulfyllyng of the law" (Taverner, Great).

That Shakespeare probably had the Bishops' Bible in mind in this passage can be seen by comparing *Love's Labor's Lost* 4.3.361–62, where the reference to Romans 13 according to the Bishops' is more obvious: "For charity itself fulfills the law, / And who can sever love from charity?"

4.2.98:   Ye white-lim'd walls!

Compare Acts 23.3: "Thou whited wall."
Compare also Matt. 23.27: "For ye are like vnto whited tombs."
If Shakespeare had Acts 23.3 in mind, it would have been according to the Geneva version. All other versions except the Rheims New Testament have "painted wal." The Rheims followed the Geneva, "thou whited wall." Again, at Matt. 23.27, only the Geneva has "whited tombs." The other versions have either "paynted tombes" (Tyndale, Matthew, Taverner) or "painted sepulchres" (Coverdale, Great, Bishops'). The Rheims has "whited sepulchres."

[5.1.71–72, 80: Matt. 5.33, Tyndale, Coverdale, Matthew, Taverner.]

5.1.147–50:   If there be devils, would I were a devil,
               To live and burn in everlasting fire,
               So I might have your company in hell,
               But to torment you with my bitter tongue!

Derived ultimately from Scripture.
Matt. 25.41: "Depart from me ye cursed, into euerlasting fire, which is prepared for the deuil and his Angels."
Rev. 20.10: "And the deuill that deceyued them, was cast into a lake of fire and brimstone, where the beast and the false prophet shalbe tormented euen day and night for euermore."

5.2.183:   The basin that receives your guilty blood.

Compare the wording of Gen. 4.11: "The earth, which hath opened her mouth to receiue thy brothers blood."
See 3.1.16, 22, above.
But compare the chapbook: "Lavinia, by his Command, held a Bowl

between her Stumps to receive the Blood" (6.43).

Since the eighteenth-century chapbook was probably derived from and was substantially the same as Shakespeare's original source for the play, Shakespeare probably borrowed this passage from his source, rather than from Scripture. It is possible that the lost source, in turn, borrowed the phrase from Scripture, but in the absence of that source, this cannot be determined.

[5.2.191: Ps. 67.6; Ezek. 34.27, Bishops'.]

5.3.197–199:   No mournful bell shall ring her burial,
                But throw her forth to beasts and birds to prey:
                Her life was beastly and devoid of pity.

Compare 2 Kings 9.36–37: "In the fielde of Izreel shall the dogs eate the flesh of Iezebel. And the carkeis of Iezebel shalbe as doung vpon the ground."

Compare also 1 Kings 21.23: "The dogs shall eate Iezebel."

But compare the following passages from Seneca's *Thyestes*:

Lye they in feeldes, a foode out floong for fleeyng foules to waste?
Or are they kept a praye, for wylde and brutyshe beasts to eate?

(6.71)

What coulde be more? to cruell beasts he cast
Perhapps their bodies to be torne, ... though them for foode
   to fowles in pastures wyde
He had out throwen, or them for pray to cruell beasts woulde flyng.

(6.67)

In both Shakespeare and Scripture, the context is that of a wicked queen who would not be given a decent burial. The passages in *Thyestes*, on the other hand, refer to the bodies of the two sons of Thyestes, which he had just eaten. But the passage in 2 Kings mentions only dogs eating the flesh of Jezebel, while both Shakespeare and Seneca's play say that birds ("fowles") and beasts would feed on the dead bodies. Thus it is uncertain which source Shakespeare had in mind, or whether he combined elements from both sources. His reference may be to *Thyestes* alone, and the similarity to 2 Kings, a coincidence.

Similar words occur in part 2 of the anonymous play *The Troublesome Reign of King John*, published in 1591: "Cast out o' door, denied his burial rite, / A prey for birds and beasts to gorge upon" (1.35–36).

Some have surmised that the author of *The Troublesome Reign* borrowed these words from Shakespeare's play, which would put the composition of *Titus Andronicus* at about 1590 or even earlier. But the relationship between the two plays is uncertain.

Romeo and Juliet

"The most excellent and lamentable Tragedie, of Romeo and Iuliet" was well known in Elizabethan times, and Shakespeare could have borrowed the tale from a number of sources. His main source was Arthur Brooke's *The Tragicall Historye of Romeus and Iuliet*, first published by Tottel in 1562 and reprinted in 1582 and 1587. Brooke appears to have been a stern Protestant moralist. In his address to the reader, he goes out of his way to inveigh against superstitious friars and "auriculer confession (the kay of whoredome, and treason)," and to exhort his readers to refrain from "the lustes of wanton fleshe." His only other surviving work is a theological treatise, *An Agreement of sundry places of Scripture seeming in shew to Iarre*, translated from the French and published in 1563. But except for the prefatory address, little of Brooke's religious bias shows up in *Romeus and Iuliet*. Friar Lawrence and the Church of Rome are treated favorably, and there are no more than twenty clear or possible biblical references throughout the poem.

Although Shakespeare followed Brooke's plot carefully and often elaborated on many details in the poem, he borrowed none of Brooke's biblical references. Both the biblical references and the many religious images in the play are Shakespeare's own. Brooke, who died the year before Shakespeare was born, claimed that he "saw the same argument lately set foorth on stage," but if so, that pre-Shakespearean play has not survived. Nor is there evidence that Shakespeare worked from an older play.

Secondary sources that Shakespeare may have consulted include Bandello's story of Romeo and Julietta (1554), and the translations and adapations of it by Pierre Boaistuau (1559) and William Painter (1567). Bandello's Italian narrative is lucid and direct, while Boaistuau made many melodramatic additions and repeatedly moralized when he translated Bandello into French. Painter's English version was a close translation of Boaistuau. But none of these works had any discernible influence on Shakespeare's biblical references. Painter's translation, included in his well-known collection of tales, *The Palace of Pleasure*, is the most likely work that Shakespeare would have read in addition to Brooke. Painter's account contains at least ten clear biblical references (to Joshua commanding the sun to stand still, to Christ weeping, to Heb. 11.36, 1 Cor. 15.52, and other texts), an equal number of less certain references, and a large number of religious images. But if

Shakespeare consulted Painter, he made no use of these references, even as he made no use of Brooke's.

Shakespeare may also have read the Italian versions of the Romeo and Juliet story by Luigi da Porto and Luigi Groto, but the few parallels between these possible sources and Shakespeare's play may be accidental and contain no biblical references. From Daniel's *Complaint of Rosamond* and Sidney's *Astrophel and Stella* Shakespeare borrowed several images, phrases, and ideas, but no Scripture.

In the list that follows, line numbers for Brooke's poem refer to volume 1 of Bullough, pages 284–363. Brooke's poem is not as dull as some claim. In spite of its weaknesses, it contains many vivid scenes and gave Shakespeare all the background material that he needed for his first major play.

For a first work, Brooke's poem shows much promise. The loss to literature by his premature death can be compared to the loss from Sidney's or even Marlowe's death. Had he lived longer, he might have become an important Renaissance poet.

1.1.15–16:   Women, being the weaker vessels.

1 Peter 3.7: "The woman, as vnto the weaker vessell."
Compare *Hamlet* 1.2.146.

1.1.65:   You know not what you do.

Compare Luke 23.34: "They know not what they doe."
Only the Geneva has "know." All other Protestant Tudor Bibles have "wote": "They wote not what they doo." But if Shakespeare had Luke 23.34 in mind in this line, that does not necessarily indicate that he echoes the Geneva rather than the other versions. Shakespeare seldom uses "wot" ("wote") throughout his plays; his overwhelming preference is for the modern word "know." The Rheims New Testament followed the Geneva at Luke 23.34: "They know not what they doe."

[1.1.65, 68: Matt. 26.52; John 18.11.]

2.2.28–32:   As is a winged messenger of heaven
              Unto the white-upturned wond'ring eyes
              Of mortals that fall back to gaze on him,
              When he bestrides the lazy puffing clouds,
              And sails upon the bosom of the air.

Compare Acts 1.9–11: "While they behelde, he was taken vp: for a cloude tooke him vp out of their sight. And while they looked stedfastly toward heauen, as he went, beholde, two men stoode by them in white apparel, which also said, ... Why stand ye gasing into heauen?"

2.2.112:   Do not swear at all.

Compare Matt. 5.34: "Sweare not at all."
Compare the homily "Against Swearing and Periury," part 1, which cautions against oaths: "He should not need to sweare at all.... When they should not sweare."

2.2.113–14:   Or if thou wilt, swear by thy gracious self,
              Which is the god of my idolatry.

Heb. 6.13: "For when God made the promes to Abraham, because hee had no greater to sweare by, he sware by him selfe."

2.3.3:   And fleckled darkness like a drunkard reels.

Compare Isa. 24.20, Great, Bishops': "The earth shal reele to and fro like a drunkarde."
Geneva: "The earth shal reele to and fro like a drunken man."
Coverdale, Matthew, Taverner: "The earth shal stacker like a dronken man."
Shakespeare appears to be closest to the Great and Bishops' Bibles, but his choice of the word "drunkard" may have been dictated by his metrical needs.
Compare Ps. 107.27: "They reele to and fro, and stacker like a drunken man."
See the comment on Ps. 107.27 at *Othello* 2.1.187–89.

2.3.27–30:   Two such opposed kings encamp them still
             In man as well as herbs, grace and rude will;
             And where the worser is predominant,
             Full soon the canker death eats up that plant.

With possible overtones of Scripture, although this was a common Renaissance concept.

Compare Gal. 5.17: "For the flesh lusteth against the Spirit, and the Spirit against the flesh: and these are contrarie one to the other, so that yee cannot do ... that ye would."

Compare Rom. 6.12–13: "Let not sinne reigne therefore in your mortal body, that ye should obey it.... But giue your selues vnto God."

Compare also Rom. 6.21, "the ende of those things is death," and 7.18–24, "I delite in the Lawe of God, concerning the inner man: but I see another Law in my members, rebelling against the Lawe of my minde."

Brooke also has several references to the conflict in man between reason and passion: "For manly reason is quite from of thy mynd outchased, / And in her stead affections lewd, and fansies highly placed" (1355–56).

"Affections foggy mist, thy febled sight doth blynde / But if that reasons beames agayne might shine into thy mynde...." (1419–20).

2.3.86:   Doth grace for grace and love for love allow.

Compare John 1.16: "Of his fulnes haue we all receiued, and grace for grace."

2.6.11–14:   The sweetest honey
            Is loathsome in his own deliciousness,
            And in the taste confounds the appetite.
            Therefore love moderately.

Compare Prov. 25.16: "If thou haue found honie, eate that is sufficient for thee, least thou be ouerful, and vomit it."

Compare also Prov. 27.7.

2.6.37:   Till Holy Church incorporate two in one.

With overtones of man and wife being made one flesh at marriage. See Gen. 2.24, Matt. 19.5–6, Mark 10.7–8, the Marriage Service, and the homily on Matrimony.

[3.1.35: Matt. 5.36.]

[3.1.56: Judges 19.20; Luke 24.36; John 20.26.]

3.1.97–98:   Ask for me to-morrow, and you shall find me a grave man.

Compare Job 7.21, Coverdale, Matthew, Taverner, Great, Bishops': "Nowe must I sleepe in the dust, and yf thou seekest me to morowe in the mornyng, I shal not be" [or, "I shall be gone"].

Geneva, Rheims: "Nowe shall I sleepe in the dust, and if thou seekest me in the morning, I shall not be."

Perhaps an unconscious echo rather than a reference. If Shakespeare had Job 7.21 in mind, he is least like the popular Geneva Bible and closer to the other versions of the day. The Rheims adopted the Geneva reading.

[3.2.59: Gen. 3.19; Eccles. 12.7.]

3.2.67: Then, dreadful trumpet, sound the general doom.

A general reference to the day of judgment.
1 Cor. 15.52: "At the last trumpet: for the trumpet shall blowe."
Compare also Matt. 24.31: "A great sounde of a trumpet," as well as the blowing of the seven trumpets at the end of the world in Rev. 8 to 11.
The closest parallel in Brooke comes from a different context, that of the Prince's sentence on Romeo: "And what appoynted payne / Is published by trumpets sound" (1275–76).

3.2.76: Wolvish ravening lamb!

Matt. 7.15: "Beware of false Prophets, which come to you in sheepes clothing, but inwardely they are rauening wolues."

[3.2.81–82: 2 Cor. 11.14.]

[3.2.85–87: Hosea 4.1–2.]

3.2.109–11:   I would forget it fain,
              But O, it presses to my memory
              Like damned guilty deeds to sinners' minds.

Ps. 51.3, Morning and Evening Prayer: "I doe knowe mine owne wickednesse, and my sinne is alway against mee."
Ps. 51.3: "For I knowledge my faultes: and my sinne is euer before me."
Compare also the General Confession, Communion Service: "The remembrance of them is grieuous vnto us, the burthen of them is intolerable."

3.3.129: Killing that love which thou hast vow'd to cherish.

Marriage Service: "I N. take thee N. to my wedded wife, ... to loue, and to cherish, till death vs depart."
"I N. take thee N. to my wedded husband, ... to loue, cherish, and to obey, till death vs depart."
Although *Romeo and Juliet* has a Catholic setting, the reference is to the Anglican marriage service. Compare 4.1.12–14, below.

[3.3.152–54: Ps. 126.6–7 (126.5–6, Geneva). But see Brooke 1447–48, 1676, 2554, 1220, where similar expressions occur.]

3.4.4: We were born to die.

Compare Wisdom 5.13: "Assoone as we were borne, wee began to draw to our ende."

[3.5.72–73: Ecclus. 38.17–23, Noble. But compare Brooke 1211–12, 1789–98. The same thought also occurs in Bandello, and especially in Boaistuau and Painter.]

3.5.116: Now, by Saint Peter's Church and Peter too. (Also 114, 154.)

A reference to the Apostle Peter. In Brooke, the church is "sainct Fraun-cis" (2006, 2200, 2693). Shakespeare changes this to Saint Peter and makes Friar Lawrence swear by Saint Francis (2.3.65; 5.3.121).

[3.5.137: Isa. 5.4.11. But see lines 211, 800, 1515 of Brooke.]

3.5.226–27: *Jul.* Speak'st thou from thy heart?
  Nurse. And from my soul too.

Compare Mark 12.30: "With all thine heart, and with al thy soule."
Compare also Matt. 22.37; Deut. 6.5.

[3.5.237–39: James 3.8–10. But see Brooke 1145–46.]

4.1.12–14: Her tears,
  Which, too much minded by herself alone,
  May be put from her by society.

When Paris informs Friar Lawrence that he and Juliet are shortly to be wed, Paris explains that her father wishes to hasten the marriage so that Juliet may no longer be alone to weep immoderately. An early marriage will provide the needed companionship or "society" for her. In the Marriage Service, this companionship or "society" is given as the third reason for which God ordained marriage. "Thirdly, for the mutuall societie, helpe, and comfort, that the one ought to haue of the other."

4.1.38:   Or shall I come to you at evening mass?

On the basis of this line, some have concluded that Shakespeare could not have been a Roman Catholic, since normally mass was not celebrated in the evening in the Catholic Church. Thus, Shakespeare's ignorance of Catholic practice is regarded as an argument in favor of his Protestantism.

While it is true that afternoon and evening masses were forbidden in the Catholic Church, the prohibition was often ignored. So much so, that a formal edict specifically forbidding them was issued at the twenty-second session of the Council of Trent (1545–63), and in 1566 Pope Pius V had to renew the ban. But afternoon masses were still observed in Germany in the following century, and in Italy evening masses continued to be observed for another three hundred years. The 19th-century liturgical writer Friedrich Brenner says that in spite of the prohibition, evening masses were still being said in Venice, Vercelli, Verona, and even in the Papal chapel in Rome. Thus the argument that Shakespeare's mention of an evening mass indicates a Protestant ignorance of Catholic customs is not conclusive.

[4.1.43: 1 Thess. 5.26; Rom. 16.16; 1 Cor. 16.20; 2 Cor. 13.12.]

4.1.55:   God join'd my heart and Romeo's, thou our hands.

Marriage Service: "Then shall the Priest ioyne their hands together, and say. Those whom God hath ioyned together, let no man put asunder."

Matt. 19.16: "Let not man therefore put asunder that, which God hath coupled together."

In both Brooke and Painter, Juliet clasps her hands and tells the friar that if she is forced to marry Paris, she would slay herself "with these two hands which you see ioyned before you" (Painter); "with these two handes which joynde unto the heavens I stretch" (Brooke, 2023). The word "joynde" apparently suggested the Marriage Service to Shakespeare, and in the play Juliet's words seem to be a clear reference to the Marriage Service.

[4.1.77–78: Matt. 4.5–6; Luke 4.9.]

4.4.27–28:   The bridegroom he is come already,
                     Make haste, I say.

Matt. 25.6: "Behold, the bridegrome commeth: go out to meete him."

[4.5.49–54: Ezek. 30.2–3, Noble. But Painter also has the expression "woefull Dayes" when Juliet is found dead.]

4.5.126–28:   When griping griefs the heart doth wound,
                       And dolcful dumps the mind oppress,
                 Then music with her silver sound—

The song Peter sings was written by Richard Edwards and published in the poetical miscellany, *The Paradyse of Daynty Deuises*, which first appeared in 1576:

> Where gripyng grief the hart would wound
>   and dolfull domps the [minde] oppresse
> There Musick with her siluer sound.... (Poem 53)

Compare Sternhold and Hopkins' metrical version of Psalm 30.5–6, which also contains the expression "gripes of griefe": "Though gripes of griefe and panges full sore, / shall lodge with vs all night...."
Psalm 30 was put into meter by John Hopkins and first published in 1549 (*STC* 2420). Edwards's poem may have been influenced by it, but the expressions "gripyng grief" and "gripes of griefe" were not uncommon in Shakespeare's day.

5.3.62:   Put not another sin upon my head.

A common biblical expression. Compare 1 Kings 2.32–33: "The Lorde shal bring his blood vpon his owne head.... Their blood shall therfore returne vpon the head of Ioab, and on the head of his seede."
1 Kings 2.37: "Thy blood shalbe vpon thine owne head."
Compare also 2 Sam. 1.16; 3.29; Josh. 2.19; Judg. 9.57; Ps. 7.16; etc.

[5.3.109–10: Job 17.13–14. Compare Brooke 2366–68.]

5.3.229–30:   I will be brief, for my short date of breath
                       Is not so long as is a tedious tale.

Compare Ps. 90.9: "We bring our yeeres to an ende, as it were a tale that is tolde."

Compare *Macbeth* 5.5.26–27 and the comments thereon.

If Shakespeare had Psalm 90 in mind, Brooke's poem may have reminded him of the Psalm, since Brooke has several passages parallel to the Friar's:

"And eke the sojorne short that I on earth must make" (2891).

"That I will make a short and eke a true dyscourse" (2907).

Compare also line 660 of Brooke, although from a different context: "And of her present state to make a tedious long discoorse." See also lines 2118–20.

[5.3.261: Ecclus. 2.4.]

Julius Caesar

Julius Caesar, Shakespeare's best-known Roman play, is based primarily on Thomas North's translation of Plutarch's *Lives*, which first appeared in 1579. Shakespeare used either that edition or the second edition of 1595; a third edition did not appear until 1603, after Shakespeare's play had been written.

Julius Caesar owes more to Plutarch's "Life of Brutus" than to the *Lives* of Caesar and of Mark Antony combined, since Brutus figures prominently throughout the play. No biblical references occur in these *Lives*.

Although North's text contains no biblical references, some of the biblical references in *Julius Caesar* may have been suggested to Shakespeare by certain phrases and expressions in North's translation. There are several perplexing passages in *Julius Caesar* that resemble both North and Scripture so closely that it is difficult to determine whether the resemblance to Scripture is accidental or whether Shakespeare consciously used Scripture to augment what he found in North. Some of the resemblances are verbal (2.1.327–28; 2.4.39–40); others involve parallel situations or ideas (1.2.20–21; 2.2.126). Both Scripture and North are quoted alongside Shakespeare's lines in these instances so that the reader can judge for himself whether Shakespeare's passage is based on North or on Scripture, or whether Shakespeare combined the two sources.

The number of other sources that Shakespeare appears to have borrowed from is legion. These include translations of Appian, Tacitus, Ovid, and Suetonius; such well-known Renaissance works as Marlowe's translation of Lucan, Kyd's translation of *Cornelia*, Elyot's *Governour*, and *The Mirrour for Magistrates*; and Latin works by Florus, Virgil, and Cicero. There are striking parallels between Shakespeare's play and Orlando Pescetti's Italian play *Il Cesare* (1594). Shakespeare probably looked at Plutarch's *Lives* of Cicero and Cato. And he was no doubt influenced by the drama of his day: the university plays on the life of Caesar; the Roman plays performed at court by child actors; the plays with Roman themes that came from the court circle centering around Mary Sidney, the Countess of Pembroke.

The extent to which these works influenced Shakespeare's play is a matter of dispute. Some think that the extant university play, *Caesar's Revenge*, produced by the students at Trinity College, Oxford, was second in importance only to Plutarch as a source for Shakespeare. Others contend that *Il*

Cesare or Appian's *Civil Wars* exerted a stronger influence on Shakespeare's play than did *Caesar's Revenge*. But none of these works seem to have had any influence on Shakespeare's biblical references. There are more biblical references in the Italian play *Il Cesare* than in any of Shakespeare's other sources, but if Shakespeare read that play, he borrowed none of its references.

Finally, it is possible that *Julius Caesar* was influenced by a lost English or Latin play; this would explain some of the play's departures from Plutarch. A lost play might also have influenced some of the biblical references that Shakespeare makes in the play.

In the list that follows, page numbers preceded by the number 5, as in (5.83), refer to volume 5 of Bullough.

1.1.35:   You blocks, you stones, you worse than senseless things!

Compare the marginal note in the Geneva Bible at Ps. 115.7–8: "They haue handes and touch not: they haue feete and walke not: neither make they a sound with their throte. They that make them are ᶠ like vnto them." Note "f" reads: "As much without sense, as blocks and stones."

Shakespeare's references to the Psalms often reflect the Prayer Book Psalter, which was read continuously in the Morning and Evening Services of the English Church. If Shakespeare's reference in this instance is to the Geneva Bible, it would indicate that his private reading of the Geneva Bible included its version of the Psalms. Compare also *Macbeth* 5.5.49 and *Titus Andronicus* 3.1.273–74.

The expression "blocks and stones," however, may have been a common one. Arthur Golding used it in his address "To the Reader," prefixed to his translation of Ovid's *Metamorphoses*: "And if wee be so drownd in vice that feeling once bee gone, / Then may it well of us bee sayd, wee are a block or stone" (113–14).

[1.2.10: Luke 7.8.]

1.2.15:   Who is it in the press that calls on me?

Compare Mark 5.30: "Hee turned him round about in the prease, and said, Who hath touched my clothes?"
See the comment on the following reference.

1.2.20–21:   *Caes.* Set him before me, let me see his face.
             Cas. Fellow, come from the throng.

Compare Mark 10.49: "Then Iesus stoode still, and commanded him to be
called: and they called the blind, saying vnto him, Be of good comfort: arise,
he calleth thee."

Shakespeare apparently combined elements from North's translation of
Plutarch and from Scripture in this passage. Caesar's being told to beware
the Ides of March comes from North. But Caesar's being called to out of a
crowd of bystanders as he heads a procession, his stopping and requesting
that whoever called him be set before him, and someone in Caesar's train
beckoning the caller to approach Caesar, are apparently borrowed from
Scripture. These details are not in North. North's text simply relates that
"there was a certaine Soothsayer that had geven Caesar warning long time
affore, to take heede of the day of the Ides of Marche" (5.83). To dramatize
that warning, Shakespeare appears to have borrowed from Scripture.

1.2.152–53:   When went there by an age since the great flood
              But it was fam'd with more than with one man?

Compare Genesis chapters 6 to 8, the account of the Flood.
Compare Gen. 10.8–9: "Cush begate Nimrod, who began to be mightie
in the earth. He was a mightie hunter before the Lord. Wherefore it is said,
As Nimrod the mighty hunter before the Lord."
Shakespeare's "great flood" refers either to the biblical Flood or to the
flood of Greek mythology. According to the latter, when Zeus decided to
destroy degenerate mankind by a flood, the only mortals saved for their
piety were Deucalion, the son of Prometheus and Clymene, and his wife,
Pyrrha (*Metamorphoses* 1; Apollodorus 1; Pausanias 1). If Shakespeare had
Greek mythology in mind, the reference would be to the flood associated
with Deucalion. But if he had Scripture in mind, the reference would be
to the Noachian Flood, and the man of fame would be Noah, or perhaps
Nimrod, who greatly distinguished himself among his contemporaries
shortly after the Flood. Shakespeare's reference is probably to the Deucalion
legend, however, since he specifically used that legend in *Coriolanus*, another Roman play: "Martius is proud; who, in a cheap estimation, is worth
all your predecessors since Deucalion" (2.1.90–92). But many persons in
Shakespeare's audience, unacquainted with Greek mythology, would have
been reminded of the Flood of Noah's day.

1.3.91:   You make the weak most strong.

Compare 2 Cor. 12.10: "For when I am weake, then am I strong."

2.1.272–73:   By all your vows of love, and that great vow
Which did incorporate and make us one.

Matt. 19.5–6: "And they twayne shalbe one flesh. Wherefore they are no more twaine, but one flesh."

Gen. 2.24: "Therefore shal man leaue his father and his mother, and shall cleaue to his wife, and they shalbe one flesh."

Portia's request to share Brutus's troubles is from Plutarch's "Life of Brutus" (5.98–99), but her appeal on the basis of their being one is from the Christian tradition. The marriage service quotes Eph. 5.31: "For this cause shall a man leaue father and mother, and shall be ioyned vnto his wife, and they two shall be one flesh." No similar passage occurs in North.

2.1.327–28:   *Bru.* A piece of work that will make sick men whole.
Lig. But are not some whole that we must make sick?

Compare Luke 5.31: "They that are whole, neede not the Physition, but they that are sicke."

Compare also Matt. 9.22: "Thy faith hath made thee whole."

"To be made whole" is a common biblical expression. See Matt. 12.13; 15.28; Mark 5.34; Luke 8.48; 17.19; John 5.6, 14; 7.23; Acts 4.9; 9.34. But North's account is similar: "Brutus, who went to see him beinge sicke in his bedde, and sayed unto him: O Ligarius, in what a time art thou sicke! Ligarius risinge uppe in his bedde, and taking him by the right hande, sayed unto him: Brutus, sayed he, if thou hast any great enterprise in hande worthie of thy selfe, I am whole" (5.96). Amyot: "Je suis sain."

2.2.18:   Graves have yawn'd and yielded up their dead.

The omens in *Julius Caesar* are primarily from Plutarch, who describes the many signs that preceded Caesar's assassination to signify that the death of an outstanding person was about to occur. Similar portents occur in Ovid, Lucan, Virgil, and Appian. The Gospels follow the same tradition when recounting the death of Christ. The opening of graves, however, occurs only in Scripture.

Matt. 27.52: "And the graues did open themselues, and many bodies of the Saints which slept, arose."

See also 1.3.74 and *Hamlet* 1.1.114–16.

[2.2.26–27: Isa. 43.13, Noble. See also Isa. 55.10–11. But the same thought occurs in many of Shakespeare's sources.]

2.2.33: The valiant never taste of death but once.

Matt. 16.28: "There bee some of them that stande here, which shall not taste of death."

See also Mark 9.1; Luke 9.27; John 8.52; Heb. 2.9 for the expression "taste of death."

The word "once," however, apparently comes from North, who says of Caesar: "When some of his frends did counsell him to have a gard for the safety of his person, and some also did offer them selves to serve him: he would never consent to it, but sayd, it was better to dye once, then alwayes to be affrayed of death" (5.78).

Compare 4.3.191, below.

2.2.126: Good friends, go in, and taste some wine with me.

The wine-tasting episode is an addition of Shakespeare. In Plutarch's "Life of Caesar," only Decius Brutus Albinus went to Caesar's house to bring him to the Senate, persuaded him to ignore the omens, and, without partaking of any food or drink, "therewithall he tooke Caesar by the hand, and brought him out of his house" (5.84). In Plutarch's "Life of Brutus," none of the conspirators went to Caesar's house to bring him; they went directly to Pompey's Porch to wait for Caesar. After a considerable delay, caused by Caesar's hesitation over the "unluckie signes of the sacrifices," Caesar arrived without anyone going after him (5.99–101). Thus, whether the drinking of wine together, which Shakespeare added, is modelled on Scripture and constitutes Caesar's "Last Supper" before his betrayal is debatable. Matt. 26.20–29. No equivalent passage can be found in any of Shakespeare's other sources.

Shakespeare, however, may have added Caesar's invitation to drink wine in order to dramatize Plutarch's emphasis on Caesar's hospitality and courtesy. Even when Caesar was a young man, Plutarch says, he was loved by the people not only because of the courteous manner in which he spoke to every man, but also because "he ever kept a good bourde, and fared well at his table, and was very liberall besides." Thus if Shakespeare added this passage in order to dramatize Caesar's reputation for hospitality, that Caesar's home was always open to his friends, then no echoes of the Last Supper are intended. North's marginal gloss when he describes Caesar's hospitality is "Caesar loved hospitalitie" (5.60).

2.4.39–40:   How weak a thing
                  The heart of woman is!

Compare Ezek. 16.30: "Howe weake is thine heart, ... a presumptuous whorish woman."

Compare Plutarch's "Life of Brutus": "I confesse, that a womans wit commonly is too weake to keepe a secret safely" (5.98). Also, "Porcia ... being too weake to away with so great and inward griefe of minde: she coulde hardlie keepe within, but was frighted with everie litle noyse and crie she hearde. ... At length, ... Porciaes weakenesse was not able to holde out any lenger, and thereuppon she sodainlie swounded" (5.100).

[3.1.106: Matt. 27.24.]

[3.2.120: Mark 15.19, Geneva.]

3.2.181:   Brutus, as you know, was Caesar's angel.

Compare Acts 12.15: "Then said they, It is his Angell."

Compare also the Medieval religious tradition of the good and bad guardian angels (Shakespeare's metaphor in Sonnet 144), based ultimately on Jesus' words at Matt. 18.10: "See that ye despise not one of these litle ones: for I say vnto you, that in heauen their Angels alwayes behold the face of my Father which is in heauen." See also Heb. 1.14; Ps. 34.7.

The closest parallel in Plutarch occurs in a completely different context. When Caesar's ghost appears to Brutus, he says, "I am thy ill angell, Brutus" (5.89, "Life of Caesar"); "I am thy evill spirit, Brutus" (5.116 "Life of Brutus"). But the ghost's words in Plutarch do not seem to be Shakespeare's primary inspiration for Antony's words at 3.2.181, since Shakespeare borrowed the words of the ghost in Plutarch for his own ghost scene, in which Caesar's ghost identifies itself as, "Thy evil spirit, Brutus" (4.3.282). Instead, it appears more likely that Shakespeare drew on biblical and religious sources for Antony's words rather than on Plutarch.

No words corresponding to Antony's at Caesar's funeral occur in Plutarch, since Plutarch has no funeral orations but briefly summarizes the substance of what Antony said.

3.2.229–30:   That should move
                    The stones of Rome to rise and mutiny.

Compare Luke 19.40: "If these should holde their peace, the stones would cry."

4.1.50–51: Some that smile have in their hearts, I fear,
Millions of mischiefs.

Ps. 28.3: "Whiche speake frendly to their neighbours, but imagine mischiefe in their hartes."
A clear reference to the Psalter. The Geneva Psalm has: "Which speake
friendly to their neighbours, when malice is in their heartes."

4.2.8–9: Hath given me some worthy cause to wish
Things done undone.

With overtones of the General Confession, Morning and Evening Prayer:
"Wee haue left vndone those things which wee ought to haue done, and we
haue done those things which wee ought not to haue done," based on Matt.
23.23, Bishops'.
Compare *Antony and Cleopatra* 3.1.14; *Othello* 3.3.204; *Coriolanus*
4.7.24–25.

4.3.86: A friend should bear his friend's infirmities.

Rom. 15.1: "We which are strong, ought to beare the infirmities of the
weake."
Shakespeare appears to have had the Geneva Bible in mind. All other
Tudor translations have "beare the fraylenesse"; the Taverner has "beare the
fraylite." Only the Geneva has "beare the infirmities." The Rheims has
"susteine the infirmities."

[4.3.90: 1 Peter 4.8.]

4.3.191: She must die once.

Compare Heb. 9.27: "It is appointed vnto men that they shall once die."
But see the comment on 2.2.33, above, where in North's translation of
Plutarch, Caesar says of himself, "It was better to dye once." Nor was
North using a biblical phrase as he translated, since the word "once" occurs
in Plutarch (*apas*), as well as in Amyot (*une fois*). Thus, it is difficult to
determine whether Shakespeare had Scripture in mind as he penned Brutus's words about Portia, or whether he followed North, where Caesar
speaks of himself.

[4.3.277–79: 1 Sam. 28.13 and Geneva note on 1 Sam. 28.14.]

5.1.48–49:   If arguing make us sweat,
             The proof of it will turn to redder drops.

Compare Luke 22.44: "Being in an agonie, ... his sweat was like droppes of bloud."

The closest parallel in North tells of "one of the Captaines, whose arme sodainly fell a sweating, that it dropped oyle of roses from him" (5.127).

[5.1.88: Gen. 35.29; 49.33; Matt. 27.50; Acts 5.10.]

[5.1.124–25: Matt. 6.34; Great, Bishops', Rheims.]

5.2.5:   And sudden push gives them the overthrow.

Some have thought that this line might be an echo of the Geneva gloss on 2 Chron. 13.15: "Euen as the men of Iudah shouted, God smote Ieroboam." The gloss on "smote" is, "gaue him the ouerthrowe."

But the expression seems to have been common. George Cavendish used the expression in *The Life and Death of Cardinal Wolsey*, written ca. 1556–58, before the Geneva Bible appeared: "By that means we may other [either] escape or elles geve them an ouerthrowe" (EETS edition 40).

Compare also *1 Henry VI* 3.2.106: "We are like to have the overthrow again."

[5.3.95–96: Ps. 37.15.]

5.5.20:   I know my hour is come.

Compare John 2.4: "Mine houre is not yet come."
Closest parallel in North: "Brutus knowing he should dye" (5.89).

5.5.41–42:   My bones would rest,
             That have but labor'd to attain this hour.

Compare Job 3.17: "There they that laboured valiantly, are at rest."
Closest parallel in North: "I will looke no more for hope, ... but will rid me of this miserable world" (5.120).

Hamlet

The Hamlet legend comes down to us from the Danish historian Saxo Grammaticus, who wrote his *Historiae Danicae* toward the end of the twelfth century. Saxo's Latin history, first published in 1514, went through several editions, but it is uncertain if Shakespeare used Saxo's account.

An important source for *Hamlet* that Shakespeare is known to have used was the *Histoires Tragiques*, a collection of tragic stories by François de Belleforest. Belleforest drew on Saxo for his Hamlet story and published it in 1570 in the fifth volume of his collection. At least six editions of volume 5 were published by 1601. The first known English translation of Belleforest's Hamlet account appeared in 1608, making it likely that Belleforest was available to Shakespeare only in French.

Although Saxo's narrative contains only one possible reference to Scripture, Belleforest makes frequent comparison to biblical persons and events as he tediously expands and comments on Saxo's narrative. Shakespeare borrowed none of Belleforest's explicit references; two of the less certain biblical references in Shakespeare, those at 3.4.173–175 and 5.2.385, may have been suggested by Belleforest.

Shakespeare's main source for *Hamlet*, however, was a lost play with the same title, generally called the *Ur-Hamlet*, which became the property of Shakespeare's company in the 1590s. He was also strongly influenced by Kyd's *Spanish Tragedy*. These two plays supplied Shakespeare with many important features that have no counterpart in either Saxo or Belleforest, including the ghost and the play-within-the-play, but they seem to have contributed little, if anything, to his use of Scripture. Certain scenes in *The Spanish Tragedy* are generously sprinkled with religious imagery, both Christian and pagan, but the 1592 edition of the play contains only seven probable references, and the scenes added to the 1602 edition contain but one additional reference, that to Judas, at 3.12A.139. The only reference which Shakespeare may have borrowed from *The Spanish Tragedy* is the reference to Genesis at 3.4.64–65.

The influence of the *Ur-Hamlet* on Shakespeare's biblical references was probably also slight. Since Kyd also appears to have written the *Ur-Hamlet*, it is likely that it contained no more references to Scripture than did its sister play, *The Spanish Tragedy*. The *Ur-Hamlet* was the main source not only for Shakespeare's play but also for *Antonio's Revenge*, written by John Marston at the same time that Shakespeare wrote *Hamlet*. The striking similarities between the two plays in plot, character, and incident on the one hand, and the lack of verbal parallels on the other, can best be explained by the playwrights' mutual dependence on the *Ur-Hamlet*, rather than on Shakespeare or Marston's borrowing from each other. Marston's play also employs many of the devices and ideas used in the *Ur-Hamlet*, but it contains no more than eight biblical references, and none of Marston's references are the same as Shakespeare's. Had any of the references in *Hamlet* and *Antonio's Revenge* been identical, that would strongly suggest that the two dramatists, working separately, had borrowed those biblical references from their common source, the *Ur-Hamlet*. But Marston's references are in no way similar to Shakespeare's. Thus it appears safe to conclude that Shakespeare did not borrow any biblical references from the *Ur-Hamlet*, and that like *The Spanish Tragedy*, the *Ur-Hamlet* made very few references to Scripture. Almost all of the numerous biblical and liturgical references that Shakespeare makes in *Hamlet* originated with him as part of his own design for the play as he reshaped and augmented his sources, and he often used them to emphasize Hamlet's scholarly and contemplative nature.

The number of secondary sources that Shakespeare made use of in *Hamlet* is large. His debt to Timothy Bright's *Treatise of Melancholie* (1586) and to Nashe's *Pierce Penilesse* (1592) is apparent. The Osric scene appears to be based on Florio's English-Italian language book, *Second Frvtes* (1591). The idea of exposing a murderer by means of a play evidently came from the anonymous play *A Warning for Faire Women* (printed 1599) that had been acted by Shakespeare's company. Marlowe, Lyly, Greene, Seneca, Plutarch, Tacitus, Ovid, and Erasmus, among others, all seem to have left some mark on the play. And much that is in *Hamlet*—pirates, ear poison, Gertrude being poisoned by mistake—should be seen against the background of events of that day. But none of these works or events exerted any discernible influence on the many biblical references that Shakespeare makes in the play. Verbal similarities exist between *A Warning for Faire Women* and several of Shakespeare's plays, including *Hamlet*, but none of the biblical references in *Hamlet* were borrowed from that play.

Hamlet, however, gives ample evidence of Shakespeare's exposure to the Homilies. In seven different passages he seems to borrow ideas or phrases from them: 1.2.135; 1.2.146; 1.3.20–24; 3.1.58; 3.1.142–46; 3.3.8–10; 5.2.359–60. Several clear references to the Prayer Book are also evident, such as the reference to the Catechism at 3.2.336, and to the Marriage Service at 3.2.251–52.

Hamlet also affords a good synopsis of which version of the Bible Shakespeare used. Most of Shakespeare's biblical references cannot be traced to one version over another, since large portions of the various English Tudor Bibles are too similar to each other to be differentiated. Yet there are four instances in *Hamlet* where his use of the popular Geneva version in strongly indicated: 3.1.77–79; 3.3.80; 5.1.229–30; and 5.2.219–20. But at 1.2.244, we have an instance in which Shakespeare clearly reflects any version except the Geneva. In the latter passage, he probably echoes one of the two authorized versions, the Bishops' or the Great Bible, although his use of the Coverdale, Matthew, or Taverner Bibles cannot be ruled out. All five of these versions read, "Therefore gapeth hel" at Isaiah 5.14, a much more vivid reading than the Geneva's "Hell hath inlarged it selfe." Shakespeare's frequent preference for the Geneva indicates that that may well have been the Bible he customarily read. But he heard the Bishops' version read at church (he may also have owned a copy) and was quick to adopt a striking image from that version to enhance his art.

In the list that follows, page numbers preceded by the number 7, as in (7.62), refer to volume 7 of Bullough.

1.1.112:   A mote it is to trouble the mind's eye.

Luke 6.42: "Let me pul out the mote that is in thine eye."
Matt. 7.3: "Why seest thou the mote, that is in thy brothers eye?"

1.1.114–16:   A little ere the mightiest Julius fell,
The graves stood tenantless and the sheeted dead
Did squeak and gibber in the Roman streets.

Matt. 27.52: "And the graues did open themselues, and many bodies of the Saints which slept, arose."
Shakespeare combines elements from Plutarch's "Life of Julius Caesar" and from Scripture in this passage. He wrote *Julius Caesar* about two years before *Hamlet*. In *Julius Caesar* Shakespeare followed Plutarch's convention of having supernatural omens appear at Caesar's death in order to signify that the death of a great person had occurred or was about to occur. ("When beggars die there are no comets seen," *Julius Caesar* 2.2.30.) The Gospels employ the same tradition by recording great omens at Jesus' death. The dead coming out of their graves at Caesar's death in both *Hamlet* and *Julius Caesar* (2.2.18), however, was an omen borrowed not from Plutarch, but from Scripture. In both plays Shakespeare combined details from Plutarch and the Bible.

1.1.117–24:   As stars with trains of fire, and dews of blood,
Disasters in the sun; and the moist star

Was sick almost to doomsday with eclipse.
And even the like precurse of fear'd events,
As harbingers preceding still the fates
And prologue to the omen coming on,
Have heaven and earth together demonstrated.

Compare Matt. 24.29: "Immediatly after the tribulations of those daies, shall the sunne be darkened, and the moone shall not giue her light, and the starres shall fal from heauen, and the powers of heauen shalbe shaken."

Compare Acts 2.19–20: "Wonders in heauen aboue, and tokens in the earth beneath, bloud, and fire, and the vapour of smoke. The Sunne shalbe turned into darkenes, and the Moone into bloud."

Compare also Joel 2.30–31; Isa. 13.10; etc.

Shakespeare's portents appear to be closer to Scripture than to the various secular sources that are sometimes cited for them. "Doomsday" suggests a biblical source, and the context of the passages at Matt. 24 and Acts 2 is that of the end of the world.

[1.1.130: Gal. 6.10; 1 Tim. 6.18; Prov. 3.27.]

1.2.70–71:   Do not for ever ...
              Seek for thy noble father in the dust.

Compare Job 7.21: "Nowe shall I sleepe in the dust, and if thou seekest me ... I shall not be found."

See also 2.2.308–309 below, and the reference at *Romeo and Juliet* 3.1.97–98.

1.2.92–102:   To persever
              In obstinate condolement is a course
              Of impious stubbornness, 'tis unmanly grief,
              It shows a will most incorrect to heaven,
              . . . .
              An understanding simple and unschool'd:
              . . . .
              Why should we in our peevish opposition
              Take it to heart? Fie, 'tis a fault to heaven,
              A fault against the dead, a fault to nature.

A common thought. But compare Ecclus. 38.23: "Seeing the dead is at rest, let his remembrance rest, and comfort thy selfe again for him."

Also 38.17: "Make a grieuous lamentation, and be earnest in mourning ...

and that, a day or two, least thou be euill spoaken of, and then comforte thy selfe for thine heauines."

Compare especially lines 95 and 101 with Ecclus. 41.4, which exhorts against excessive mourning: "Why wouldest thou be against the pleasure of the most High?"

[1.2.105: Gen. 4.8–10. Compare 3.3.36–38, below.]

1.2.131: The Everlasting.

Compare Baruch 4.14, 20 and 5.2 for the term "the Euerlasting" with reference to God. Baruch 4.20: "I will call vpon the Euerlasting."

1.2.131–32:   Or that the Everlasting had not fix'd
              His canon 'gainst self-slaughter!

While there is no specific command in Scripture against suicide per se, the Sixth Commandment, "Thou shalt not kill" (Ex. 20.13), or, according to the Prayer Book, "Thou shalt doe no murther," was generally interpreted to also forbid self-slaugher. In the account of Razis's suicide, the Geneva note at 2 Maccabees 14.41 reads: "As this priuate example ought not to be followed of the godlie, because it is contrary to the word of God, although the autor seeme here to approue it."

The Bishops' Bible glosses this text: "This fact is not to be approoued, for that it is contrary to gods commaundement, Thou shalt not kil. Exo. 20. Deute. 5." See also the Bishops' gloss at 1 Maccabees 6.46. The term 'canon" includes canon law, the Church's attitude toward suicide. See also *Cymbeline* 3.4.76–78.

1.2.133–34:   How weary, stale, flat, and unprofitable
              Seem to me all the uses of this world!

Compare Eccles. 1.14: "I haue considered all the workes that are done vnder the sunne, and beholde, all is vanitie, and vexation of the spirit."

Perhaps an analogy rather than a reference. Although there is no verbal similarity, weariness of life and its vain pursuits is an important theme in Ecclesiastes, a book that Shakespeare knew well.

1.2.135:   'Tis an unweeded garden.

Compare the homily "Of the State of Matrimonie": "Though it bringeth forth weedes, ... apply thy selfe to weede out by little and little the noysome weedes."

1.2.146:   Frailty, thy name is woman!

The homily "Of the State of Matrimonie" three times refers to the frailties of women: "She is the weaker vessell, of a fraile heart. ... And therefore considering these her frailties. ..." "The woman is the more fraile partie." "But consider thou againe that the woman is a fraile vessel, and thou art therefore made the ruler and head ouer her, to beare the weakenesse of her ... in her weakenesse and subiection."

These references are largely based on 1 Peter 3.7: "Giuing honour vnto the woman, as vnto the weaker vessell."

[1.2.185: Num. 24.4, Geneva, gloss c; Eph. 1.18, Tyndale, Matthew, Taverner, Great, Bishops'.]

1.2.244:   Though hell itself should gape.

Isa. 5.14, Bishops': "Therefore gapeth hel."
Geneva: "Hell hath inlarged it selfe."
The Coverdale, Matthew, Taverner, and Great Bibles read exactly like the Bishops', and Shakespeare's reference could be to any of these versions. The Bishops' Bible, however, was the version that Elizabeth's government stipulated should be read in the churches after it was published in 1568, and Shakespeare probably had that version in mind.

[1.3.12–14: 1 Cor. 3.16–17; 6.19.]

1.3.20–24:   For on his choice depends
               The safety and health of this whole state,
        · · · · · · · · · · · · · ·
               ... that body
               Whereof he is the head.

An oft-rehearsed theme in Elizabethan England. Compare part 3 of the homily "Concerning Good Order, and Obedience to Rulers and Magistrates": "This is Gods ordinance, ... that the whole body of euery Realme, and all the members and parts of the same, shall be subiect to their head, their king."

See 3.3.8–10, below.

1.3.47–50:   Do not ...
Show me the steep and thorny way to heaven,
Whiles ...
Himself the primrose path of dalliance treads.

Compare Matt. 7.13–14: "It is the wide gate, and broade way that leadeth to destruction: ... The gate is straite, and the waye narrow that leadeth vnto life."

Compare Wisdom 2.7–8.

Compare *Macbeth* 2.3.18–19 and *All's Well* 4.5.54–55 for parallel expressions.

[1.3.47–51: Matt. 23.2–4.]

1.3.53:   A double blessing is a double grace.

Compare the Geneva note on Isa. 40.2: "Double grace, whereas she deserued double punishment."

Compare Ecclus. 26.15: "A shamefast and faithfull woman is a double grace." "Double grace," however, was not an uncommon expression.

Carter claims that Polonius's words find their closest parallel in an alleged note in the Geneva Bible at Isa. 40.2 (actually note "f" on 40.3): "This was fully accomplished when John the Baptist brought tidings of Jesus Christe's comming, who was the true deliverer of His Church from sinne and Satan; *hence this double blessing of the Forerunner and the Messiah announced the sufficient or double grace of the forgiveness of God.*" (Italics added.) But the portion of the note which Carter thinks Shakespeare had in mind, the portion in italics, does not appear in any Geneva Bible at Isaiah 40. I have checked almost every edition of the complete Geneva Bible that was ever published between 1560 and 1644, and the portion of the note in italics appears in none of them.

Carter claims that he used the 1598 edition of the Geneva Bible for the Old Testament and the 1557 edition of the Geneva for the New (Whittingham's New Testament). Only two editions of the Geneva Bible appeared in 1598 (*STC* 2171, 2172), and the note that Carter purports to quote appears in neither of them. Nor does that note appear in any of the "1599" editions. All but one (*STC* 2173) of these editions were actually published after 1599 on the Continent, in Amsterdam and Dort, although their title pages declare them to have been published in London in 1599.

The Geneva note that Carter claims to quote simply does not exist. For a more complete discussion of this passage, see my note, "Shakespeare and the Geneva Bible," in *Studies in Bibliography* 38 (1985): 201–3.

[1.3.68: James 1.19.]

[1.3.72: Ecclus. 19.28.]

1.4.39:   Angels and ministers of grace defend us!

Heb. 1.14: "Are they not all ministring spirites, sent forth to minister?"
Ps. 104.4: "He maketh his angels spirites: and his ministers a flaming fire."
See also Heb. 1.7.

1.5.3:   When I to sulph'rous and tormenting flames. ...

A general reference to religious descriptions of torment that derive ultimately from Scripture.
Rev. 14.10: "Shalbe tormented in fire and brimstone [sulphur]."
See also Rev. 20.10; 21.8.

1.5.11–13:   And for the day confin'd to fast in fires,
             Till the foul crimes done in my days of nature
             Are burnt and purg'd away.

A clear reference to the Roman Catholic doctrine of purgatory that rests largely on church tradition rather than on Scripture.

1.5.22:   To ears of flesh and blood.

A common expression. But compare Matt. 16.17: "Flesh and bloud hath not reueiled it vnto thee."
Eph. 6.12: "Wee wrestle not against fleshe and bloud."
See also Gal. 1.16; Heb. 2.14.

1.5.49–50:   The vow
             I made to her in marriage.

A general reference to the Anglican marriage service.

[1.5.54–55: 2 Cor. 11.14.]

1.5.72–73: Most lazar-like, with vile and loathsome crust
            All my smooth body.

Derived ultimately from the parable of the rich man and Lazarus. That parable was the source of the word "lazar," a person afflicted with a loathsome disease, especially leprosy.

Luke 16.20: "A certeine begger named Lazarus, which was laied at his gate full of sores."

Compare also *The Faerie Queene*, 1.4.3.(6).

1.5.92: All you host of heaven!

The phrase "host of heaven" comes from Scripture. (Heb. *tsva hashamayim.*)

Isa. 34.4: "All the hoste of heauen shalbe dissolued."

1 Kings 22.19: "All the hoste of heauen stood about him."

Acts 7.42: "To serue the host of heauen."

See also Neh. 9.6.

1.5.165: And therefore as a stranger give it welcome.

Compare Heb. 13.2: "Bee not forgetful to lodge strangers: for thereby some haue receiued Angels into their houses vnwares."

Compare also Matt. 25.35.

[1.5.189: John 18.37?]

2.2.178–79: Is to be one man pick'd out of ten thousand.

Compare Eccles. 7.30 (7.28, AV): "I haue found one man of a thousande."

2.2.303–307: What a piece of work is a man, how noble in reason, how
              infinite in faculties, in form and moving, how express and
              admirable in action, how like an angel in apprehension, how
              like a god! the beauty of the world; the paragon of animals.

Compare Ps. 8.4–6: "What is man that thou art so myndful of hym: and the sonne of man that thou visitest hym? Thou makest hym lower then the angels: to crowne hym with glory and worshyp. Thou makest hym to haue dominion of the woorkes of thy handes: and thou hast put al thinges in subiection vnder his feete. Al sheepe and oxen: yea, and the beastes of the feelde."

See also Heb. 2.6–7.

2.2.308:   Yet to me what is this quintessence of dust?

Compare Gen. 3.19: "Thou art dust, and to dust shalt thou returne."
Compare Eccles. 3.20: "All was of the dust, and all shal returne to the dust."
Burial Service: "We therefore commit his body to the ground, earth to earth, ashes to ashes, dust to dust."

2.2.403–12:   *Ham.* O Jephthah, judge of Israel. ...

. . . .

Pol. If you call me Jephthah, my lord, I have a daughter that I love passing well.

A reference to Judge Jephthah, who vowed that if God would give him victory, he would sacrifice whomever first came out of his house to greet him on his return. As a result, he sacrificed his only daughter. Judges 11.30–40. In lines 407–408, 416, and 418, however, Hamlet quotes from a ballad about Jephthah.

Homily "Against Swearing and Periury," part 2: "And Iephtah when God had giuen to him victorie of the children of Ammon, promised (of a foolish deuotion) vnto God, to offer for a sacrifice vnto him, that person which of his owne house should first meete with him after his returne home. By force of which fonde and vnaduised oath, hee did slay his owne and onely daughter. ... Thus the promise which hee made (most foolishly) to God ... most cruelly hee performed."

[2.2.527–32: Ps. 143.2; 130.3; Morning Prayer.]

2.2.598–600:   The spirit that I have seen
                May be a dev'l, and the dev'l hath power
                T' assume a pleasing shape.

2 Cor. 11.14: "Satan him selfe is transformed into an Angel of light." When Saul consulted the Witch of Endor to speak with dead Samuel, the Geneva note on "it was Samuel" at 1 Sam. 28.14 reads: "To his imagination, albeit it was Satan, who to blind his eyes tooke vpon him the forme of

Samuel, as he can do of an Angel of light." The Bishops' Bible adopted the first part of the Geneva note: "To his imagination: albeit it was Sathan in deede."

Hamlet's fears that the spirit he had seen was the devil reflect the Protestant view that spirits or ghosts which appeared to men were either angels or devils. A ghost seeking revenge would be a devil according to this view. The Catholic view appears 1.5.11–13: ghosts were the souls of those in purgatory.

3.1.58:   Take arms against a sea of troubles.

Compare the homily "Of the State of Matrimonie": "So shall we passe through the dangers of the troublous sea of this world."

The expression "sea of troubles," however, seems to have been fairly common in Shakespeare's day. The eloquent preacher Henry Smith, whose *Sermons* were frequently published, called this life "a sea of troubles" in his sermon "The Trial of the Righteous." The expression even appears in Aeschylus's play, *The Persians*, line 433: "A mighty sea of troubles (*pélagos kakon*) has burst upon the Persians."

[3.1.70: Job 3.18.]

3.1.77–79:   But that the dread of something after death,
The undiscover'd country, from whose bourn
No traveller returns.

Job 10.21–22: "Before I goe and shall not returne, euen to the lande of darkenesse and shadowe of death: into a land, ... darke as darkenes it selfe."

Job 16.22: "I shall go the way, whence I shall not returne."

Job 7.9–10: "Hee that goeth downe to the graue, shall come vp no more. He shall returne no more to his house."

Wisdom 2.1: "Neither was any knowen that hath returned from the graue."

Shakespeare appears to be decidedly closer to the Geneva Bible in this reference. Coverdale, Matthew, the Great, and the Bishops' Bibles have either "not turne agayne" or "nor turneth agayne" in all three texts in Job. Only the Geneva has "shall not returne" or "shall returne nomore." Taverner has "whence I shall not retourne" in Job 10.21, but Shakespeare is far more likely to have had the Geneva in mind, which has "returne" in all three passages in Job.

3.1.142–46:   I have heard of your paintings, well enough. God hath given you one face, and you make yourselves another. You jig and amble, ... and make your wantonness your ignorance.

Compare the homily "Against Excesse of Apparell": "Who can paint her face and curle her hayre ... as though shee could make her selfe more comely then God hath appointed the measure of her beauty ... to reforme that which God hath made." Again: "So were the daughters of ... Jerusalem, whom Esai the Prophet threatneth, because they walked with stretched out neckes and wandering eyes, mincing as they went, and nicely treading with their feet."

The homily's reference to Esai is Isa. 3.16. Disapproval of cosmetics and fancy apparel was a common sermon theme, and many writers, including Nashe in *Pierce Penilesse*, attacked the use of cosmetics.

[3.1.160: Isa. 6.5.]

3.2.13–14:   It out-Herods Herod.

Primarily a reference to the mystery plays, in which Herod is depicted as a raging tyrant. In the Coventry miracle play on Herod, a stage direction reads: "Here Erode ragis in the pagond and in the strete also." It is fairly certain that Shakespeare had seen the Coventry cycle during his childhood. The Bible's account of Herod is at Matt. 2.1–20.

[3.2.59: Job 20.10, Geneva.]

3.2.63–65:   Since my dear soul was mistress of her choice
              And could of men distinguish her election,
              Sh' hath seal'd thee for herself.

"Sealed" and "election" are definite religious terms that find their origin in Scripture.
  Eph. 4.30: "Grieue not the holy Spirit of God, by whom ye are sealed."
  2 Cor. 1.22: "Who hath also sealed vs."
  Rom. 11.5: "Through the election of grace."
  Rom. 11.28: "As touching the election, they are beloued."
  1 Thess. 1.4: "Knowing, beloued brethren, that ye are elect of God."
  See also Eph. 1.13; 2 Peter 1.10; etc.

[3.2.200: 1 John 2.17.]

[3.2.204–205: Ecclus. 13.22.]

3.2.251–52:   *Oph.* Still better, and worse.
                Ham. So you mistake your husbands.

Both Q2 and F1 have "mistake." The First Quarto has "must take," which, in the context of the previous line, would be a clearer reference to the Marriage Service: "I N. take thee N. to my wedded husband, to haue and to hold from this day forward, for better for worse, ... till death vs depart." For the reference to the Marriage Service to be apparent in Q2 and F1, "mistake" would have to be understood as "mis-take," that women for better or for worse make poor choices when taking husbands, a cynical observation on marriage.

3.2.336:   By these pickers and stealers.

Catechism: "To keepe my hands from picking and stealing."
Compare Titus 2.9–10: "Let seruants be subiect to their masters, ... neither pykers."

[3.2.396: Ps. 59.7.]

3.3.8–10:   Most holy and religious fear it is
              To keep those many many bodies safe
              That live and feed upon your Majesty.

A common theme in Shakespeare's day, often repeated in the homilies.
Compare part 1 of the homily "Concerning Good Order, and Obedience to Rulers and Magistrates": "Take away Kings, Princes, Rulers ... and such estates of Gods order, no man shall ride or goe by the high way vnrobbed, no man shall sleepe in his owne house or bedde vnkilled, no man shall keepe his wife, children, and possession in quietnesse, ... and there must needes follow all mischiefe, and vtter destruction both of soules, bodies. ..." Compare 1.3.20–24, above.

3.3.36–38:   O, my offense is rank, it smells to heaven,
              It hath the primal eldest curse upon't,
              A brother's murther.

A reference to Cain's murder of Abel. Gen. 4.10–11: "The voyce of thy brothers blood cryeth vnto me from the earth. Nowe therefore thou art cursed from the earth, which hath opened her mouth to receiue thy brothers blood from thine hand."

3.3.45–46:   Is there not rain enough in the sweet heavens
　　　　　　To wash it white as snow?

Ps. 51.7: "Washe me, and I shalbe whyter then snowe."
Isa. 1.18: "Though your sinnes were as crimsin, they shalbe made white as snowe."

3.3.80:   'A took my father grossly, full of bread.

Ezek. 16.49: "Behold, this was the iniquitie of thy sister Sodom, Pride, fulnes of bread, and abundance of idlenes."
Shakespeare appears to have the Geneva version in mind in this passage. The Coverdale, Matthew, Taverner, Great, and Bishops' Bibles all have "fulnesse of meate."

3.4.15:   You are the Queen, your husband's brother's wife.

Richmond Noble thinks that these words of Hamlet echo the "Table of Kindred and Affinity" in the Prayer Book, which stipulated that "A woman may not marry with her Husband's Brother," and that Hamlet's words would remind Shakespeare's audience that "Elizabeth's legitimacy depended on the illegality of her father's marriage with his brother's widow. The audience would thus sympathize with Hamlet's strong feelings" (205).
　　Henry VIII had divorced Katherine on grounds of incest because she had previously been married to his brother, Arthur. In *Hamlet*, Gertrude's marriage to Claudius is several times referred to as incest (1.2.157; 1.5.42, 83; 3.3.90; 5.2.325).
　　However, both Saxo and Belleforest stressed the incest theme. Saxo relates that Hamlet's uncle "took the wife of the brother he had butchered, capping unnatural murder with incest" (7.62; Saxo's Latin: "Trucidati quoque fratris uxore potitus incestum parricidio adjecit"). Belleforest expands Saxo and several times mentions the "incestuous adulterie and parricide murther" (*d'adultere incestueux*), and that Hamlet's mother would be punished for "joyning incestuously in marriage with the tyrannous murtherer of her husband" (7.87, 88, 94). Thus the references to incest in the play are basic to

Shakespeare's sources, and were not intended as a comment on Elizabeth's legitimacy.

Moreover, although the original "Table of Kindred and Affinity" prohibited a woman from marrying her husband's brother (that stipulation was removed in 1907), the Table was not part of the Elizabethan or even of the Jacobean Prayer Book. It was drawn up by Archbishop Parker in 1563 and was given full status of law by Canon 99 in 1604, which ordered that the "Table shall be in euery Church publikely set vp and fixed at the charge of the Parish." It was added to the Prayer Book for the first time in 1681, although some editions of the Prayer Book appeared after 1681 without the Table.

Shakespeare's audience was certainly acquainted with the Church's prohibitions against incest, since each marriage had to conform to the Church's regulations prohibiting the marriage of close relatives, and Hamlet's impassioned words to his mother were intended to remind her that she was guilty of incest. But the incest theme in *Hamlet* came from Shakespeare's sources. Reflections on Elizabeth's legitimacy, if any, would be secondary.

In Scripture, marriage relationships that were unlawful are listed in Leviticus 18. Verse 16 forbids marrying one's sister-in-law: "Thou shalt not discouer the shame of thy brothers wife: for it is thy brothers shame." See also Lev. 20.21: "The man that taketh his brothers wife, committeth filthinesse, because he hath vncouered his brothers shame."

Claudius's marriage to Gertrude cannot be justified as a Levirate marriage (Deut. 25.5–10), wherein a man was allowed to marry his deceased brother's wife. A Levirate marriage was possible only if the previous marriage had been childless. Its purpose was to provide an heir for the dead brother, so "that his name be not put out of Israel" (25.6). That situation does not exist in *Hamlet*.

3.4.34–35:   Leave wringing of your hands. Peace, sit you down,
              And let me wring your heart.

Compare Morning and Evening Prayer: "Rent your hearts and not your garments," based on Joel 2.13, Bishops': "Rent your hartes, and not your garmentes." At best an analogy rather than a reference.

[3.4.61–62: John 6.27; Eph. 4.30.]

3.4.64–65:   Here is your husband, like a mildewed ear,
              Blasting his wholesome brother.

Gen. 41.5–7: "Seuen eares of corne grewe vpon one stalke, ranke and goodly. And loo, seuen thinne eares, and blasted with the east winde, sprang vp after them: and the thinne eares deuoured the seuen ranke and full eares."
    See also Gen. 41.22–24.
    Compare the similar reference in *The Spanish Tragedy*, 4.2.17–18: "An eastern wind, commix'd with noisome airs, / Shall blast the plants and the young saplings."
    Compare also *Lear*, 5.3.24–25.

3.4.81:   O shame, where is thy blush?

    Compare 1 Cor. 15.55: "O death, where is thy sting? O graue, where is thy victorie?"
    Burial Service: "Death, where is thy sting? Hell, where is thy victory?"
    Compare *Troilus and Cressida* 5.2.67: "O beauty, where is thy faith?"

    [3.4.103–104: Ps. 34.7; Matt. 4.6; Ps. 91.11–12; Luke 4.10.]

3.4.126–27:   His form and cause conjoin'd, preaching to stones,
                    Would make them capable.

    Compare Luke 19.40: "If these should holde their peace, the stones would cry."
    Compare also Matt. 3.9: "God is able of these stones to rayse vp children vnto Abraham."

3.4.149:   Confess yourself to heaven.

    Most likely a reference to the exhortation before Communion in the Prayer Book to "confesse your selues to Almightie God," taking care not to run afoul of the 1559 Act of Uniformity, which forbade disrespectful use of the Prayer Book in plays. See the comment on *Othello* 2.3.111–112.

3.4.169–70:   And either [....] the devil or throw him out
                    With wondrous potency.

    A word seems to be missing in line 169. The Second Quarto has, "And either the deuill, or throwe him out," while F1 omits these lines completely. Of the many suggested emendations, the Oxford edition of Shakespeare has

"And master ev'n the devil or throw him out." Reference to the many exorcisms mentioned in the New Testament seems clear.

Compare Matt. 8.16: "They brought vnto him many that were possessed with deuils: and he cast out the spirits."
Matt. 9.33: "When the deuill was cast out."
Mark 3.15: "Power to ... cast out deuils."
See also Mark 1.34, 39; 6.13; etc.

3.4.173–75:   But heaven hath pleas'd it so
. . . .
That I must be their scourge and minister.

Compare Rom. 13.4: "For hee is the minister of God: ... for he is the minister of God to take vengeance on him that doth euil."
Submission to secular rulers as God's duly constituted ministers was a theme that Elizabeth's government stressed. Paul's words at Romans 13 are quoted in part 1 of the homily "Concerning Good Order, and Obedience to Rulers and Magistrates," and part 1 of the homily "Against Disobedience and Wilfull Rebellion."
But compare Belleforest: "Amleth, qui est le ministre et executeur de si juste vengeance." The anonymous 1608 English translation of Belleforest: "Hamlet, the minister and executor of just vengeance" (7.116). Thus Belleforest, rather than Scripture or the homilies, may have been Shakespeare's primary source for Hamlet's words.

4.2.5–6:   *Ros.* What have you done, my lord, with the dead body?
            Ham. Compounded it with dust, whereto 'tis kin.

With overtones of the biblical 'dust to dust.'
Gen. 3.19: "Thou art dust, and to dust shalt thou returne."
Eccles. 3.20: "All was of the dust, and all shal returne to the dust."
Burial Service: "Earth to earth, ashes to ashes, dust to dust."

4.2.22–24:   *Ros.* I understand you not, my lord.
            Ham. I am glad of it, a knavish speech sleeps in a foolish ear.

Compare Ecclus. 22.10: "Who so telleth a foole of wisdome, is as a man, which speaketh to one that is a sleepe: when he hath tolde his tale, he saith, What is the matter?"

4.2.28–30:   *Ham.* .... The King is a thing—
             Guil. A thing, my lord?
             Ham. Of nothing.

Compare Ps. 144.4: "Man is like a thing of nought."
Compare Geneva note "g" on Micah 1.7: "As a thing of nought."
The expression, however, was common.

4.3.16–18, 33:   *King.* Now, Hamlet, where's Polonius?
                 Ham. At supper.
                 King. At supper? where?
                 · · · · · · · · · ·
                 Ham. In heaven.

A clear echo of the biblical supper promised to those who inherit the
kingdom of heaven.
    Compare Rev. 19.9: "Blessed are they which are called vnto the Lambes
supper."
    Compare Luke 14.15–16: "Blessed is he that eateth bread in the kingdome
of God. Then said he to him, A certaine man made a great supper, and bade
many."
    Compare also Matt. 22.2–4; Rev. 3.20.
    Compare *2 Henry VI* 5.1.214: "For you shall sup with Jesu Christ to-
night."

4.3.48:   I see a cherub that sees them.

The term "cherub" comes from Scripture. This is the only passage in
which Shakespeare uses "cherub" in the singular. See *Macbeth* 1.7.22 for a
discussion of Shakespeare's references to cherubim.

4.3.52:   Man and wife is one flesh.

Eph. 5.31: "For this cause shall a man leaue father and mother, and shall
cleaue to his wife, and they twaine shalbe one flesh."
    Gen. 2.24: "Therefore shal man ... cleaue to his wife, and they shalbe one
flesh."
    Marriage Service: "For this cause shall a man leaue father and mother, and
shall be ioyned vnto his wife, and they two shall be one flesh."
    See also Matt. 19.5–6; Mark 10.7–8.

4.5.43–44:   Lord, we know what we are, but know not what we may be.

Compare 1 John 3.2: "Now are we the sonnes of God, but yet it doeth not appeare what we shalbe."

4.5.132–34:   To hell, allegiance! vows, to the blackest devil!
Conscience and grace, to the profoundest pit!
I dare damnation.

"The profoundest pit" is probably a reference to "the bottomles pit" of Rev. 9.1; 11.7; 17.8; and 20.1, especially when made parallel with hell, the devil, and damnation.

5.1.30–31:   Gard'ners, ditchers, and grave-makers; they hold up Adam's profession.

5.1.36–37:   The Scripture says Adam digg'd.

Gen. 2.8, 15: "The Lord God planted a garden Eastward in Eden, and there he put the man whom he had made ... that he might dresse it and keepe it."
Gen. 3.23: "Therefore the Lorde God sent him foorth from the garden of Eden, to tyll the earth."

5.1.35–36:   How dost thou understand the Scripture? The Scripture says
. . . .

Compare Gal. 4.21, 22, 27, 30: "Do ye not heare the Law? For it is written .... But what saith the Scripture?"
Compare Rom. 4.3: "For what saith the Scripture?"
Common theological expressions that originate with Scripture.

[5.1.74: Wisdom 2.2.]

5.1.76–7:   As if 'twere Cain's jaw-bone, that did the first murder!

Gen. 4.8: "Kain rose vp against Habel his brother, and slew him." An ancient English tradition that goes back at least to the ninth century has it that Cain killed Abel with the jawbone of an ass. That tradition was incorporated into Medieval drama and appears in several mystery plays, including the Wakefield play, *The Killing of Abel*, in which Cain slays Abel with a "cheke-bon."

5.1.126:   'Tis for the dead, not for the quick.

2 Tim. 4.1: "The quicke and dead."
See also 1 Peter 4.5; Acts 10.42.
The Apostles' Creed, Morning and Evening Prayer: "He shall come to iudge the quicke and the dead."
The Nicene Creed, Communion Service: "He shall come againe with glory to iudge both the quicke and the dead."
See also 5.1.251, below.

5.1.209–10:   Alexander returneth to dust, the dust is earth.

See above at 4.2.5–6.

5.1.229–30:   She should in ground unsanctified been lodg'd
              Till the last trumpet.

1 Cor. 15.52: "At the last trumpet: for the trumpet shall blowe, and the dead shal bee raised vp."
1 Thess. 4.16: "The Lord him selfe shal descend from heauen ... with the trumpet of God: and the dead in Christ shal rise first."
The Geneva Bible was the first version to use "trumpet" in the above texts, followed by the Rheims. All other versions have "trompe" ("trumpe") in all three instances.

[5.1.233: Eccles. 12.6, Bishops'. Compare *Titus Andronicus* 1.1.83.]

5.1.240–42:   I tell thee, churlish priest,
              A minist'ring angel shall my sister be
              When thou liest howling.

Compare Matt. 8.12: "The children of the kingdome shalbe cast out into vtter darkenes: there shalbe weeping and gnashing of teeth."
For "a minist'ring angel," compare Heb. 1.14, discussing angels: "Are they not all ministring spirites, sent forth to minister?"
Compare also Matt. 21.31; 13.42.

5.1.251: Now pile your dust upon the quick and dead.

Burial Service rubric at time of burial: "Earth shall be cast vpon the body by some standing by."
See 5.1.126, above.

5.1.259: *Laer.* The devil take thy soul!
         Ham. Thou pray'st not well.

With possible overtones of Matt. 5.44 to pray for those who would hurt us: "Blesse them that cursse you: doe good to them that hate you, and pray for them which hurt you, and persecute you."
Another possibility is that Hamlet chides Laertes for invoking the devil.

[5.2.10–11: Prov. 16.9; 19.21.]

5.2.40: Like the palm might flourish.

Ps. 92.11 (92.12, Geneva): "The ryghteous shal florishe lyke a palme tree."
See *Timon of Athens* 5.1.10–11.

5.2.219–20: There is special providence in the fall of a sparrow.

Matt. 10.29: "Are not two sparowes sold for a farthing, and one of them shal not fal on the ground without your Father?"
Shakespeare is closest to the Geneva and Taverner Bibles. Other than the Rheims New Testament, which probably borrowed the Geneva reading (as it often does), only the Geneva and Taverner Bibles have "fal on the ground." All other versions have "light on the ground." Shakespeare probably had the Geneva in mind.
See also Luke 12.6–7.

5.2.219–24: We defy augury. ... If it be now, 'tis not to come; if it be not to come, it will be now; if it be not now, yet it will come—the readiness is all. Since no man, of aught he leaves, knows what is't to leave betimes, let be.

The Folio reads: "The readinesse is all, since no man ha's ought of what he leaues. What is't to leaue betimes?" The Folio reading lends itself to comparison with 1 Tim. 6.7: "For we brought nothing into the world, and it is certaine, that we can carie nothing out," and to the Burial Service adaptation of that text: "Wee brought nothing into this world, neither may wee cary any thing out of this world."

The Riverside Shakespeare, however, adheres closely to the Second Quarto of 1604, which is punctuated thus: "The readines is all, since no man of ought he leaues, knowes what ist to leaue betimes, let be." While the Folio reading appears to be a reference to 1 Tim. 6.7, the Quarto portrays a more fatalistic frame of mind for Hamlet. According to the Quarto, Hamlet is convinced that certain events are predestined to occur and there is little that one can do to forestall these events except to be ready for them when they occur, whether sooner or later. Thus since no man knows when is the best time to leave life, let events occur when they will, be they great or small.

[5.2.234–37: Rom. 7.15, 17, 20.]

[5.2.317–18: Prov. 11.5.]

5.2.347:   Absent thee from felicity a while.

Perhaps an echo of the penultimate prayer in the Burial Service, in which those who have been "deliuered from the burden of the flesh" are said to be "in ioy and felicitie."

5.2.358:· The rest is silence.

Compare Ps. 115.17: "The dead praise not thee, O Lord: neyther al they that goe downe into the scilence."
Compare 2 Esdras 7.32: "So shall the dust [restore] those that dwell therein in silence."

5.2.359–60:   Good night, sweet prince,
              And flights of angels sing thee to thy rest!

Compare Luke 16.22: "Dyed, and was caryed by the Angels into Abrahams bosome."
Compare the homily "Against the Feare of Death," part 1: "Death, which sent Lazarus the poore miserable man by Angels anon vnto Abrahams bosome, a place of rest, pleasure, and consolation." Part 2 of the same homily: "And Lazarus, ... did not death highly profit and promote him, which by

the ministery of Angels sent him vnto Abrahams bosome, a place of rest, ioy, and heauenly consolation?"

5.2.385:   Fall'n on th' inventors' heads.

   Compare Ps. 7.17 (7.16, Geneva): "For his trauaile shal come vpon his owne head: and his wickednesse shal fal vpon his owne pate."

   Shakespeare's primary source, however, may have been Belleforest, who used this expression twice. When recounting how Hamlet changed the letter ordering his death, the 1608 translation of Belleforest says that Hamlet was able "to turne the death they had devised against him upon their owne neckes" (7.102). Belleforest's French, however, has "heads": "Tourner sur eux la mort ordonnee pour sa teste." When the execution order was carried out against Hamlet's companions, Belleforest's marginal comment is: "Trahison tombe sur la teste de celuy qui la veut faire." The English reads, "Treachery falls on the head of him who wishes to perform it" (7.107, n. 3).

Troilus and Cressida

The story of Troilus and Cressida was well known in the sixteenth century both in England and on the Continent, and the number of pre-Shakespearean works that dealt with that theme was large. In Shakespeare's day, English versions of the story could be found in prose, poetry, ballad, and drama. Shakespeare's principal sources for the play were Chaucer's *Troilus and Criseyde*, Chapman's 1598 translation of Homer, an early, unrevised edition of Caxton's *Recuyell of the Historyes of Troye*, and Lydgate's *The Hystorye Sege and Dystruccyon of Troye*. Henryson's *Testament of Cresseid* and Golding's translation of the *Metamorphoses* were the most important of Shakespeare's secondary sources, although Shakespeare's usual wide reading of all pertinent material prior to penning a play included Robert Greene, Virgil's *Aeneid*, and other works.

The many medieval stories which dealt with the fall of Troy further complicate the problem of Shakespeare's sources. Shakespeare used many Homeric details not in Chapman; he must, therefore, have read at least one of the full Latin or French translations of Homer made in the sixteenth century, probably that of Hugues Salel, which went through several editions. Nor can Shakespeare's direct use of Homer be ruled out in view of the many dual language Greek-Latin editions of Homer that were available.

Shakespeare found few biblical references in these works. The war story comes primarily from Homer, but no biblical references can be expected in Homer or in close translations of Homer. The love story was borrowed primarily from Chaucer, and religious imagery is frequent in Chaucer: the lovers meet at a religious service; stricken with love, Troilus fervently prays to the "God of Love"; an abundance of Christian and pagan theological terms and religious customs are repeatedly applied to the love of Troilus and Criseyde. But just as Shakespeare's treatment of the love story differs vastly from Chaucer's, so does his use of Scripture. Chaucer's poem of over 8,000 lines contains at most some fifteen biblical references, less than half of which are certain, but except for a few similarities, there are no clear borrowings of biblical references from Chaucer. Nor were Shakespeare's references taken from Lydgate. Although written by a monk, Lydgate's 30,000 line poem is, with a few exceptions (the digressions on idolatry in books 2 and 4, and the Envoy), almost completely devoid of biblical references. Shakespeare borrowed none of the few references that do appear in Lydgate.

Several pre-Shakespearean plays dealt with the same theme, but all of them are lost. As early as 1516, the "Story of Troylus and Pander" was staged before Henry VIII by the Children of the Chapel Royal at the royal residence in Eltham, Kent. Nicholas Grimald (1519–62) is said to have written a Latin comedy called *Troilus ex Chaucero*. Henslowe records that the Troy (not Troilus) story was played by the Admiral's Men four times in 1596, and that on April 7, 1599 he advanced the playwrights Dekker and Chettle three pounds for their upcoming book "Troyeles & creasse daye." The British Library has an Admiral's Men's plot outline, which records the entrances and exits of thirteen scenes of a Troilus and Cressida play, probably the stage director's plot outline of Dekker and Chettle's 1599 play. Shakespeare may have written his play to meet the competition from the Admiral's Men's play, but it is unlikely that any of these lost plays influenced his biblical references.

Troilus and Cressida appears to have a surprisingly large number of biblical references for a play with a classical setting, but less than half of the items in the following list are certain references. Many of the entries marked "Compare ... " are probably not strict references, but striking analogies that are worth noting; a few seem to possess accidental verbal similarities to Scripture, similarities which may or may not have been conscious on Shakespeare's part.

Page numbers preceded by the number 6, as in (6.113), refer to volume 6 of Bullough. Book and line numbers of Chaucer's *Troilus and Criseyde* are to Robinson's *The Works of Geoffrey Chaucer*, second edition.

[1.1.61: Ezek. 27.17; Luke 10.34.]

[1.2.198: Matt. 25.29.]

[1.3.20–22: Zech. 13.9; Mal. 3.3; Job 23.10; Heb. 12.5–7.]

[1.3.27–30: Matt. 3.12.]

1.3.31:   With due observance of thy godlike seat.

Compare Matt. 5.34, Bishops': "For it is Gods seate."
Compare Matt. 23.22, Bishops': "The seate of God."
Compare Heb. 1.8, Bishops': "Thy seate, O God, shalbe for euer."
The Geneva has "throne" rather than "seate" in the above texts, and the Rheims adopted the Geneva reading. All other sixteenth-century Bibles

have "seate," although Taverner has "trone" at Matt. 23.22. Thus if Shakespeare borrowed the phrase "godlike seat" from Scripture, he was least like the popular Geneva Bible and closer to the other versions of his day.

But compare Chapman's translation of Homer, one of Shakespeare's principal sources, which has parallel expressions: "Godlike sonn," "godlike framde," "godlike men," and "godlike in counsels" (6.113, 114, 128, 129).

1.3.78–137:   The specialty of rule hath been neglected.
. . . .
The heavens themselves, the planets, and this centre
Observe degree, priority, and place.
. . . .
... But when the planets
In evil mixture to disorder wander,
What plagues and what portents, what mutiny!
. . . .
Take but degree away, untune that string,
And hark what discord follows....
... The bounded waters
Should lift their bosoms higher than the shores,
. . . .
And the rude son should strike his father dead.

Compare the homily "Concerning Good Order, and Obedience to Rulers and Magistrates": "Almighty GOD hath created and appointed all things in heauen, earth, and waters, in a most excellent and perfect order. In Heauen, hee hath appointed distinct and seuerall orders and states of Archangels and Angels. In earth hee hath assigned and appointed Kings, Princes ... in all good and necessary order. The water aboue is kept, and rayneth downe in due time and season. The Sun, Moone, Starres ... doe keepe their order.... Take away Kings, Princes, Rulers, Magistrates, Judges, and such estates of GODS order, no man shall ride or goe by the high way vnrobbed, no man shall sleepe in his owne house or bedde vnkilled, no man shall keepe his wife, children, and possession in quietnesse,... and there must needes follow all mischiefe."

Compare also the homily "Against Disobedience and Wilfull Rebellion." We should not conclude, however, that Shakespeare's only source for Ulysses's speech on order and degree was the *Book of Homilies*. There are similar passages in Chapman's translation of Homer, Elyot's *Governour*, Hooker's *Ecclesiasticall Politie*, in Montaigne's essays, Cicero's *Tusculans*, and elsewhere. Shakespeare was writing within a well-known tradition, and the speech was a collection of commonplaces.

[1.3.94–101: Luke 21.25–26.]

[1.3.240: Judges 18.19. Compare *Othello* 2.1.221.]

1.3.240–42:   Lay thy finger on thy lips!
              The worthiness of praise distains his worth,
              If that the prais'd himself bring the praise forth.

A common saying, and there are many proverbs to the same effect.
Compare Prov. 27.2: "Let another man prayse thee, and not thine owne
mouth: a stranger, and not thine owne lippes."
Compare also 2.3.156–57.

[2.1.14: 1 Cor. 5.8.]

2.1.70–71:   I will buy nine sparrows for a penny.

Compare Matt. 10.29: "Are not two sparowes sold for a farthing?"
Compare also Luke 12.6: "Are not fiue sparowes boght for two farth-
ings?"

2.1.80:   The eye of Helen's needle.

Compare Matt. 19.24: "To goe through the eye of a needle."
See also Mark 10.25; Luke 18.25.

[2.1.118–19: Prov. 13.20.]

2.2.56–57:   'Tis mad idolatry
             To make the service greater than the god.

Compare Matt. 23.17, 19: "Ye fooles and blinde, whether is greater, the
gold, or the Temple that sanctifieth the gold? Ye fooles and blinde, whether
is greater, the offring, or the altar which sanctifieth the offring?"
At best an analogy rather than a reference.

2.2.81–83:   Why, she is a pearl,
             Whose price hath launch'd above a thousand ships,
             And turn'd crown'd kings to merchants.

Compare Matt. 13.45–46: "The kingdome of heauen is like to a marchant man that seeketh good pearles, who hauing founde a pearle of greate price, went and sold all that he had, and bought it."

The parable of the "pearle of greate price" was well known in Shakespeare's day and caused the pearl to become a favorite metaphor for anything of great value. The title page of all New Testament editions of the Bishops' Bible that were published apart from the Old Testament bore the words: "The pearle which Christ commaunded to be bought: Is here to be found, not els to be sought." Most editions give Matthew 13 as the source of the motto.

The description of Helen as a "pearl" may also owe something to Greene. In 1587, Robert Greene published *Euphues his Censure to Philautus*, a collection of stories and debates that took place during a truce in the Trojan War. Before a combined audience of Trojans and Greeks, Ulysses speaks of Helen as a "Pearle," "a supposed Jem," "a peece." In the play, Troilus speaks of her as "a pearl," while Diomedes speaks of her as a "piece" at 4.1.63, although in considerably different contexts than in Greene. Thus, while Shakespeare's primary reference seems to be to Jesus' parable of the pearl of great price, that comparison could have been suggested by Greene.

[2.2.92:   Matt. 23.15.]

2.2.104:   Virgins and boys, mid-age and wrinkled eld.

Compare Ps. 148.12: "Young menne and maidens, olde menne and children."

2.2.172–73:   Have ears more deaf than adders to the voice
          Of any true decision.

Ps. 58.4–5: "Like the deafe Adder that stoppeth her eares. Whiche refuseth to heare the voyce of the charmer."

[2.2.174: Rom. 13.7, Rheims.]

[2.2.184–86: Rom. 2.14.]

2.3.33:   Lazars.

Derived ultimately from the parable of the rich man and Lazarus.

Luke 16.20–21: "There was a certeine begger named Lazarus, which was laied at his gate full of sores,... and the dogs came and licked his sores."

2.3.241:   Praise him that gat thee, she that gave thee suck.

Luke 11.27: "Blessed is the wombe that bare thee, and the pappes which thou hast sucked."
See also Luke 23.29.
A clear biblical reference, perhaps suggested to Shakespeare by verbal similarities in both Homer and Lydgate. According to Homer, when Hector's mother Hecuba attempted to persuade him not to engage in combat with Achilles, she "stript nak't her bosome, shew'd her breasts, and bad him reverence them, / And pittie her" (6.144).
Lydgate relates how Hector's wife Andromache took her infant son, who "at the pappes whyte / For very yonge that tyme was soukynge," approached Hector, and

> With hir pappes also hangynge oute,
> Hir lytell childe in hir armes twayne,
> Afore hir lorde gan to wepe and playne,
> Besechynge hym of routhe and pyte,

not to go into the field (6.175–77).

2.3.244:   He that disciplin'd thine arms to fight.

Compare Ps. 144.1: "Blessed be the Lorde my strength: whiche teacheth my handes to warre, and my fingers to fight."
Geneva: "Which teacheth mine hands to fight, and my fingers to battell."

3.1.8:   The Lord be prais'd!

Spoken of Paris, but an obvious play, with a tone of ridicule, on a cant religious phrase. The words "prayse the Lorde," "prayse ye the Lorde," and "praysed be the Lorde" occur frequently in Scripture, particularly in the Psalms, which gave rise to the expression. See Ps. 103.20–21; 104.1, 35; 113.1; 115.18; 117.1; 135.1–3, 21; 146.1; 147.1, 12; 148.1–7, 12–13; 150.1–6.

3.1.15:   You are in the state of grace.

Another play on a cant religious phrase that derives ultimately from Scripture. Compare Eph. 2.5, 8: "By grace are ye saued through faith, ... it is the gift of God."

Compare Titus 2.11: "The grace of God, that bringeth saluation vnto al men, hath appeared."

See also Romans 5.15, 21; 1 Cor. 15.10; 2 Cor. 6.1; Heb. 4.16.

Similar expressions occur in Chaucer: "God have yow in his grace!" (5.1631) See also 1.1005; 2.243; 3.1349 of Chaucer's poem.

3.1.101–102:   They two are twain.

Spoken of Cressida and of Helen's husband, Paris.

Contrast these words with Jesus' description of husband and wife at Matt. 19.5–6: "And they twayne shalbe one flesh. Wherefore they are no more twaine, but one flesh."

3.1.133:   Generation of vipers.

Matt. 3.7; 12.34; Luke 3.7: "Generations of vipers."
Matt. 23.33: "Generation of vipers."

Most editions of the Geneva Bible have "generations" in the first three texts (Matt. 3.7; 12.34; Luke 3.7) and "generation" at Matt. 23.33. All other Protestant translations have "generacion" in all four texts, although Taverner has "progenye" at Matt. 3.7. But this does not necessarily indicate that Shakespeare was following one of the latter versions. Since Shakespeare's subject is singular, "Is love a generation of vipers?" it would be more natural for him to prefer "generation" rather than "generations." Thus the evidence from this passage is too inconclusive and cannot be used to determine which version of the Bible Shakespeare had in mind. The Rheims New Testament has "brood" or "broodes" in all four texts.

3.2.69:   Fears make devils of cherubins.

Derived ultimately from Scripture, where cherubim are frequently mentioned.

See Macbeth 1.7.22 for a discussion of Shakespeare's references to cherubim.

[3.3.74–78: Ecclus. 13.22; Prov. 14.20; 19.4.]

[3.3.96–98: Ps. 49.6.]

3.3.154–55:   For honor travels in a strait so narrow,
                    Where one but goes abreast. Keep then the path.

With clear overtones of Matt. 7.13–14: "Enter in at the straite gate: ... because the gate is straite, and the waye narrow that leadeth vnto life, and fewe there be that finde it."

[3.3.161–63: Isa. 51.23.]

3.3.211–13:   And all the Greekish girls shall tripping sing,
                    "Great Hector's sister did Achilles win,
                    But our great Ajax bravely beat down him."

With clear overtones of 1 Sam. 18.6–7: "The women came out of all cities of Israel, singing and dauncing ... with timbrels.... And the women sang by course in their play, and sayde, Saul hathe slaine his thousand, and Dauid his ten thousand."

The account in 1 Samuel may have been suggested to Shakespeare by Chaucer's account of Troilus returning from battle: "And ay the peple cryde, 'Here cometh oure joye, / And, next his brother, holder up of Troye!'" (2.643–44)

4.1.58:   With such a hell of pain.

Compare Ps. 18.4: "The paynes of hel came about me: the snares of death ouertooke me."
Compare Ps. 116.3: "The snares of death compassed me rounde about: and the paines of hel gate holde vpon me."
A clear reference to the Psalter. The Geneva has "sorowes of death" and "griefes of the graue."
See *Othello* 1.1.154.

4.1.76–77:   Fair Diomed, you do as chapmen do,
                    Dispraise the thing that they desire to buy.

Compare Prov. 20.14: "It is naught, it is naught, saith the buyer: but when he is gone apart, he boasteth."

At best an analogy rather than a reference.

4.2.85–86:   Would thou hadst ne'er been born!

Compare Matt. 26.24: "It had bene good for that man, if he had neuer bene borne."
A common saying, but with clear overtones of Jesus' words. The parallel expressions in Chaucer are somewhat different: "Allas, that I was born!" (3.1103); "In corsed tyme I born was" (5.1699).
See also 3.1073, 1222, 1423; 5.690, 700, 1275–76 of Chaucer's poem.

4.2.96:   I have forgot my father.

Compare Ps. 45.11 (45.10, Geneva): "Hearken (O daughter) and consyder,... forget also thyne owne people, and thy fathers house."
Compare Matt. 19.5: "For this cause, shal a man leaue father and mother."
Compare 1 Esdras 4.21: "And neither remembreth father nor mother."
Perhaps an analogy rather than a reference. Compare Chaucer 4.666–68 for a similar thought.

4.4.80:   A kind of godly jealousy.

2 Cor. 11.2: "I am ielous ouer you, with godlie ielousie."
Closest parallel in Chaucer:

> Therwith the wikked spirit, God us blesse,
> Which that men clepeth the woode jalousie,
> Gan in hym crepe.
>
> (5.1212–14)

Shakespeare is considerably closer to Scripture than to Chaucer.

[4.4.89–91: 2 Cor. 11.3, 14; Gen. 3.1–6.]

4.4.145:   With a bridegroom's fresh alacrity.

Compare Ps. 19.5: "Whiche commeth foorth as a brydegrome out of his chamber, and reioyceth as a giant to runne his course."

4.5.65–66:   What shall be done
              To him that victory commands?

Compare 1 Sam. 17.26: "What shall be done to the man that killeth this Philistim?"

Compare also Esther 6.6: "What shalbe done vnto the man, whom the King will honour?"

5.1.65:   A lazar.

Sec 2.3.33, above.

5.2.67:   O beauty, where is thy faith?

Compare 1 Cor. 15.55: "O death, where is thy sting? O graue, where is thy victorie?"

Compare the reference at *Hamlet* 3.4.81.

Compare also Luke 8.25: "Then he said vnto them, Where is your faith?"

Compare Chaucer 5.1674–76:

> O lady myn, Criseyde,
> Where is youre feith, and where is youre biheste?
> Where is youre love? where is youre trouthe?

5.3.63:   Thy wife hath dreamt, thy mother hath had visions.

Compare Joel 2.28: "Your olde men shal dreame dreames, and your yong men shall see visions."

Compare Acts 2.17: "Your young men shall see visions, and your olde men shall dreame dreames."

A clear echo of Scripture which was probably suggested to Shakespeare by his sources. In *The Hystorye Sege and Dystruccyon of Troye* Lydgate writes of Hector's wife,

> And she that nyght, as made is mencioun,
> Hadde in hir slepe a wonder visioun,
> I not, in soth, what I may it nevene,
> Outher a dreme or verraily a sweuene,
> . . . .
> Hir pitous dreme.
>
> (3.4909–12, 4969)

Caxton has: This Andrometha sawe that nyght a mervayllous vysion....
Hector blamed his wyf sayng that men shold not beleve ne
gyve fayth to dremes .... Andrometha wente unto the
kynge Pryant and to the quene and tolde to them the veryte
of her vysion.

(6.204)

5.4.33–35:   I think they have swallow'd one another. I would laugh at that
miracle—yet in a sort lechery eats itself.

The words, "I would laugh at that miracle," might be a reference to the
miracle of Aaron's rod, which swallowed the rods of Egypt's magicians.
Exodus 7.12: "They cast downe euerie man his rod, and they were turned
into serpents: but Aarons rod deuoured their rods."

5.5.9:   And stands Colossus-wise, waving his beam.

Perhaps with overtones of the giant Goliath, whose "speare was like a
weauers beame." 1 Sam. 17.7.
Compare *The Merry Wives of Windsor* 5.1.22.

Othello

Shakespeare's main source for the plot of *Othello* was Geraldi Cinthio's *Hecatommithi*, first published in 1565, which contains 110 tales about love and marriage. The introduction contains ten short tales, and then follow ten Decades of ten stories each. The story that Shakespeare borrowed occurs in Decade 3, story 7, the account of the valiant Moor and Disdemona.

Shakespeare read Cinthio either in the original Italian or in a 1584 French translation of Cinthio by Gabriel Chappuys; Cinthio was not translated into English until 1753. No biblical references occur in Cinthio's narrative.

Shakespeare followed Cinthio's plot closely throughout most of *Othello*. For the murder scene, however, he turned to a completely different story by Bandello, the account of an Albanian captain who killed his beautiful wife lest anyone should enjoy her after his death. Bandello's account was translated into English by Geoffrey Fenton (*Certaine Tragicall Discourses*, 1567) from the French of Belleforest. Fenton greatly expanded Belleforest, even as Belleforest had enlarged Bandello's account, and Fenton appears to have influenced Shakespeare's use of Scripture in *Othello* at 2.1.64–65 and particularly in the murder scene at 5.2.347 and 5.2.358–59. Fenton's influence at 5.2.347 is especially important, and strongly argues that Shakespeare wrote "Iudean" rather than "Indian" in that passage.

Other sources from which Shakespeare borrowed various details include Philemon Holland's translation of Pliny's *Natvrall Historie* (1601), Richard Knolles' *Historie of the Turkes* (1603), John Pory's *A Geographical Historie of Africa* (1600), and Sir Lewes Lewkenor's *The Commonwealth and Government of Venice* (1599); but none of these had any influence on Shakespeare's biblical references.

Othello affords ample evidence of the effects of the profanity laws on Shakespeare's plays. In 1606 Parliament passed *An Act to Restrain the abuses of Players*, "for the preventing and avoiding of the great abuse of the holy Name of God, in Stage-plays, Enterludes, May-games, Shews, and such-like." It provided that if any person in a stage play should "jestingly or prophanely speak, or use the holy Name of God, or of Jesus Christ, or of the Holy Ghost, or of the Trinity," he should be fined ten pounds for each offense.

The First Quarto of *Othello* contains many oaths that were prohibited by the Act, and most of these were expurgated in the Folio. The Quarto is generally believed to have been based on a copy of Shakespeare's foul papers, and Shakespeare apparently had no qualms about using such expressions as "By God," "'Zounds," "By'r lady," "'Sblood," and "God bless the mark!" Since the Quarto appeared in 1622, long after the Act of 1606, the prohibition apparently did not apply to the press, only to the stage. The Folio text, on the other hand, was based in part on the promptbook, the acting version of the play, in which the objectionable oaths were removed. Thus Emilia's cry "O God! O heavenly God!" in the Quarto becomes "Oh Heauen! Oh heauenly Powres!" in the Folio.

In the first four acts of the play, a large number of the biblical and liturgical references (nineteen out of forty-six, or 41 percent) are spoken by Iago, and only twelve by Othello. The situation changes in act 5, where thirteen references are spoken by Othello, but none by Iago. Thus forty-four of the sixty-two references in the play are spoken by Othello and Iago. Desdemona utters seven references.

In the list that follows, page numbers to Cinthio, Bandello, and Fenton preceded by the number 7, as in (7.242) refer to vol. 7 of Bullough.

[1.1.43–44: Matt. 6.24; Luke 16.13; James 3.1.]

1.1.65:   I am not what I am.

Compare Ex. 3.14: "I am that I am."
Compare 1 Cor. 15.10: "I am that I am."

1.1.70–71:   And though he in a fertile climate dwell,
             Plague him with flies.

The fourth plague on Egypt was the plague of flies. Ex. 8.21–23.
See also Gen. 47.6.
Geneva chapter heading, Exodus chapter 8: "Egypt is plagued with noysome flyes."

1.1.108–109:   You are one of those that will not serve God, if the devil bid
               you.

A reversal of the devil's proposal that Jesus worship him instead of God, and of Jesus' answer: "Thou shalt worshippe the Lord thy God, and him onely shalt thou serue." Matt. 4.10.

1.1.154: Though I do hate him as I do hell-pains.

    Ps. 18.4: "The paynes of hel came about me: the snares of death ouertooke me."
    Ps. 116.3: "The snares of death compassed me rounde about: and the paines of hel gate holde vpon me."
    A reference to the Psalter. The Geneva has "sorowes of death" and "griefes of the graue."
    See also *Troilus and Cressida* 4.1.58.

1.2.9–10:   That with the little godliness I have
               I did full hard forbear him.

    Compare Col. 3.13: "Forbearing one another, and forgiuing one another."
    Compare Eph. 4.2, Tyndale, Matthew, Coverdale, Taverner, Great, Bishops': "Forbearyng one another." Geneva, Rheims: "Supporting one another."

1.2.59:   Keep up your bright swords.

    Compare Matt. 26.52: "Put vp thy sword into his place."
    Compare John 18.11: "Put vp thy sword into the sheath."
    The setting closely parallels the Gospel accounts. A band with torches and armed with swords comes by night to arrest Othello. The circumstances of Jesus' arrest are much the same. Matt. 26.47.
    In Cinthio's tale, there is no elopement and no attempt is made to arrest Othello. Desdemona marries Othello with her parents' knowledge but against their wishes because she and Othello ("the Moor") deeply love each other. Shakespeare adds the arrest scene, which increases the likelihood that in doing so, he patterned Othello's arrest on Christ's.

    [1.3.67: Josh. 1.8; Heb. 9.19.]

1.3.81:   Rude am I in my speech.

    2 Cor. 11.6: "Though I be rude in speaking."

Closest parallel in Shakespeare's sources: "The vntuned harshnesse of my disioynted stile" (Lewkenor's Epistle Dedicatory).

1.3.94–95:   A maiden, never bold;
             Of spirit so still and quiet.

1 Peter 3.4–5, on women, who should have "a meeke and quiet spirit."

1.3.147–50: But still the house affairs would draw her thence,
             Which ever as she could with haste dispatch,
             She'ld come again, and with a greedy ear
             Devour up my discourse.

Luke 10.39–40: "Marie, which also sate at Iesus feete, and hearde his preaching. But Martha was combred about much seruing."
Here, again, as at 1.2.59, the parallelism is to be found in the setting rather than in the actual words. The fact that in this instance also, Shakespeare adds this scene to what he found in Cinthio, increases the likelihood that he modelled this addition on the well-known account of Jesus at supper at the home of Mary and Martha. In *Othello* Desdemona corresponds to both Martha and Mary, being occupied with domestic duties and at the same time greedily listening to Othello's words.

1.3.177:   Destruction on my head.

A common biblical expression. Compare 1 Kings 2.33: "Their blood shall therefore returne vpon the head of Ioab, and on the head of his seede."
Compare Ezek. 9.10: "Will recompence their wayes vpon their heads."
See also Joshua 2.19; Judges 9.57; 2 Sam. 1.16; 1 Kings 2.37; Ps. 7.17 (7.16 Geneva); etc.

[1.3.185–87: Gen. 2.24; Matt. 19.5; Mark 10.7; Eph. 5.31. But see Fenton, 7.255, 258.]

1.3.347–49: The food that to him now is as luscious as locusts, shall be to
             him shortly as acerb as the coloquintida.

Matt. 3.4: "His meate was also locustes and wilde honie."
Rev. 10.9–10: "It was in my mouth as sweete as honie: but when I had eaten it, my bellie was bitter."
See also Mark 1.6.

2.1.64–65:   And in th' essential vesture of creation
              Does tire the ingener. (Folio)

Ps. 102.25–27: "The heauens are the woorke of thy handes. They shal perishe, but thou shalt endure: they al shal waxe olde as dooth a garment. And as a vesture shalt thou change them, and they shalbe changed."

The Psalmist stresses God's everlastingness when he says that God will outlast the constellations, for they will wax old and perish in the same way that a garment wears out and needs to be changed. The sense of the passage in the Folio is to liken Desdemona's perfection to a work of art that exhausts its creator.

The Quarto reads: "And in the essentiall vesture of creation, / Does beare all excellency."

However, compare Fenton: "For touchinge her bewtie, seaming of suche wonderfull perfection that it was thoughte nature was dryven to the ende of her wittes in framinge a pece of so great excellancie.... Being blessed therwith so plentifully at the handes of th' Almighty, that it was doubted to the writers of that tyme whether God or nature deserved the greatest prayse in forminge so perfecte a creature" (7.254–55).

Both the Folio and Quarto reflect Fenton's influence. Line 64 of either text, however, seems to be a clear reference to Psalm 102. Cinthio simply has: "A virtuous Lady of wondrous beauty" (7.242).

2.1.187–89:   And let the laboring bark climb hills of seas
              Olympus-high, and duck again as low
              As hell's from heaven!

Compare Ps. 107.23–26: "They that goe downe to the sea in shippes: and occupie their businesse in great waters ... the stormie wynde aryseth: whiche lyfteth vp the waues thereof. They are caryed vp to the heauen, and downe agayne to the deepe."

Perhaps an analogy rather than a reference. Shakespeare appears to echo the next verse, Ps. 107.27, in *Romeo and Juliet* 2.3.3. He may, therefore, have known this Psalm well.

[2.1.221: Judges 18.19.]

2.1.299:   Till I am even'd with him, wife for wife.

With overtones of the "eye for eye, tooth for toothe, hande for hand, foote for foote" principle of the Mosaic Law. See Ex. 21.23–25; Lev. 24.20; Deut. 19.21.

2.3.71–72:   A soldier's a man;
             O, man's life's but a span.

Ps. 39.6: "Beholde, thou hast made my dayes as it were a spanne long."
Geneva (39.5): "Thou hast made my dayes as an hand breadth."
Compare *Timon of Athens* 5.3.3.

2.3.102–104:   Well, God's above all; and there be souls must be sav'd, and
               there be souls must not be sav'd.

Rom. 9.18: "Therefore he hath mercie on whome he will, and whom he
will, he hardeneth."
Rom. 9.22–23: "What and if God ... suffer with long pacience the vessels
of wrath, prepared to destruction ... that he might declare the riches of his
glorie vpon the vessels of mercie, which he hath prepared vnto glorie?"

2.3.106–107:   For mine own part ... I hope to be sav'd.

Rom. 8.24: "For wee are saued by hope."

2.3.111–112:   God forgive us our sins!

Luke 11.4: "And forgiue vs our sinnes."
Matt. 6.12: "And forgiue vs our dettes."
Prayer Book: "And forgiue vs our trespasses."
The form of the Lord's Prayer that Shakespeare heard most often, the form
that would have been most natural for him to use, was the one which
appeared in the Prayer Book. That version of the Lord's Prayer was read
daily in both the Morning and Evening Services of the English Church. But
the Act for the Uniformity of Common Prayer of 1559 prohibited disrespectful use of the Prayer Book in any interlude, play, song, or rhyme. Thus
when drunken Cassio quotes the Lord's Prayer, Shakespeare is careful not to
use the Prayer Book version lest he run afoul of the law. That seems to be the
overriding consideration in the above reference, rather than a conscious use
of Luke's version of the Lord's Prayer according to the Geneva Bible.

2.3.296–97:   It hath pleas'd the devil drunkenness to give place to the devil
              wrath.

Eph. 4.27: "Neither giue place to the deuil."

The Geneva Bible was the first version to read "giue place to the deuil." Earlier versions had "geue place vnto the backebyter." The Bishops' Bible followed the Geneva: "Neyther geue place to the deuyl."

2.3.309–310:   Good wine is a good familiar creature, if it be well us'd.

Ecclus. 31.27–28: "Wine soberly drunken, is profitable for the life of man.... Wine measurably drunken and in time, bringeth gladnes and cherefulness of the minde."

2.3.342–44:   And then for her
To win the Moor, were't to renounce his baptism,
All seals and symbols of redeemed sin.

Eph. 4.30: "The holy Spirit of God, by whom ye are sealed vnto the day of redemption."

Eph. 1.13–14: "Ye were sealed with the holy Spirit of promise ... vntill the redemption."

See also 2 Cor. 1.22; Acts 2.38.

Tomson note on 1 Cor. 7.14: "Baptisme is added as the seale of that holines."

Here Iago uses common theological terms.

2.3.351–53:   When devils will the blackest sins put on,
They do suggest at first with heavenly shows,
As I do now.

With clear overtones of Satan as an angel of light, which Shakespeare refers to several times in his plays. 2 Cor. 11.14: "For Satan him selfe is transformed into an Angel of light."

Compare *Love's Labor's Lost:* "Devils soonest tempt, resembling spirits of light" (4.3.253).

Compare also *Hamlet* 2.2.598–600; *Richard III* 1.3.337; *King John* 3.1.208–209.

See also the devil's temptation of Christ in Matt. 4.1–11 and Luke 4.1–13.

2.3.360:   So will I turn her virtue into pitch.

Compare Ecclus. 13.1: "He that toucheth pitche, shalbe defiled with it."
See *1 Henry IV* 2.4.410–14, where the reference to Ecclus. 13.1 is more
obvious.

3.3.117:   My lord, you know I love you.

Compare these words of Iago's with Peter's threefold reply to Christ at
John 21.15–17: "Yea Lord, thou knowest that I loue thee."

[3.3.137–38: Prov. 20.9.]

3.3.155–59:   Good name in man and woman,...
              Is the immediate jewel of their souls.
              Who steals my purse steals trash;...
              . . . .
              But he that filches from me my good name....

Prov. 22.1: "A good name is to bee chosen aboue great riches."
Ecclus. 41.12: "Haue regarde to thy name: for that shall continue with
thee aboue a thousande treasures of golde."
Eccles. 7.3 (7.1, AV): "A good name is better then a good oyntment."
Homily "Against Contention," part 1: "The one taketh away a mans
good name, the other taketh but his riches, which is of much lesse value and
estimation then is his good name."
Homily "Against Adultery," part 2: "Is not that treasure, which before all
other is most regarded of honest persons, the good fame and name of man
and woman, lost through whoredome?"

3.3.172–73:   Poor and content is rich, and rich enough,
              But riches fineless is as poor as winter.

Compare 1 Tim. 6.6–8: "Godlines is great gaine, if a man be content with
that he hathe.... Therefore when we haue foode and rayment, let vs there-
with be content."

3.3.203–204:   Their best conscience
               Is not to leave't undone, but keep't unknown.

Matt. 23.23, Bishops': "These ought ye to haue donne, and not to leaue
the other vndonne." (Also Tyndale, Matthew, Taverner, Great.)

Geneva: "These ought ye to haue done, and not to haue left the other."

Coverdale: "These ought to haue bene done, and not to leaue the other behinde."

Prayer Book, Morning and Evening Prayer: "Wee haue left vndone those things which wee ought to haue done, and we haue done those things which wee ought not to haue done." The Morning and Evening Prayer, recited daily, would have been Shakespeare's most likely source.

See also *Julius Caesar* 4.2.8–9; *Antony and Cleopatra* 3.1.14; *Coriolanus* 4.7.24–25.

3.3.322:   Trifles light as air.

Carter claims that Iago's words are a reference to Scripture Paraphrase 26:

> How long to streams of false delight
>   Will ye in crowds repair?
> How long your strength and substance waste
>   On trifles, light as air?

Paraphrases of various passages of Scripture were appended to the metrical Psalter used by the Church of Scotland. Paraphrase 26 is a metrical version of Isa. 55.2. However, none of these paraphrases had yet appeared in Shakespeare's day.

The complete Scottish Psalter in meter first appeared in 1564, the year of Shakespeare's birth, and was based largely on the newly completed English metrical Psalter of 1562 by Sternhold and Hopkins. Both Psalters prefixed and appended a number of religious songs and metrical passages to the core of 150 Psalms. The Scripture Paraphrases referred to by Carter, however, first appeared in 1745 and were occasionally appended to the Scottish Psalter. But not until 1781 did the Church of Scotland officially sanction the *Translations and Paraphrases, in verse, of Several Passages of Sacred Scripture*, commonly called *The Paraphrases*, which thereafter were frequently added to its metrical Psalter.

Many editions of the Scottish Psalter were published during Shakespeare's lifetime, and he may well have seen some of them, but none contained *The Paraphrases*, which were still a century and a half in coming. Thus Iago's words could not have been based on Scripture Paraphrase 26, although the similarity is striking.

For a more complete discussion of this passage, see my note in *Notes and Queries* 225 (April, 1980): 169–70.

[3.3.323–24: 2 Peter 1.19–21; 1 Cor. 15.3–4.]

[3.3.361: Mark 8.36–37.]

3.3.381–83:   *Oth*.... Thou shouldst be honest.
              Iago. I should be wise—for honesty's a fool
              And loses that it works for.

Compare Luke 16.8: "And the Lorde commended the vniust stewarde, because hee had done wisely. Wherefore the children of this worlde are ... wiser then the children of light." The Unjust Steward was wise though dishonest.
Compare *Timon of Athens* 4.3.497–506.

[3.4.126: Heb. 1.14.]

3.4.146–48:   For let our finger ache, and it endues
              Our other healthful members even to a sense
              Of pain.

1 Cor. 12.25–26: "In the body ... if one member suffer, al suffer with it."

3.4.197:   I pray you bring me on the way a little.

Compare Gen. 18.16: "Abraham went with them to bring them on the way."
"To bring on the way," however, was a common expression.

4.1.8:   The devil their virtue tempts, and they tempt heaven.

Compare the devil's second temptation of Jesus and Jesus' answer at Matt. 4.7: "Thou shalt not tempt the Lord thy God."
See also Luke 4.12; Deut. 6.16.
See 1.1.108–109 above.

[4.1.182–83: Zech. 7.12.]

4.1.234:   Fire and brimstone!

An expression which ultimately derives from Scripture. See Luke 17.29

and Rev. 14.10, 20.10, and 21.8: "Fire and brimstone."
  See also Gen. 19.24; Ps. 11.6; Ezek. 38.22; Rev. 9.17–18.

4.1.270:   He's that he is.

  Compare Ex. 3.14: "I am that I am."
  See also 1.1.65 above.

4.2.15–16:   If any wretch have put this in your head,
         Let heaven requite it with the serpent's curse!

  A reference to God's curse on the serpent in Eden at Gen 3.14: "The Lord
God saide to the serpent, Because thou hast done this, thou art cursed aboue
al cattell."
  Emilia tells Othello that to slander Desdemona's innocence would be as
great a crime as that of the serpent in Eden.

4.2.25–26:   Let me see your eyes;
         Look in my face.

  Perhaps based on the idea that the guilt of an adulterous woman can be
detected by the look on her face and especially by looking into her eyes.
  Compare Ecclus. 26.9: "The whoredome of a woman may be knowen in
the pride of her eyes, and eye liddes."

4.2.42, 124:   Alas the heavy day!
          Alas the day!

  Compare Joel 1.15: "Alas: for the day."
  Compare Jer. 30.7: "Alas, for this day."

4.2.47–53:   Had it pleas'd heaven
         To try me with affliction, had they rain'd
         All kind of sores and shames on my bare head,
         Steep'd me in poverty to the very lips,
         Given to captivity me and my utmost hopes,
         I should have found in some place of my soul
         A drop of patience.

A reference to Job, who was reduced to poverty and shame, afflicted with disease, and yet maintained patience.

Job 2.7–10: "Smote Iob with sore boyles, from the sole of his foote vnto his crowne.... In all this did not Iob sinne with his lippes."

James 5.11: "Ye haue heard of the patience of Iob."

4.2.57–62:   But there,...
                Where either I must live or bear no life;
                The fountain from the which my current runs
                Or else dries up: to be discarded thence!
                Or keep it as a cestern for foul toads
                To knot and gender in!

Prov. 5.15–18: "Drinke the water of thy cisterne, and of the riuers out of the middes of thine owne well. Let thy fountaines flowe foorth, and the riuers of waters in the streetes. But let them be thine, euen thine onely, and not the strangers with thee. Let thy fountaine be blessed, and reioyce with the wife of thy youth."

Shakespeare seems to have the Geneva Bible in mind in this reference. The Bishops' has neither "cisterne" nor "fountaine" ("fountaines"): "Drinke of the water of thine owne wel, and of the riuers that run out of thyne owne spring. Let thy welles flowe.... Let thy wel be blessed, and be glad with the wyfe of thy youth." Coverdale, Matthew, Taverner, and the Great Bibles all parallel the Bishops'. The Geneva gloss on "fountaine" in verse 18 is: "Thy children which shal come of thee in great abundance, shewing that God blesseth marriage and curseth whoredome."

Shakespeare may also have had the homily "Against Idlenesse" in mind, which corresponds to the Geneva at verse 15: "The wiseman also exhorteth vs to drinke the waters of our owne cesterne, and of the riuers that runne out of the middes of our owne well." The homily "Against Idlenesse" first appeared in 1563 in *The Seconde Tome of Homelyes*; the Geneva Bible had appeared three years earlier.

4.2.63:   Thou young and rose-lipp'd cherubin.

Derived ultimately from Scripture, where cherubim are frequently mentioned. The word first appears at Gen. 3.24, and occurs many times thereafter. The lid of the ark (the mercy seat) had two cherubim on it, and various curtains in both the tabernacle and the temple were embroidered with cherubim. See Ex. 25.18–22; 37.7–9; 26.1, 31; Ezek. 10.4–7; Heb. 9.5. See *Macbeth* 1.7.22 for a discussion of Shakespeare's references to cherubim.

4.2.69:   Would thou hadst never been born!

Matt. 26.24: "It had bene good for that man, if he had neuer bene borne."
See also Mark 14.21.

At 3.3.362 Othello threatens Iago that if Iago does not provide him with ocular proof of Desdemona's unfaithfulness, "Thou hadst been better have been born a dog." In Cinthio's narrative the Moor says: "If you do not make me see with my own eyes what you have told me, be assured, I shall make you realize that it would have been better for you had you been born dumb" (7.246). Othello's words to Iago at 3.3.362 were clearly based on the Moor's words to the Ensign in Cinthio, and although similar to Othello's words to Desdemona at 4.2.69, this latter passage appears to be a biblical reference, there being no corresponding words in Cinthio between the Moor and his wife.

4.2.82–85:   No, as I am a Christian.
             If to preserve this vessel for my lord
             From any other foul unlawful touch
             Be not to be a strumpet, I am none.

1 Thess. 4.3–4: "That yee should absteine from fornication, that euery one of you should know how to possesse his vessel in holines and honor."
1 Sam. 21.5: "Certainly women haue bene separate from vs ... and the vessels of the yong men were holy,... how much more then shall euery one be sanctified this day in the vessel?"

4.2.90–92:   You, mistress,
             That have the office opposite to Saint Peter,
             And keeps the gate of hell!

Matt. 16.18–19: "Thou art Peter, and vpon this rocke I will builde my Church: and the gates of hell shall not ouercome it. And I wil giue vnto thee the keyes of the kingdome of heauen."

4.2.103–104:   I cannot weep, nor answers have I none
               But what should go by water.

Editors of *Othello* generally assume that Desdemona's words, "what should go by water," refer to tears, that her answer can only be "expressed in tears," although she had just said, "I cannot weep." It is likely, however, that the reference is to the ancient Hebrew ritual of purification by water from the charge of adultery.

In Numbers 5.11–31 a ritual is outlined to determine a wife's innocence or guilt in case her husband "be moued with a ielous minde" that his wife had committed adultery against him. She was to be brought before the priest and made "to drinke the bitter and cursed water, and the cursed water, turned into bitternesse, shall enter into her" (5.24). If guilty, the water would cause her belly to swell "and her thigh shall rot." If not guilty, she would be declared clean. The ritual concludes: "This is the lawe of ielousie ... when a man is moued with a ielous minde being ielous ouer his wife, then shall he bring the woman before the Lorde, and the Priest shall do to her according to al this lawe" (5.29–30).

Thus Desdemona appears to say that neither tears nor words can exonerate her, so great was Othello's jealousy. The charge of adultery against her could only "go by water." Nothing less than that ancient water ritual would prove her innocent in Othello's mind.

[4.2.111–12: 1 Thess. 2.7.]

4.2.152–53:   If e'er my will did trespass 'gainst his love,
              Either in discourse of thought or actual deed.

A paraphrase of the General Confession, Communion Service: "Wee knowledge and bewaile our manifold sinnes and wickednes, which we from time to time most grieuously haue committed, by thought, word, and deede, against thy diuine Maiestie."

Also the exhortation before Communion: "Offended, either by will, word, or deed."

4.3.64, 68–70:   *Des.* Wouldst thou do such a deed for all the world?
                 Emil. The world's a huge thing; it is a great price
                 For a small vice.

With overtones of Satan offering Jesus "all the Kingdomes of the world, and the glorie of them," if Jesus would but fall down and worship him. Matt. 4.8–9.

Compare also Matt. 16.26: "What shall it profite a man, though he should winne the whole worlde, if hee lose his owne soule?"

[5.2.7–8: 2 Sam. 21.17; Job 18.5.]

[5.2.8: Ps. 104.4 ("flaming minister").]

5.2.21–22: This sorrow's heavenly,
It strikes where it doth love.

Compare Heb. 12.6: "For whome the Lorde loueth, he chasteneth."

5.2.26–27: If you bethink yourself of any crime
Unreconcil'd as yet to heaven and grace.

Compare 2 Cor. 5.20: "Be reconciled to God."

5.2.32: I would not kill thy soul.

Compare Matt. 10.28: "Feare ye not them which kill the bodie, but are not able to kill the soule."

5.2.46: Peace, and be still.

Mark 4.39: "Peace, and be still."

5.2.59–61: Never lov'd Cassio
But with such general warranty of heaven
As I might love.

A general reference to the Christian admonition to "loue one another." See 1 John 3.11; 1 Thess. 4.9; Rom. 13.8; etc.

[5.2.87: Prov. 12.10.]

5.2.99–101: Methinks it should be now a huge eclipse
Of sun and moon, and that th' affrighted globe
Did yawn at alteration.

Typical of the signs that signify the deaths of outstanding persons. At Christ's death, the Gospels record an eclipse, an earthquake, the opening of the graves, and the dead coming out of their graves. Matt. 27.45, 51–53; Mark 15.33; Luke 23.44–45.

See also *Julius Caesar* 2.2.1–40, based on Plutarch, who follows the same convention.

5.2.129:   She's like a liar gone to burning hell.

Compare Rev. 21.8: "All lyers, shal haue their parte in the lake, which burneth with fire and brimstone."

5.2.132:   She turn'd to folly, and she was a whore.

Deut. 22.21: "For she hath wrought follie in Israel,by playing the whore."

5.2.134:   She was false as water.

Compare Gen. 49.4, said to Reuben for defiling his father's bed: "Thou wast light as water."
Tyndale, Matthew, Taverner, Great, Bishops': "Vnstable as water."
Coverdale: "Thou passest forth swyfely as the water."

[5.2.145–46: Matt. 13.46.]

5.2.196:   'Tis proper I obey him; but not now.

With clear overtones of both the Marriage Service and the homilies. Marriage Service: "Wilt thou haue this man to thy wedded husband?... Wilt thou obey him, and serue him?" "I N. take thee N. to my wedded husband, to haue and to hold,... to loue, cherish, and to obey."
Homily "Of the State of Matrimonie": "But as for their husbands, them must they obey.... A good wife by obeying her husband, shall beare the rule.... For, obey thy husband,... and so shalt thou honour God."
Compare also Eph. 5.22: "Wiues, submit your selues vnto your husbandes."
Compare 1 Peter 3.5–6: "Holy women ... were subiect to their husbands. As Sarra obeyed Abraham."

5.2.220:   I will speak as liberal as the north.

Compare Ezek. 1.4: "A whirlewinde came out of the North."
Compare Job 37.9: "The cold [cometh] from the North winde."
Geneva note on "North winde": "In Ebrewe it is called the scattering winde, because it driueth away the cloudes and purgeth the ayre."
Quarto: "I'le be in speaking, liberal as the ayre."

5.2.347, Folio: Like the base Iudean.

Most likely a reference to Judas Iscariot, who betrayed Jesus. Matt. 26.14–16.

The First Folio text of *Othello* is considered the superior text by most editors, but in this line, the Riverside editors preferred the First Quarto, which has "Like the base Indian." "Indian" was a much more familiar word than "Iudean" in Shakespeare's day, and more likely to have been used. A copyist or typesetter would be more likely to change "Iudean" to the more familiar "Indian" when confronted with a puzzling word than to change "Indian" to "Iudean."

Strongly favoring "Judean" over "Indian" is the fact that, while Shakespeare followed Cinthio throughout most of the play, he completely abandoned Cinthio in the murder scene, and followed a different murder account that he found in Bandello and in Fenton's English translation and adaptation of Bandello. Fenton twice compares the murder to Judas's betrayal of Christ: "Wherewith, after he had embraced and kissed her, in such sorte as Judas kissed our Lorde the same night he betraied him, he saluted her with ten or xii estockados [stabs]." Then after killing himself, he commended "his soule to the reprobate socyetie of Judas and Cayne" (7.260–61).

Shakespeare followed not only Fenton's expanded English version of Bandello, but also consulted Bandello's narrative in the original Italian. Bandello's account of the murder relates that when the housemaid called the neighbors, they broke down the door and found "the treacherous husband lying face downward on the almost lifeless body of his unhappy wife.... The wife, returning somewhat to consciousness,... made confession, pardoning her husband with all her heart, not being willing to let anyone speak ill of him, but accusing nobody but her own misfortune" (7.261–62). Shakespeare closely followed this pattern of the murder, rather than Cinthio's. In Cinthio the Moor and the Ensign kill Desdemona with a stocking filled with sand, break her skull, and then cause part of the ceiling to fall to make it appear that the fallen rafters had killed her. In Cinthio the Moor is exiled and dies much later at the hands of Desdemona's relatives.

Since Shakespeare followed Bandello and Fenton so closely in the murder scene, it is only logical that he also followed Fenton's comparison of the murder to Judas's betrayal of Christ. To argue that, with Fenton's account before him, Shakespeare changed the comparison from Judas to an Indian is hardly logical. The Q1 typesetter, unacquainted with Fenton, and confronted with the unfamiliar and puzzling word "Iudean," might well have changed it to the familiar word "Indian." But it seems clear that the generally superior Folio text is correct in this instance also, and that "Iudean" is what Shakespeare wrote, a reference to Judas, who belonged to the same tribe as Jesus. See 5.2.348, below.

For a more complete discussion of this passage, see my note, "Like the Base Judean," in *Shakespeare Quarterly* 31 (1980): 93–95.

5.2.347–48:   Threw a pearl away
              Richer than all his tribe.

A reference to the "pearle of great price" of Matt. 13.46. Jesus' parable of the "pearle of great price" was well known in Shakespeare's day. The motto on the title page of all separately-issued Bishops' New Testaments was, "The pearle which Christ commaunded to be bought: Is here to be found, not els to be sought."

5.2.348:   Richer than all his tribe.

Since both Judas and Jesus belonged to the same genealogical tribe, Judas threw away the most precious jewel of his tribe by betraying Jesus.

Assuming that "Iudean" is the correct reading in the previous line, this reference may indicate Shakespeare's use of a Tomson New Testament. Judas Iscariot was the only apostle from the tribe of Judah; the other eleven were Galileans. The gloss on "Iscariot" in Tomson's New Testament at Matt. 10.4 is, "A man of Kerioth. Nowe Kerioth was in the tribe of Iudah, Iosh. 15.25." No other version contains the Tomson gloss on Matt. 10.4.

Tomson's New Testament appeared in 1576 (*STC* 2878), and from 1576 until 1604, when *Othello* was most likely written, thirty editions of Tomson's New Testament were published, more than twice as many as all other versions of the New Testament that were published in England during that time.

Starting in 1587, the Tomson New Testament also began to be bound with various editions of the Geneva Old Testament to form a Geneva-Tomson Bible (*STC* 2146). Of the forty editions of the complete Geneva Bible published in England between 1587 and 1604 (excluding the spurious "1599" Geneva Bibles published on the Continent), eleven included the Tomson rather than the Geneva New Testament.

5.2.355–56:   I took by th' throat the circumcised dog,
              And smote him—thus.

Compare 1 Sam. 17.35: "I went out after him and smote him, . . . I caught him by the beard, and smote him, and slue him."

5.2.358–59: I kiss'd thee ere I kill'd thee. No way but this,
Killing myself, to die upon a kiss.

Again, parallel to Judas, who betrayed Jesus with a kiss and afterwards killed himself. Matt. 26.48–49; 27.4–5.

See the comment on 5.2.347 above.

Fenton: "Wherewith, after he had embraced and kissed her, in such sorte as Judas kissed our Lorde the same night he betraied him, he saluted her with ten or xii estockados [stabs]" (7.260).

The false kiss of Judas is also referred to in *Love's Labor's Lost* 5.2.600; *As You Like It* 3.4.8–9; and *3 Henry VI* 5.7.33.

King Lear

Shakespeare's main source for *Lear* was the anonymous play *The True Chronicle History of King Leir, and his three daughters, Gonorill, Ragan, and Cordella*, first published in 1605. Henslowe's diary records that *Leir* was acted as early as April 1594, but it was probably not a new play even then. That Shakespeare had read the old play seems certain; what is not certain is whether he read a manuscript of the play or a printed copy of *Leir* as soon as it was published.

Unlike that of Shakespeare's play, the action of *Leir* takes place in a Christian world, and the play has strong Christian overtones. Leir wishes to abdicate because his wife has just died, and he wants to think about the welfare of his soul with prayers and beads. He hopes that his late wife is now "possest of heavenly joyes," and that she rides "in triumph 'mongst the Cherubins." After being rejected, Cordella feels nought but love and Christian forgiveness for her father, although he had called her a "bastard Impe" and considered Gonorill and Ragan "the kindest Gyrles in Christendome." On becoming Queen of France, she goes "to the Temple of my God, / To render thanks for all his benefits." When Leir and Perillus are almost murdered by a messenger from Gonorill, Perillus exclaims:

> Oh just *Jehova*, whose almighty power
> Doth governe all things in this spacious world,
> How canst thou suffer such outragious acts
> To be committed without just revenge?

To which Leir replies,

> Ah, my true friend in all extremity,
> Let us submit us to the will of God:
> Things past all sence, let us not seeke to know;
> It is Gods will, and therefore must be so.   (1649–58)

The play also contains references to the Litany and the Magnificat. Few of the sources that Shakespeare used for his plays contain so many biblical references and religious images. *Leir* contains some thirty clear biblical references, thirteen possible references or passages with strong biblical echoes, and many religious images.

Shakespeare borrowed none of *Leir's* references. In a few instances, for example, at 1.2.106–112, 1.4.301–303, 3.6.79–81, and 4.2.34–36, Shakespeare's references to Scripture may have been suggested by a phrase or a parallel situation in the old play, but for the most part, Shakespeare's biblical references are his own.

Other sources for Shakespeare include Holinshed, book 2 of *The Faerie Queene*, Sidney's *Arcadia*, and *The Mirrour for Magistrates*. He may also have consulted Geoffrey of Monmouth's *Historia Regum Britanniae* and Camden's *Remaines Concerning Britaine*. But none of these works affected Shakespeare's biblical references. There are less than five biblical references in the portions of these works that deal with the Lear story, and Shakespeare used none of them. He evidently read Florio's 1603 translation of Montaigne shortly before he wrote *Lear*, since there are over one hundred verbal echoes of Florio,—over one hundred words and phrases in *Lear* that also occur in Florio's translation—that Shakespeare used for the first time. But Shakespeare borrowed no biblical references from Montaigne. The only passage in *Lear* that may be a biblical reference and may have been inspired by a similar thought in Montaigne occurs at 3.4.102–103.

A large number of religious names and images in *Lear* were borrowed from Dr. Samuel Harsnett's *A Declaration of Egregious Popish Impostures*. Harsnett, Chaplain to the Bishop of London, had already exposed a Puritan exorcist. In 1603 he published the *Declaration* to warn against "wandring Iesuits," Catholic exorcists who pretended that they could exorcise demons by using relics, holy water, and other means. The names of the devils that "Poor Tom" mentions as he raves, his repeated references to the "foul fiend," and the devil described to Gloucester at 4.6.69–72 are all based on Harsnett. The biblical references that can be found in Edgar's utterances (such as at 3.4.80–83) were added by Shakespeare, but Harsnett exerted an important influence on the religious imagery in the play.

Lear is sometimes interpreted as a Christian allegory, especially on the basis of Cordelia's words,

> O dear father,
> It is thy business that I go about,
>
> (4.4.23–24)

and the words of Cordelia's attendant,

> Thou hast one daughter
> Who redeems nature from the general curse
> Which twain have brought her to.
>
> (4.6.205–207)

The former, it is claimed, puts Cordelia in the role of a Christ figure (Luke

2.49), while the latter is interpreted as an allegorical reference to the ransom, wherein Christ's death atoned for the sins of Adam and Eve.

The play's many references to providence and the questions it raises about heaven's concern for men may have been influenced by books 2 and 3 of the *Arcadia*, 1590. Gloucester's well-known comment at 4.1.36–37, "As flies to wanton boys are we to th' gods, / They kill us for their sport," may have been based on book 3, chapter 10 of the *Arcadia*, where Cecropia says that to think the gods are concerned about men is as reasonable "as if flies should thinke, that men take great care which of them hums sweetest, and which of them flies nimblest." The closest parallel in the old play is the Messenger's statement,

> I weigh no more the murdring of a man,
> Then I respect the cracking of a Flea,
> When I doe catch her byting on my skin.   (1214–16)

Book 2 of the *Arcadia*, with its account of the blinded Paphlagonian king, who trusted his treacherous bastard son and turned against his loyal son, was Shakespeare's source for the Gloucester subplot in *Lear*.

Line numbers in *Leir* are those in Bullough, vol. 7, pages 337–402.

[1.1.84: Gen. 49.12.]

1.1.91–92:   I cannot heave
          My heart into my mouth.

Compare Ecclus. 21.26: "The heart of fooles is in their mouth: but the mouth of the wise is in their heart."

Closest parallel in *Leir*: "I cannot paynt my duty forth in words" (277).

1.1.96–98:   You have begot me, bred me, lov'd me: I
          Return those duties back as are right fit,
          Obey you, love you, and most honor you.

Compare the Catechism: "To loue, honour, and succour my father and mother."

Compare Eph. 6.1–2: "Children, obey your parents in the Lord: for this is right. Honour thy father and mother."

See also Ex. 20.12; Deut. 5.16.

Leir: "But looke what love the child doth owe the father, / The same to you I beare, my gracious Lord" (279–80).

[1.1.99–104: With faint overtones of the Marriage Service, Gen. 2.24, Matt. 19.5–6, etc. In one of Shakespeare's possible sources (Camden's *Remaines Concerning Britaine*), the reference is explicit. Bullough, 7.322.]

[1.1.233–34: Matt. 26.24; Mark 14.21.]

1.1.250:   Fairest Cordelia, that art most rich being poor.

2 Cor. 8.9: "Our Lord Iesus Christ, that he being riche, for your sakes became poore."
2 Cor. 6.10: "As poore, and yet make many riche."

1.1.281–82:   Who covers faults, at last with shame derides.
              Well may you prosper!

Compare Prov. 28.13: "He that hideth his sinnes, shall not prosper."
All other Tudor versions parallel the Geneva. The Authorized Version of 1611 alone has "couereth": "Hee that couereth his sinnes, shall not prosper."

[1.2.103–104: Matt. 24.29.]

1.2.106–112:   Love cools, friendship falls off, brothers divide: in cities, mutinies; in countries, discord; in palaces, treason; and the bond crack'd 'twixt son and father. This villain of mine comes under the prediction; there's son against father: ... there's father against child.

1.2.144–46:   Unnaturalness between the child and the parent, death, dearth, dissolutions of ancient amities. . . .

Matt. 10.21: "The brother shall betray the brother to death, and the father the sonne, and the children shal rise against their parents, and shal cause them to die."
Matt. 24.12: "The loue of many shalbe colde."
See also Mark 13.8, 12; Luke 12.52–53; 21.16; Micah 7.6.
"Comes under the prediction" evidently refers to Jesus' prediction about

the signs that would foretell the end of the world.

Compare the homily "Against Disobedience and Wilfull Rebellion," part 3: "The brother to seeke, and often to worke the death of his brother, the sonne of the father, the father to seeke or procure the death of his sons,... and by their faults to disinherite their innocent children."

Compare the following passages in *Leir*: "This wicked age, / When children thus against their parents rage" (753–54).

"O times! O monstrous, vilde, / When parents are contemned of the child!" (761–62)

"But trust strangers rather, / Since daughters prove disloyall to the father" (767–68).

Although these passages in *Leir* are not echoes of Scripture, they may have suggested to Shakespeare the biblical references which he makes in 1.2 of *Lear*. Particularly the expressions "This wicked age" and "O times!" followed by outcries against rebellious children, may have suggested to Shakespeare the biblical passages describing the end of the world, when children and parents would turn against each other.

1.4.15–16:   To converse with him that is wise and says little.

Compare Ecclus. 9.17: "Let thy talke be with the wise."
Compare Prov. 13.20: "He that walketh with the wise, shall be wise."
Compare Prov. 17.27–28: "He that hath knowledge, spareth his wordes.... Euen a foole (when he holdeth his peace) is counted wise."

[1.4.16, "to fear judgment": Ps. 1.6 (1.5, Geneva); Jer. 8.7, Noble.]

[1.4.270–71: 1 Sam. 21.13.]

1.4.288:   How sharper than a serpent's tooth it is.

Compare Ps. 140.3: "They haue sharpened their tongues like a serpent."
Closest parallel in *Leir*: three references to Gonorill and/or Ragan as "viperous," "vipers," and "viper" (811, 2558, 2584).

1.4.301–303:   Old fond eyes,
                 ... I'll pluck ye out,
                 And cast you.

Matt. 5.29: "Wherefore if thy right eye cause thee to offende, plucke it out, and cast it from thee."

Compare *Leir*, in which Ragan says of Cordella: "And with these nayles scratch out her hatefull eyes" (1906).

[2.2.65–66: Prov. 27.22.]

2.4.67–68: We'll set thee to school to an ant, to teach thee there's no laboring i' th' winter.

Prov. 6.6, 8: "Go to the pismire, O sluggarde: beholde her wayes, and be wise. Prepareth her meat in the sommer, and gathereth her foode in haruest."
See also Prov. 30.25.
Although the Taverner also has "pysmere," most other English Bibles of Shakespeare's Day (Coverdale, Matthew, Great, Bishops') have "emmet." The Douay of 1610 has "emmote." Only the Authorized Version of 1611 has, "Go to the Ant, thou sluggard," in this well-known passage. Some consider this to be evidence of Shakespeare's influence on the Authorized Version. (Compare 1.1.281–82 above and 4.2.78–80.) However, although the Douay has "emmote" at Prov. 6.6, it alone has "antes" in the related Scripture at Prov. 30.25: "The antes, a weake people, which prepareth in the haruest meate for themselues," and this may have been an influence on the Authorized Version in both Prov. 6.6 and 30.25.
However Florio used "Antes-neast" in his 1603 translation of Montaigne (see 3.4.102–103 below), while Shakespeare used "pismires" at *I Henry IV* 1.3.240. Shakespeare's only other use of "ant" also occurs in *I Henry IV*, at 3.1.147.
Baldwin thinks that the reference is to Aesop's fable of the fly and the ant rather than to Scripture. (*William Shakspere's Small Latine & Lesse Greeke* 1.620–21.)

[2.4.160–61: Ps. 140.3.]

[2.4.189, 191 ("heavens … are old"): Ps. 102.25–26.]

3.1.5–6: Bids the wind blow the earth into the sea,
Or swell the curled waters 'bove the main.

Compare Ps. 46.2–3: "Though the earth be moued: and though the hylles be caryed into the middest of the sea. Though the waters thereof rage and swel."

At best an analogy rather than a reference. It was a common Renaissance concept that when order and degree were violated, land and sea would forsake their ordained boundaries and seek to overwhelm each other.

[3.2.37: James 5.11.]

3.4.80–83:   Obey thy parents, keep thy word's justice, swear not, commit not with man's sworn spouse, set not thy sweet heart on proud array.

"Poor Tom's" garbled version of the Ten Commandments, the Sermon on the Mount, and related Scriptures.
   Eph. 6.1: "Children, obey your parents."
   Ex. 20.12, Deut. 5.16: "Honour thy father and thy mother."
   Matt. 5.33–34: "Thou shalt not forsweare thy selfe, but shalt performe thine othes.... Sweare not at all."
   Ex. 20.14: "Thou shalt not commit adulterie."
   1 Tim. 2.9: "... that they aray them selues in comely apparell, with shamefastnes and modestie, not with ... gold, or pearles, or costly apparell."
   See also 1 Peter 3.3–4; James 5.12.
   Edgar's words also have overtones of the Catechism in which the Ten Commandments are rehearsed. Compare the Catechism's "to bee true and iust in all my dealing," with "keep thy word's justice."

3.4.85:   Proud in heart.

Compare Prov. 16.5: "All that are proude in heart."
   See also Prov. 21.4; 28.25: "A proude heart."
   Compare Ps. 101.5 (101.4): "A frowarde hart shal depart from me."
   Compare Ps. 101.5, Geneva: "A proude looke and high heart." (The Psalter has "A proud looke and high stomacke" in the latter text, 101.7 in the Psalter.)

3.4.87–90:   Did the act of darknesse with her;... one that slept in the contriving of lust, and wak'd to do it.

Compare the homily "Against Whoredome and Vncleannesse," part 2: "Here the holy Apostle exhorteth vs to cast away the workes of darkenesse,... which are all ministers vnto that vice, and preparations to induce and bring in the filthy sinne of the flesh. Hee calleth them the deedes and

workes of darkenesse, not onely because they are customably in darkenesse...." "Doeth not the whoremonger giue his minde ... to serue his
lusts and carnall pleasures? Doeth not the adulterer give his minde ... that
hee may bee the more able to maintaine his harlots and whores, and to continue in his filthy and vnlawfull loue?"
    See also Rom. 13.12–14.

3.4.102–103:   Is man no more than this? Consider him well.

    Compare Heb. 2.6: "What is man, that thou shouldest bee mindfull of
him? or the sonne of man that thou wouldest consider him?"
    Compare Ps. 8.4: "What is man that thou art so myndful of hym: and the
sonne of man that thou visitest hym?"
    If Shakespeare had Scripture in mind in this passage, and if his reference is
to Heb. 2.6 rather than to Ps. 8.4, then he echoes the Geneva Bible. Only the
Geneva has "consider him" at Heb. 2.6. The other versions have "visitest
him." Taverner has "doest vyset hym."
    Some think that Shakespeare borrowed this passage not from Scripture
but from Florio's 1603 translation of Montaigne: "Miserable man: whom if
you consider well, what is he?" The complete quotation is: "This many-
headed, divers-armed, and furiously-raging monster, is man; wretched,
weake and miserable man: whom if you consider well, what is he, but a
crawling, and ever-moving Antes-neast?" (Book 2, chapter 12, "An Apolo-
gie of Raymond Sebond," 274.)
    This passage is one of the more striking parallels between Shakespeare and
Montaigne.

3.6.79–81:   I do not like the fashion of your garments. You will say they
             are Persian, but let them be chang'd.

    Dan. 6.8: "Seale the writing, that it be not changed according to the lawe
of the Medes and Persians, which altereth not." (Also 6.12, 15.)
    Closest parallel in *Leir*: "I thought as much to have met with the Souldan
of Persia, / As to have met you in this place" (425–26).
    Lear's words are a reference to the immutability of the laws of the Medes
and Persians, which had become proverbial in Shakespeare's day on account
of their mention in Scripture. (Compare Esther 8.8.) The sense of Lear's
words is that, in spite of the "Persian" nature of Poor Tom's garments, Lear
wants them changed. The passage in *Leir*, on the other hand, is from an
altogether different context.

    [3.7.5, 57: Matt. 5.29. Compare 1.4.301–303 above.]

3.7.58, of Lear: His anointed flesh.

A reference to the expression "the Lord's anointed," applied to kings.
1 Sam. 26.9: "The Lords anointed."
See also 2 Sam. 1.14; 12.7; etc.
Leir: "Beware, how thou dost lay thy hand / Upon the high anoynted of the Lord" (1695–96).

4.1.33:   Which made me think a man a worm.

Compare Job 25.6: "Howe much more man, a worme, euen the sonne of man, which is but a worme?"
See also Job 17.14; Ps. 22.6.

4.2.34–36:   She that herself will sliver and disbranch
             From her material sap, perforce must wither,
             And come to deadly use.

John 15.6: "If a man abide not in me, he is cast forth as a branche, and withereth: and men gather them, and cast them into the fire, and they burne."
Compare *Leir*: COR.... If so the stocke be dryed with disdayne,
             Withered and sere the branch must needes remaine.
             KING [of France]. But thou art now graft in another
               stock;
             I am the stock, and thou the lovely branch:
             And from my root continuall sap shall flow.   (1242–46)

Shakespeare is considerably closer in meaning to the passage in John 15. He may have transformed the *Leir* passage into a more explicit biblical reference.

[4.2.38–39: Titus 1.15.]

4.2.51:   That bear'st a cheek for blows.

Compare Matt. 5.39: "Whosoeuer shall smite thee on thy right cheeke, turne to him the other also."
Compare Luke 6.29: "Vnto him that smiteth thee on the one cheeke, offer also the other."

4.2.78–80:   This shows you are above,
             You justicers, that these our nether crimes
             So speedily can venge!

Compare Luke 18.7–8: "Shal not God auenge his elect?... I tell you he wil auenge them quickely."

Authorized Version: "He will auenge them speedily." Coverdale has "shortly," but all other versions have "quickly." Only the Authorized Version has "speedily." See the comment on 2.4.67–68, above.

Leir: "The heavens are just, and hate impiety, / And will (no doubt) reveale such haynous crimes" (1909–10).

4.4.3–5:   Crown'd with rank femiter and furrow-weeds,
           With hardocks, hemlock, nettles, cuckoo-flow'rs,
           Darnel, and all the idle weeds.

Compare the homily, "Of the Misery of All Mankinde," part 2: "We ... bring foorth but weedes, netles, brambles, briers, cockle, and darnel."

Compare *Leir*: "Though you name yourselfe the thorn, / The weed, the gall, the henbane & the wormewood ..." (2069–70).

Perhaps an analogy rather than a reference to the homily, since the comparison of an undesirable state to weeds and an unweeded garden was common.

4.4.23–24:   O dear father,
             It is thy business that I go about.

Luke 2.49: "I must go about my fathers busines."

[4.6.73–74: Matt. 19.26; Luke 18.27.]

4.6.98–100:   To say "ay" and "no" to every thing that I said! "Ay," and
              "no" too, was no good divinity.

2 Cor. 1.18–19: "Our worde toward you, was not Yea, and Nay. For ... Iesus Christ ... was not Yea, and Nay: but in him it was Yea."

Compare James 5.12: "Let your yea, be yea, and your nay, nay."

Compare Matt. 5.37: "Let your communication be, Yea, yea: Nay, nay. For whatsoeuer is more then these, commeth of euil."

[4.6.100–102: Matt. 7.27.]

4.6.109–111:   I pardon that man's life. What was thy cause?
Adultery?
Thou shalt not die. Die for adultery? No.

A reference to the death penalty for adultery as set forth in Lev. 20.10;
Deut. 22.22; John 8.4–5; and elsewhere.

[4.6.134–35: Ps. 102.25–27.]

4.6.178–83:   We came crying hither.
Thou know'st, the first time that we smell the air
. We wawl and cry. I will preach to thee. Mark.
. . . .

When we are born, we cry that we are come
To this great stage of fools.

Compare Wisdom 7.3: "When I was borne, I receyued the common ayre
... crying and weeping at the first as all other doe."
Compare Wisdom 7.6: "All men then haue one entrance vnto life, and a
like going out." (Resembling stage imagery.)

4.6.205–207:   Thou hast one daughter
Who redeems nature from the general curse
Which twain have brought her to.

A favorite passage for those who seek to give a Christian interpretation to
Lear. These words are applied allegorically to Christ, who redeemed mankind from the sin of Adam and Eve.
Compare *Leir*: "Ah, good my Lord, condemne not all for one: / You have
two daughters left" (908–909).
Leir had just complained how Gonorill had broken "natures sacred law"
(898).

4.7.38:   To hovel thee with swine and rogues forlorn.

Compare the parable of the Prodigal Son at Luke 15, in which the son was
sent "to feede swine. And he would faine haue filled his belly with the
huskes, that the swine ate" (15.15–16).
Milward thinks that Cordelia's reference to Lear as "poor perdu!" four
lines earlier is another reference to the parable of the Prodigal Son, of whom
it was said, "he was lost, but he is found" (15.24, 31). "Perdu," however,

also meant a sentinel or sentry on duty at a dangerous outpost, and Cordelia asks, "Was this a face ... to watch—poor perdu!— / With this thin helm?"

[4.7.71: John 18.11: Matt. 20.23; 26.42.]

[5.3.16–17: Dan. 2.29; Ps. 139.2–3, Noble.]

5.3.22–23:   He that parts us shall bring a brand from heaven,
             And fire us hence like foxes.

Judges 15.4–5: "Samson went out, and tooke three hundreth foxes, and tooke firebrands, and turned them taile to taile, and put a firebrand in the middes betweene two tailes. And when he had set the brandes on fire, he sent them out into the standing corne."
But compare Harsnett: "Fire him out of his hold, as men smoke out a Foxe out of his burrow" (p. 97).

5.3.24–25:   The good-years shall devour them, flesh and fell,
             Ere they shall make us weep! We'll see 'em starv'd first.

Lear's words appear to allude to Pharaoh's dream of seven "good" years of plenty followed by seven years of famine (Gen. 41.1–36). Lear tells Cordelia that although their enemies have won the day, even in their "good yeeres" (Gen. 41.35), her sisters will not enjoy their victory, but will starve and be "deuoured" (Gen. 41.7, 24) as if living in the seven years of famine.
Compare the reference to Gen. 41 in *Hamlet* 3.4.64–65.

5.3.137–38:   And from th' extremest upward of thy head
              To the descent and dust below thy foot.

Compare 2 Sam. 14.25: "From the sole of his foote euen to the top of his head there was no blemish in him."
Most likely an analogy rather than a reference.

[5.3.171–74: Wisdom 12.23; 11.16 (*sic* 11.13); Jer. 2.19, Noble.]

[5.3.186: 1 Cor. 15.30–31.]

5.3.264–65:   *Kent.* Is this the promis'd end?
                    Edg. Or image of that horror?

The reference is to the foretold end of the world.
Matt. 24.3, 6: "What signe shalbe ... of the end of the worlde.... Ye shall heare of warres, and rumors of warres:... the end is not yet."
See also Matt. 24.7–14.
Compare 1 Peter 4.7: "The end of al things is at hand. Be ye therefore sober."
See 1.2.106–112 above.

[5.3.303–305: See note on 4.7.71 above.]

5.3.308:   Thou'lt come no more.

Compare Job 7.9–10: "Hee that goeth downe to the graue, shall come vp no more. He shall returne no more."
Shakespeare refers to Job 7.6 in *The Merry Wives of Windsor* 5.1.22–23, increasing the likelihood that he may also be referring to Job 7 in this passage.

Macbeth

Shakespeare chose the subject of Macbeth to please King James, his company's patron, whose Scottish background made him thoroughly familiar with that story. Shakespeare incorporated several topics into the play which he knew were of interest to the king, and he may have read several of James's published works before writing the play. The king constantly referred to Scripture for authority in his writings, and some of the biblical references in *Macbeth* may have been inspired by the king's use of the same references in his works. The alleged correspondences between Shakespeare's references and those of the king, however, have sometimes been exaggerated.

Shakespeare's principal source for the play was Holinshed's *Chronicles*. Holinshed, in turn, based his Scottish history mainly on the *Scotorum Historiae* (1527) of Hector Boethius (Boece). Shakespeare may also have read Boece either in the original Latin or in John Bellenden's Scottish translation of Boece (ca. 1536). Holinshed seldom has many biblical references. The Holinshed material that is relevant for *Macbeth* contains only two clear references: "avarice is the root of all mischiefe" (Bullough 7.502), from 1 Tim. 6.10, and the expression "gift of prophesie" (7.508), probably from the Geneva version of 1 Cor. 13.2. A third possible reference is Holinshed's placing the slaying of the king "a little before cocks crow" (7.482), perhaps a reference to Matt. 26.34, 74–75 and parallel Gospel accounts.

Shakespeare borrowed only the second reference, "gift of prophesie" (4.3.157). Although some claim that the play's well-known expression "man that's born of woman" is a clear reference to Job 14.1 and to the Burial Service quotation of Job, the use of that expression was not a reference to Scripture on the part of either Shakespeare or Holinshed, since it had always been an important element of the original Macbeth story. The prediction that Macbeth would not be slain by any man born of woman can be found in all the Macbeth narratives, including the earliest extant accounts written almost two centuries before Shakespeare's time.

The most important secondary sources which Shakespeare may have consulted were the Latin history of Scotland *Rerum Scoticarum Historia* (1582) by George Buchanan, the tutor of King James; *De Origine ... Scotorum* (1578) by John Leslie, Bishop of Ross; and several of Seneca's tragedies that had been translated into English, especially *Medea, Agamemnon,* and *Hercules Furens*. None of these works influenced Shakespeare's biblical references. Shakespeare borrowed some important ideas and key phrases from Seneca, including the well-known phrase "hurlye burlye." But while the English translators of Seneca occasionally employed biblical expressions (Studley borrowed "twynklyng of an eye" from 1 Cor. 15.52 in his translation of *Agamemnon*), Shakespeare borrowed none of those biblical phrases.

Other works which Shakespeare appears to have read or to have had in mind when writing *Macbeth* include Reginald Scot's *Discouerie of Witchcraft* (1584), P. de Loyer's *Treatise of Specters* (1605), Samuel Daniel's *The Queenes Arcadia* (1606), and Marston's *Sophonisba* (1606). Biblical references are frequent throughout Scot's lengthy work on witchcraft, but it would be difficult to demonstrate that any of Shakespeare's references were borrowed from Scot.

Another influence on *Macbeth* that has generally been overlooked was the anonymous play *A Warning for Faire Women*, written about 1590 and first published in 1599. Shakespeare knew the play well; his company had performed it several times, and it gave him some important ideas and phrases. The biblical reference to Luke 19.40 at 2.1.58 may have been inspired by the anonymous play.

Some have argued that the relationship between Macbeth and his wife was inspired by the account of King Ahab and Queen Jezebel in 1 Kings 21, but these arguments are unconvincing. Holinshed was Shakespeare's prime source for the story of Macbeth's being incited by his wife to murder the king. Shakespeare borrowed not only from that regicide account, but also from Holinshed's account of Donwald, whose wife urged him to slay King Duff. Even less convincing are suggestions that the slaughter of Macduff's children was inspired by Herod's Slaughter of the Innocents or that the knocking in the Porter scene is based on Luke 11.9, "Knocke, and it shalbe opened vnto you." These suggestions are too far-fetched to be given serious consideration. The spirit and context of the Porter scene and of Jesus' words are hardly similar, and there is insufficient linguistic similarity to claim that Shakespeare's passage is a verbal echo of the text in Luke.

In the list that follows, page numbers preceded by the number 7, as in (7.482), refer to volume 7 of Bullough.

1.2.40:   Or memorize another Golgotha.

Matt. 27.33: "They came vnto the place called Golgotha."
See also Mark 15.22; John 19.17.

[1.2.47: 2 Kings 11.12.]

[1.3.25: Isa. 54.11, Geneva.]

1.3.107:   What, can the devil speak true?

Compare John 8.44: "The deuil,... there is no trueth in him. When he speaketh a lie, then speaketh hee of his owne: for he is a liar."
See also 5.5.42–43 below.

1.3.123–25:   To win us to our harm,
               The instruments of darkness tell us truths,
               ... to betray 's.

Compare 2 Cor. 11.14: "For Satan him selfe is transformed into an Angel of light."
Compare also the temptation of Jesus wherein the devil quoted Scripture to mislead Jesus. Matt. 4.1–10; Luke 4.1–12.
Shakespeare has a parallel thought in *The Merchant of Venice*, 1.3.98: "The devil can cite Scripture for his purpose."
Compare King James's *Daemonologie*: The devil "will make his schollers to creepe in credite with Princes, by fore-telling them manie greate thinges; parte true, parte false: For if all were false, he would tyne credite at all handes; but alwaies doubtsome, as his Oracles were" (22).
The king also quotes 2 Cor. 11.14: "That the Diuel is permitted at somtimes to put himself in the liknes of the Saintes, it is plaine in the Scriptures, where it is said, that *Sathan can trans-forme himselfe into an Angell of light*" (4).
Shakespeare could have had the king's treatise in mind when he wrote this passage, but at the same time, it must be recognized that these were commonly held views about the tactics that Satan uses to seduce the faithful.

1.4.23–26:   Your Highness' part
               Is to receive our duties; and our duties
               Are ... servants;
               Which do but what they should.

Compare Luke 17.10: "When ye haue done all those things,... say, We are vnprofitable seruants: wee haue done that which was our duetie to doe." Perhaps an analogy rather than a reference.
Compare King James's work, *Basilicon Doron*: "But saying (as Christ commandeth vs all) when wee haue done all that we can, *Invtiles servisumus*." Margin: "Luke 17.10" (26).

1.4.28–29:   I have begun to plant thee, and will labor
To make thee full of growing.

In Scripture the righteous are frequently compared to flourishing trees
that the Lord has planted, and this may well have been Shakespeare's inspiration for this image. The phrase does not occur in Holinshed.

Compare Jer. 12.2: "Thou hast planted them,... they growe, and bring
forth fruit."

Compare Ps. 92.11–12 (92.12–13, Geneva): "The ryghteous shal florishe
lyke a palme tree: and shal spreade abroade lyke a Cedar in Libanus. Such as
be planted in the house of the lord: shal florishe."

Compare Ps. 1.3: "He shalbe lyke a tree planted by the water."

See also Jer. 17.8; 11.17.

[1.5.23–25: See 5.1.68, n.]

[1.5.65–66: Matt. 10.16. (Or perhaps referring to representations of the serpent in Eden with
a human face encircled with flowers. Cf. *Romeo and Juliet* 3.2.73.)]

1.6.1–10:   This castle hath a pleasant seat ...
. . . .
This guest of summer,
The temple-haunting marlet, does approve,
By his lov'd mansionry, that the heaven's breath
Smells wooingly here;...
... this bird
Hath made his pendant bed and procreant cradle.
. . . .
The air is delicate.

Compare Ps. 84.1, 3, Sternhold and Hopkins:

How pleasant is thy dwelling place,
O Lord of hostes to me:
The tabernacles of thy grace,
how pleasant Lord they be:
The sparrowes find a roome to rest,
and saue themselues from wrong:
And eke the swallowe hath a nest,
wherein to keepe her young.

Prayer Book Psalter: "O howe amiable are thy dwellinges: thou Lorde of
hostes. Yea the sparowe hath founde her an house, and the swalow a neast,

where she may lay her young."

Psalm 84.1, 3 is also referred to in the homily "Of Good Works," but the passage in *Macbeth* is most likely an analogy rather than a reference. "Temple-haunting": refers to the bird's tendency to build its nest in churches.

[1.6.28: 1 Chron. 29.14, 16.]

1.7.1–2: If it were done, when 'tis done, then 'twere well
It were done quickly.

Compare John 13.27: "That thou doest, do quickely."
Closest parallel in Holinshed: "Shewed him the meanes wherby he might soonest accomplish it" (7.481).

1.7.7: The life to come.

Compare the Prayer Book, Nicene Creed: "The life of the world to come."

1.7.19: Will plead like angels, trumpet-tongu'd.

The New Testament frequently depicts angels blowing trumpets.
Rev. 8.2, 6: "I saw the seuen Angels,... and to them were giuen seuen trumpets. Then the seuen Angels, which had the seuen trumpets, prepared them selues to blowe the trumpets."
Chapters 8 to 11 of Revelation describe the events that occurred when each of the angels blew his trumpet.
Matt. 24.31: "He shall sende his Angels with a great sounde of a trumpet."

1.7.20: The deep damnation of his taking-off.

Part 2 of the homily "Against Disobedience and Wilfull Rebellion": 'Surely no mortall man can express with wordes,... the horrible and most dreadfull damnation that such [rebels] be worthy of.'
Holinshed: "How heinous a thing it is to pollute their hands in the sacred blood of their prince" (7.484).
See 2.3.64–65 below.

1.7.22:   Heaven's cherubin.

Derived from the many instances where cherubim are mentioned in Scripture. The word first appears at Gen. 3.24 and occurs frequently thereafter. The lid of the ark (the mercy seat) had two cherubim on it, and various curtains in both the tabernacle and the temple were embroidered with cherubim. See Ex. 25.18–22; 37.7–9; 1 Kings 6.23–32; Ps. 80.1; 99.1; Ezek. 10.1–20; Heb. 9.5.

In Hebrew, "cherubim" is the plural of "cherub." But in Latin, the form most frequently employed in the liturgy was "cherubin," as in the *Te Deum*. When the Latin form was adopted into English it was treated as a singular, and the plural became "cherubins." Thus "cherubin" and "cherubins" were the original English singular and plural forms.

In the sixteenth century, acquaintance with Old Testament Hebrew led Bible translators to substitute "cherub" as the singular and "cherubims" as the plural. Coverdale generally has "cherub" for the singular and "cherubins" for the plural, although the plural appears as "cherubes" at Gen. 3.24. The Great Bible generally has "cherub" and "cherubins," but the plural also appears as "cherubs," most often in 1 Kings 6. The Geneva consistently has "cherub" for the singular and "cherubims" for the plural. The Bishops' Bible generally has "cherub" and "cherubims" although the singular appears as "cherubim" (without the final *s*) at Ex. 25.19, and the plural appears as "cherubs" seven times in 1 Kings 6 and a few times elsewhere.

With only one exception, Shakespeare has "cherubin" for the singular and "cherubins" for the plural. The one exception occurs in *Hamlet* (4.3.48), where "cherub" occurs as the singular. Thus Shakespeare's usage is the popular older usage rather than that of any particular version. Nonetheless, the influence of the newer trend is apparent in *Hamlet*.

1.7.22–23:   Heaven's cherubin, hors'd
             Upon the sightless couriers of the air.

Compare Ps. 18.10: "He rode vpon the Cherubims and dyd flee: he came fleeyng [flying] vpon the wynges of the wynde."
See also 2 Sam. 22.11.

2.1.56:   Thou sure and firm-set earth.

Ps. 93.2: "He hath made the rounde world so sure: that it can not be moued."
Geneva (93.1): "The world also shall be established, that it cannot be

mooued."

Shakespeare's reference is to the Psalter. See *Antony and Cleopatra* 5.1.15–17, where Shakespeare again has the Psalter reading of Ps. 93.2 in mind.

2.1.58: The very stones prate of my whereabout.

Luke 19.40: "If these should holde their peace, the stones would cry."
Shakespeare's primary source for this reference may have been the anonymous play *A Warning for Faire Women*: "Yet will the very stones / That lie within the streetes cry out vengeance" (sig. G1ʳ).
See my note, "Echoes of *A Warning for Faire Women* in Shakespeare's Plays," in *Philological Quarterly* 62 (1983): 521–25.

[2.1.58: Hab. 2.11.]

2.2.56: Hah! they pluck out mine eyes.

Compare Matt. 18.9: "If thine eye cause thee to offende, plucke it out, and cast it from thee."
Compare also Matt. 5.29; Mark 9.47.

2.2.64: A little water clears us of this deed.

Compare Matt. 27.24: "Pilate ... tooke water and washed his hands before the multitude, saying, I am innocent of the bloud of this iust man."
Compare also Deut. 21.6–7.
Perhaps an analogy rather than a reference.

2.3.4: I' th' name of Belzebub.

Matt. 12.24–27: "Beelzebub the prince of deuils."
See also Mark 3.22; Luke 11.15–19; Matt. 10.25.

2.3.18–19: That go the primrose way to th' everlasting bonfire.

Matt. 7.13: "It is the wide gate, and broade way that leadeth to destruction: and manie there bee which goe in thereat."

Matt. 18.8: "Be cast into euerlasting fire."

Rev. 20.10: "Was cast into a lake of fire and ... shalbe tormented euen day and night for euermore." See also Rev. 20.15.

Wisdom 2.7–8: "Let vs fil our selues with costly wine and oyntments, and let not the floure of life passe by vs. Let vs crowne our selues with rose buddes afore they be withered."

Compare *All's Well*, 4.5.54–55: "The flow'ry way that leads to the broad gate and the great fire."

King James referred to Matt. 7.13 in *A Fruitfull Meditation* (1603): "Therefore our Maister saith ... Wide is the waye that leadeth to destruction, and many enter thereat" (sig. B5ᵛ).

Shakespeare primarily had Scripture in mind. The context of the king's printed sermon is considerably different.

2.3.64–65:   O horror, horror, horror! Tongue nor heart
             Cannot conceive nor name thee!

Part 2 of the homily "Against Disobedience and Wilfull Rebellion": "Surely no mortall man can expresse with wordes, nor conceiue in minde the horrible and most dreadfull damnation that such [rebels] be worthy of."

See 1.7.20 above.

2.3.68:   The Lord's anointed temple.

1 Sam. 26.9, 11, 16: "The Lords anointed."

See also 1 Sam. 24.11 (24.10, AV); 2 Sam. 1.14, 16; Lam. 4.20.

The phrase is also used in the Homilies. See part 2 of the homily "Against Disobedience and Wilfull Rebellion."

2.3.67–69:   Hath broke ope
             The Lord's anointed temple, and stole thence
             The life o' th' building!

Compare Rev. 11.19: "Then the Temple of God was opened in heauen, and there was seene in his Temple the Arke of his couenant."

The ark of the covenant in the Holy of Holies can be aptly described as "the life o' th' building."

Compare also John 2.19–21; 1 Cor. 3.17; 6.19; 2 Cor. 6.16 which speak of the human body as a temple.

2.3.77–79:   Up, up, and see
The great doom's image! Malcolm! Banquo!
As from your graves rise up, and walk like sprites.

A general reference to the day of judgment.
Compare Rev. 20.12–13: "I sawe the dead, both great and smal stand before God."
Compare John 5.28–29: "All that are in the graues, shal heare his voice. And they shal come foorth."

2.3.82–83:   Such a hideous trumpet calls to parley
The sleepers of the house.

Evidently a continuation of the preceding resurrection image: the dead rising to the sound of God's trumpet.
1 Cor. 15.52: "At the last trumpet: for the trumpet shall blowe, and the dead shalbee raised."
1 Thess. 4.16: "The Lord him selfe shal descend from heauen with ... the trumpet of God: and the dead in Christ shal rise."

[2.3.98–99: Lev. 20.18.]

[2.3.130: Ps. 18.35; 31.17 (31.15, Geneva); Isa. 49.2.]

[2.4.1: Ps. 90.10.]

2.4.6–10:   By th' clock 'tis day,
And yet dark night strangles the travelling lamp.
· · · · · · · · · · · · · · · · · · · ·
... darkness does the face of earth entomb,
When living light should kiss it.

Typical of the supernatural omens that accompany the deaths of great persons, as at the death of Christ.
Luke 23.44–45: "And it was about the sixt houre: and there was a darkenes ouer al the land, vntill the ninth houre. And the sunne was darkened."
See also Matt. 27.45; Mark 15.33.
Closest parallel in Holinshed: "For the space of six moneths togither, after this heinous murther thus committed, there appeered no sunne by day, nor moone by night in anie part of the realme, but still was the skie covered with continuall clouds" (7.483).

Shakespeare is considerably closer to the biblical pattern than to Holin-shed. See also *Julius Caesar* 2.2.13–31 and *Othello* 5.2.99–101.

2.4.40–41:   God's benison go with you, and with those
             That would make good of bad, and friends of foes!

From the general Christian context of doing good to others, even one's foes.

Rom. 12.17, 20–21: "Recompense to no man euil for euil.... If thine ene-mie hunger, feede him: if he thirst, giue him drinke.... Be not ouercome of euil, but ouercome euil with goodnes."

Matt. 5.44: "Loue your enemies: blesse them that cursse you: doe good to them that hate you, and pray for them which hurt you, and persecute you."

See also 1 Peter 3.9; 1 Thess. 5.15.; Matt. 5.9, 39.

Contrast 2.4.41 with Isa. 5.20: "Wo vnto them that speake good of euill, and euill of good."

3.1.67–68:   And mine eternal jewel
             Given to the common enemy of man.

"Mine eternal jewel" refers to Macbeth's soul. "The common enemy of man" is a general reference to the devil.

Compare 1 Peter 5.8: "Your aduersarie the deuil."

Compare Rev. 12.9: "The deuill and Satan ... which deceiueth all the worlde."

For the loss of one's soul, compare Mark 8.36: "What shal it profite a man, though he should winne the whole world, if he lose his soule?"

One of the many instances in the play where no specific biblical reference is involved but where the passage has strong overtones of Christian beliefs that derive from Scripture. Line 67 might echo the "pearle of great price" of Matt. 13.46. See *Othello* 5.2.347–48.

3.1.87–88:   Are you so gospell'd,
             To pray for this good man?

Luke 6.27–28: "Loue your enemies.... Blesse them that curse you, and pray for them which hurt you."

See also Matt. 5.44; Rom. 12.14; 1 Cor. 4.12.

Compare 2.4.40–41 above.

3.1.96–99: Every one,
             According to the gift which bounteous nature
             Hath in him clos'd; whereby he does receive
             Particular addition.

Compare Eph. 4.7: "Vnto euerie one of vs is giuen grace, according to the measure of the gift."

Compare Matt. 25.15: "Vnto one hee gaue fiue talentes, and to another two, and to another one, to euery man after his owne habilitie."

Compare 1 Peter 4.10: "Let euerie man as hee hath receiued the gift, minister the same one to another."

Compare *Basilicon Doron*: "Imploying euery man according to his gifts" (77). Both Shakespeare and King James are probably echoing Scripture independently. "Each one according to his gift (ability)" was a common expression in Shakespeare's day.

3.2.4–5: Nought's had, all's spent,
           Where our desire is got without content.

Compare Ecclus. 40.18: "To labour and to be content with that a man hath, is a sweete life."

See also 1 Tim. 6.6; Eccl. 4.6; Ps. 106.15.

[3.4.21: Matt. 7.25.]

3.4.121: It will have blood, they say; blood will have blood.

Compare Gen. 9.6: "Whoso sheadeth mans blood, by man shal his blood be shed."

Compare also Gen. 4.10; Ex. 21.12; Lev. 24.17.

The Mirrour for Magistrates, Tragedy of Thomas, Duke of Gloucester, 203: "Blood wyll haue blood."

Compare also *A Warning for Faire Women*: "Measure for measure, and lost bloud for bloud" (sig. G3ʳ).

A common expression based on a well-known principle that was probably enunciated most clearly in Scripture.

3.4.122: Stones have been known to move and trees to speak.

Perhaps a reversal of Luke 19.40: "The stones would cry." Compare 2.1.58 above. But more likely a reference to the *Aeneid* 3.22–46, where the ghost of Polydorus speaks from a tree, or to another nonbiblical source. Compare *The Faerie Queene* 1.2.30–42.

4.1.52–55:   Though you untie the winds, and let them fight
             Against the churches; though the yesty waves
             Confound and swallow navigation up;
             Though bladed corn be lodg'd, and trees blown down.

Compare Rev. 7.1: "I saw foure Angels ... holding the foure winds of the earth, that the windes should not blow on the earth, neither on the sea, neither on any tree."

4.1.80:   None of woman born.

See below at 5.3.6.

4.1.110:   Show his eyes, and grieve his heart.

Compare 1 Sam. 2.33: "To make thine eyes to faile, and to make thine heart sorowfull."

4.1.125–28:   But why
              Stands Macbeth thus amazedly?
              Come, sisters, cheer we up his sprites,
              And show the best of our delights.

1 Sam. 28.21–25: "Then the woman came vnto Saul, and sawe that hee was sore troubled, and saide vnto him, ... I pray thee, ... let me set a morsell of bread before thee, that thou maiest eat and get thee strength, and go on thy iourney."

These details seem to be borrowed from the biblical account of the witch of Endor. In the Bible narrative, after the witch had delivered a message of doom to King Saul, Saul was greatly troubled and the witch attempted to comfort him. None of these details occur in Holinshed or in any of Shakespeare's sources. But these lines are not Shakespeare's. Most authorities consider 4.1.125–32 to be an interpolation, probably by Middleton.

4.1.133–34:   Let this pernicious hour
              Stand aye accursed in the calendar!

Compare Job 3.1–8: "Iob ... cursed his day ... and said, Let the day perish, wherein I was borne.... Let that day bee darkenesse.... Let darkenesse possesse that night.... Let them that curse the day,... curse it."

4.2.12:   All is the fear, and nothing is the love.

Compare 1 John 4.18: "There is no feare in loue, but perfect loue casteth out feare:... he that feareth, is not perfect in loue."

4.2.31–32:   *L. Macd....* What will you do now? How will you live?
              Son. As birds do, mother.

Matt. 6.26: "Behold the foules of the heauen: for they sowe not, neither reape."

[4.2.69: Matt. 18.6.]

4.3.22:   Angels are bright still, though the brightest fell.

A general reference to Satan, who in Shakespeare's time was often identified with the Lucifer of Isaiah 14.
Part 1 of the homily "Against Disobedience and Wilfull Rebellion": "Lucifer,... who by rebelling against the Maiestie of GOD, of the brightest and most glorious Angel, is become the blackest and most foulest fiend and deuill."
Isa. 14.12: "How art thou fallen from heauen, O Lucifer, sonne of the morning?"
Luke 10.18: "I sawe Satan, like lightening, fall downe from heauen."
See also 2 Peter 2.4; Jude 6; Rev. 12.9.
Shakespeare probably had the homily in mind.

[4.3.45: Josh. 10.24; Ps. 108.13.]

4.3.55–56:   Not in the legions
              Of horrid hell can come a devil more damn'd.

Compare Luke 8.30: "He said, Legion, because many deuils were entred into him."
Compare Mark 5.9: "My name is Legion: for we are many."

4.3.109–111:   The queen ...

     . . . . . .

        Died every day she liv'd.

Compare 1 Cor. 15.31: "I dye dayly."

4.3.120–21:   But God above
        Deal between thee and me!

Compare 1 Sam. 24.16 (24.15, AV): "The Lord therefore be iudge, and iudge betweene thee and me."

Compare Gen. 31.49–50: "The Lord looke betweene me and thee.... God is witnes betweene me and thee."

Compare also 1 Sam. 20.23.

Compare King James's *Basilicon Doron*: "I take the greate GOD to recorde, that this booke shall one day be a witnes betwixt me and you." ("The Epistle" sig. B1ʳ.)

[4.3.127: Ex. 20.17.]

[4.3.129–30: 1 Cor. 13.6.]

4.3.157:   He hath a heavenly gift of prophecy.

Compare 1 Cor. 13.2: "Though I had the gift of prophecie."

Tyndale, Coverdale, Matthew, Taverner, Great: "Though I coulde prophesy."

Bishops': "Though I haue prophecie."

Rheims: "If I should haue prophecie."

But Holinshed, Shakespeare's primary source, has: "He was inspired with the gift of prophesie" (7.508). Shakespeare most likely borrowed the expression "gift of prophecy" from Holinshed. Holinshed, in turn, may have been influenced by the Geneva Bible.

[4.3.159: John 1.14.]

[4.3.176–79: 2 Kings 4.26, Bishops' (Noble).]

4.3.218–19:   All my pretty chickens, and their dam,
        At one fell swoop?

Compare Deut. 22.6: "If thou finde a birdes nest ... and the dam sitting vpon the yong,... thou shalt not take the dam with the yong."

4.3.237–38:   Macbeth
                Is ripe for shaking.

Compare Nahum 3.12: "Like figtrees with the first ripe figs: for if they be shaken, they fall into the mouth of the eater."
Compare Rev. 6.13: "As a figge tree casteth her greene figs, when it is shaken of a mightie winde."

[5.1.17–18: Matt. 18.16, Geneva.]

[5.1.68: General Confession, Morning Prayer. Compare *Julius Caesar* 4.2.8–9.]

[5.1.74: 2 Chron. 16.12.]

5.3.6:   Man that's born of woman.

Compare Job 14.1: "Man that is borne of woman."
Burial Service: "Man that is borne of a woman."
While some authorities think that Shakespeare borrowed this line from Job 14.1, his primary source was the Macbeth story as he found it in Holinshed and as Holinshed found it in his sources. Holinshed three times repeats the words of a "certeine witch" (other than the three weird sisters, according to Holinshed), that Macbeth would never be slain by "man borne of anie woman" (7.500, 504, 505). Since the witch's prediction was a basic feature of the original Macbeth narrative from its very beginning, that narrative must be considered Shakespeare's primary source. But Shakespeare was probably aware that the expression strongly echoed both Job 14.1 and the Prayer Book.

[5.3.27: Isa. 29.13; Matt. 15.8; Mark 7.6.]

5.5.17–18:   She should have died hereafter;
                There would have been a time for such a word.

It appears that "word" in line 18 refers to the word "died" in the previous line. Macbeth's meaning is that it would have been fitter had Lady Macbeth died later, since, with a battle impending, there was no time to attend to her death. If so, Macbeth's words could be an allusion to Eccles. 3.1–2: "To all thinges there is ... a time.... A time to be borne, and a time to dye."

5.5.23:   The way to dusty death.

Ps. 22.15: "The dust of death."
Burial Service: "We therefore commit his body to the ground, earth to earth, ashes to ashes, dust to dust."
Gen. 3.19: "Thou art dust, and to dust shalt thou returne."
See also part 1 of the homily "Of the Misery of all Mankinde," which quotes Gen. 3.19.

5.5.23:   Out, out, brief candle!

Job 18.6: "His candle shalbe put out with him."
Job 21.17: "How oft shall the candle of the wicked bee put out?"
Compare also Ps. 18.27 (18.28, Geneva).

5.5.24:   Life's but a walking shadow.

Ps. 39.7 (39.6, Geneva): "Man walketh in a vayne shadowe."
Job 8.9: "Our dayes vpon earth are but a shadowe."
Ps. 144.4: "Man ... passeth away like a shadowe."
Wisdom 2.5: "Our time is as a shadow that passeth away."
Job 14.1–2: "Man ... is cut downe: he vanisheth also as a shadow."
Burial Service: "Hee fleeth as it were a shadow."

5.5.26–27:   It is a tale
              Told by an idiot.

Compare Ps. 90.9: "We bring our yeeres to an ende, as it were a tale that is tolde."
Coverdale, Matthew, Taverner, and the Great Bibles have readings identical to the Prayer Book Psalter.
Geneva: "We haue spent our yeeres as a thought."
Bishops': "We spende our yeeres as (in speaking) a woorde."
If Shakespeare had this Psalm in mind, he most likely reflects the Psalter which was read daily in the service of the Anglican Church.
However, Shakespeare may simply be using a common expression rather

than making a biblical reference. Holinshed uses a parallel expression in "The Historie of King Edward the Fift." When Buckingham urged the people to make the Duke of Gloucester king rather than the Prince of Wales (Edward the Fifth), his speech was ill received. The reason, Holinshed explains, was that the people "neuer had in their liues heard so euill a tale so well told" (Holinshed 3/730).

Moreover, Tilley records the following parallel proverbs:

T 38: "A good tale ill told is marred in the telling."
T39: "A good tale is none the worse to be told twice."
T42: "One tale is good until another be told."

5.5.42–43:   Th' equivocation of the fiend
              That lies like truth.

Compare John 8.44: "The deuil,... there is no trueth in him. When he speaketh a lie, then speaketh hee of his owne: for he is a liar."
See 1.3.107 above.

[5.5.48–49: Rev. 9.6.]

5.5.49:   And wish th' estate o' th' world were now undone.

Compare the superscription to Ps. 127 in the Geneva Bible: "He sheweth that the whole estate of the worlde ... standeth by Gods mere prouidence."
If Shakespeare echoes the Geneva Bible in this passage, it would indicate that his private reading of the Geneva Bible included the Geneva version of the Psalms. Compare *Julius Caesar* 1.1.35 and *Titus Andronicus* 3.1.273–74 for other possible references to the Geneva Psalms. Shakespeare's references to the Psalms generally echo the Psalter, the Prayer Book version of the Psalms used in the Anglican Church.
"Estate of the world," however, may have been a familiar expression in Shakespeare's day.

5.7.11:   Thou wast born of woman. (Also 5.7.3; 5.8.13, 31.)

See 5.3.6 above.

5.8.5–6:   My soul is too much charg'd
           With blood of thine already.

Compare Deut. 21.8: "Lay no innocent blood to the charge of thy people."
More likely a verbal echo rather than a reference.

Antony and Cleopatra

The story of Antony and Cleopatra, like that of Romeo and Juliet or of Troilus and Cressida, was one of the best-known love stories in Shakespeare's day. Chaucer, Lydgate, and Spenser had written about it; Chaucer placed Cleopatra first in his *Legend of Good Women*. Many Continental writers, including Boccaccio and Cinthio, related the story.

Shakespeare's primary source was Plutarch's "Life of Antony" as translated by Thomas North from the French of Jacques Amyot. Shakespeare followed North's text closely, even more closely than he followed North in *Julius Caesar* and *Coriolanus*, but he found no biblical references in North's text. Shakespeare borrowed several expressions and phrases from North's "Life of Antony" which appear to be based on Scripture (as at 3.6.13), but these expressions originate with Plutarch, and the resemblance to Scripture is accidental.

Cinthio was the first to turn the story into drama with his *Cleopatra*, ca. 1542, and in 1552 the Frenchman Etienne Jodelle wrote his play *Cléopâtre Captive*. More important as a source for Shakespeare was Robert Garnier's play *Marc-Antoine*, translated into English in 1592 by Mary Sidney, the Countess of Pembroke. The most important influence on Shakespeare after North, however, was probably Samuel Daniel's closet drama, *The Tragedie of Cleopatra*, 1594. Other works which Shakespeare consulted include the 1578 translation of Appian's *Civil Wars* by W. B., and Daniel's *Letter from Octavia to Marcus Antonius*, first published in 1599.

Shakespeare's debt to most of these works is clear. From Appian he borrowed facts and phrases that appear in none of his other sources, including Plutarch. Distinctive words and expressions borrowed from Mary Sidney's translation of Garnier, Daniel's *Letter from Octavia*, and especially from Daniel's closet drama, make it clear that Shakespeare had read those works. He may even have read Jodelle's play in French. Yet the influence of these works on Shakespeare's biblical references in *Antony and Cleopatra* was slight. In all of these secondary sources there are only about twelve biblical references, half of which occur in Daniel's play and *Letter*, but Shakespeare used none of them. Occasionally a phrase or an image in one of these sources is similar to Scripture and may have suggested a biblical reference to Shakespeare (1.4.27; 2.5.10–13; 3.6.66–68; 4.15.85), but most of the references in *Antony and Cleopatra* are his own.

Shakespeare's use of the book of Revelation in *Antony and Cleopatra* is outstanding. The Apocalypse seems to have supplied him with some of the most vivid images in the play. Since only three chapters of Revelation were read during Morning and Evening Prayer in the Anglican Church (chapter 19 on All Saints Day, November 1; chapters 1 and 22 on the Feast of St. John, December 27), Shakespeare must have read privately much of Revelation shortly before or during the composition of the play.

The references to Exodus in 3.13 are also noteworthy. The setting of much of the play is Egypt, and Shakespeare appropriately drew on the Exodus account of the Ten Plagues.

In the list that follows, page numbers preceded by the number 5, as in (5.387), refer to volume 5 of Bullough. Page numbers may be followed by line numbers, as in (5.415.315).

1.1.17:   Then must thou needs find out new heaven, new earth.

Rev. 21.1: "I saw a new heauen, and a new earth."
2 Peter 3.13: "We looke for newe heauens, and a newe earth."
Isa. 65.17: "I will create new heauens and a new earth."
Of the three texts which contain the expression 'new heauen, and a new earth,' Shakespeare is probably indebted to Revelation. Only Rev. 21.1 has "heauen" rather than "heauens." Revelation is also favored in view of Shakespeare's use of the Apocalypse throughout the play. See 3.6.66–68; 3.13.145–47; 4.14.106–107; 5.2.79–86.

1.1.35:   Kingdoms are clay.

Daniel 2.42: "As the toes of the feete were parte of yron, and parte of clay, so shall the kingdome bee partly strong, and partly broken."

1.1.35:   Our dungy earth.

Compare Ps. 83.10: "As the doung of the earth."
Compare Jer. 8.2; 16.4: "Shalbe as doung vpon the earth."

[1.1.35–37: Eccles. 3.18–20; 3.12, 13, 22.]

1.2.28–29: Let me have a child at fifty, to whom Herod of Jewry may do homage.

Matt. 2.7–8: "Then Herode priuily called the Wisemen, ... and sent them to Beth-lehem, saying, Goe, and search diligently for the babe ... that I may come also, and worship him."

The reference to Herod is obvious. But Charmian's words, "Let me have a child at fifty," do not appear to have overtones of Luke's account of Elizabeth, the mother of John the Baptist, who bore John when past the age of childbearing (Luke 1.7, 57). Rather, it reflects that attitude of mind, still prevalent in certain cultures, in which women thought it extremely flattering to give birth to a child at an advanced age. In the anonymous play *Histrio-Mastix* (ca. 1589; published 1610), when the hostess says that unless she is paid, "Ile beare no Longer," Posthaste puns, "What and be vnder fifty?" (sig. H1ʳ). Shakespeare was probably acquainted with *Histrio-Mastix*, which figured prominently in the "war of the theaters."

[1.2.129–30: Ecclus. 33.26.]

1.4.27: The dryness of his bones.

Compare Prov. 17.22: "A sorrowfull minde dryeth the bones."
Compare Ezek. 37.11: "Our bones are dryed."
Compare Mary Sidney's *The Tragedie of Antonie*, a translation of Robert Garnier's *Marc-Antoine*: "Suck their mary [marrow] drie" (5.387.1185). But Shakespeare's line is considerably closer to Scripture. If Shakespeare is referring to Scripture in this passage, Mary Sidney's play may have suggested the reference to him.

[2.1.5–8: James 4.3; Rom. 8.26; 2 Cor. 12.8–9.]

2.2.143–45 [Of Agrippa's proposal that Antony marry Octavia]:

> May I never
> (To this good purpose, that so fairly shows)
> Dream of impediment!

Compare Sonnet 116, which is generally recognized as echoing the language of the Prayer Book: "Let me not to the marriage of true minds / Admit impediments."
Prayer Book, Marriage Service: "I require and charge you ... that if either

of you doe know any impediment, why yee may not bee lawfully ioyned together in Matrimonie, that yee confesse it."

2.5.10–13:   Give me mine angle, we'll to th' river; there,
             . . . .
             … my bended hook shall pierce
             Their slimy jaws.

Compare the wording of Job 40.20–21 (Job 41.1–2, AV): "Canst thou drawe out Liuiathan with an hooke?… Canst thou perce his iawes with an angle?"

The above passage from Shakespeare's play appears to have overtones of Job, although the lines which follow (2.5.15–18) are based on Plutarch. North's translation relates how in their "foolishe sportes," Cleopatra arranged for divers to put salted fish on Antony's hook while he was fishing (5.276–77). But the words "pierce" and "jaws" do not occur in North and seem to be based on Job.

3.1.14:   Better to leave undone.

Compare the General Confession, Morning and Evening Prayer: "Wee haue left vndone those things which wee ought to haue done."

Compare *Othello* 3.3.203–204; *Coriolanus* 4.7.24–25; *Julius Caesar* 4.2.8–9.

See also Matt. 23.23 Bishops'.

3.3.2–5:   *Alex.* Good Majesty!
           Herod of Jewry dare not look upon you
           But when you are well pleas'd.
               Cleo.   That Herod's head
           I'll have.

Matt. 14.6, 8: "The daughter of Herodias daunced before them, and pleased Herode. And she … said, Giue me here Iohn Baptists head in a platter."

Historically, the Herod who beheaded John was the son of Herod the Great mentioned at 1.2.28–29. Herod the Great was Cleopatra's contemporary; he lived from 73 to 4 B.C., while Cleopatra lived from 69 to 30 B.C. John the Baptist was beheaded some sixty years after Cleopatra's death. Shakespeare was probably aware of the anachronism, since Herod the Great is mentioned several times in Plutarch's "Life of Antony" as a contemporary of both Antony and Cleopatra, but Shakespeare was more interested in the apt use of a familiar incident.

3.6.13, Folio: King of Kings.

Compare Rev. 19.16: "He hath vpon his garment, and vpon his thigh a name written THE KING OF KINGS, AND LORDE OF LORDES."
Compare Rev. 17.14: "For he is Lord of Lordes, and King of Kings."
Shakespeare's reference is to North's translation of Plutarch, rather than to Scripture. The First Folio, the sole authority for the play, has "King of Kings," but most editors have emended the line to read "kings of kings" for grammatical consistency: "His sons he there proclaim'd the kings of kings." North has "kings of kings" (as do Plutarch and Amyot): "He called the sonnes he had by her, the kings of kings" (5.290). If Shakespeare followed North and wrote "kings of kings," then the typesetter, acquainted with the biblical expression, may unconsciously have changed it to "King of Kings."
The expression "kings of kings" also appears in *The Tragedie of Antonie,* Mary Sidney's English translation of Robert Garnier's *Marc-Antoine:* "The kings of kings proclaming them to be" (5.393.1435).

[3.6.46–47: Luke 19.3–4.]

3.6.66–68:   He hath given his empire
Up to a whore, who are now levying
The kings o' th' earth for war.

Compare Rev. 17.1–2: "Come: I will shewe thee the damnation of the great whore that sitteth vpon manye waters, with whome haue committed fornication the Kings of the earth."
Compare Rev. 19.19: "And I saw ... the Kings of the earth, and their warriers gathered together to make battel."
The expression "The kynges of the earth" also occurs at Ps. 2.2, but Shakespeare probably had Revelation in mind in this passage, even as he refers to Revelation throughout the play (1.1.17; 3.13.145–47; 4.14.106–107; 5.2.79–86).
Closest parallel in North: "He had before given it uppe unto a woman" (5.295). North's text may have suggested the account in Revelation 17 to Shakespeare. If so, then Shakespeare combined North's text with Revelation 17, and perhaps with Revelation 19.19.

3.6.73:   Herod of Jewry.

See above at 1.2.28–29 and 3.3.2–5.
But in Shakespeare's main source, North's translation of Plutarch, the expression "Herodes king of Jury" occurs in the same context: a catalogue of the kings that Antony had enlisted to support him in his war against Octavius (5.296). Many in Shakespeare's audience, unacquainted with Plutarch, would have been reminded of Herod the Great from Scripture or from the mystery plays. But Shakespeare's source was North's text, not Scripture.
The same point applies to "Archelaus / Of Cappadocia" in Shakespeare's list of kings (3.6.69–70). Shakespeare's source was North's "Archelaus king of Cappadocia" (5.296), although some in Shakespeare's audience might have been reminded of the Archelaus mentioned at Matt. 2.22.

3.6.87–89:   And the high gods,
             To do you justice, makes his ministers
             Of us.

Compare Rom. 13.4, 6: "For hee is the minister of God for thy wealth.... For they are Gods ministers."
To support their doctrine that civil governments are God's ministers instituted to execute punishment on evildoers, Elizabeth's government often quoted Romans 13, particularly in the homilies "Concerning Good Order, and Obedience to Rulers and Magistrates" and "Against Disobedience and Wilfull Rebellion."
Compare Richmond's prayer in *Richard III* 5.3.108–113:

O Thou whose captain I account myself,
Look on my forces with a gracious eye;
. . . .
Make us thy ministers of chastisement.

Compare the Geneva note on 2 Chron. 9.8: "Kings are the lieutenantes of God, which ought to graunt vnto him the superioritie, and minister iustice to all."

3.13.67–69:   It much would please him,
              That of his fortunes you should make a staff
              To lean upon.

Compare Isaiah 36.6.: "Thou trustest in this broken staffe of reede on Egypt, whereupon if a man leane, it will goe into his hand, and pearce it: so is Pharaoh King of Egypt, vnto all that trust in him."

Caesar's messenger urges Cleopatra to desert Antony, ruler of Egypt, and lean instead on Caesar. Rabshakeh's words in Isaiah 36.6 are similar.

Compare also 2 Kings 18.21; Ezek. 29.6–7.

The similarity to Scripture may be accidental, yet there is no corresponding passage in any of Shakespeare's other sources.

3.13.94:   A lion's whelp.

Compare Gen. 49.9: "A Lions whelpe."

3.13.126–28:   O that I were
               Upon the hill of Basan, to outroar
               The horned herd!

Ps. 22.12: "Fat bulles of Basan close me in on euery syde."

Ps. 68.15: "As the hyl of Basan, so is Gods hyl: euen an high hyl as the hyl of Basan."

See also Ezek. 39.18; Amos 4.1; Deut. 32.14.

3.13.145–47:   When my good stars, that were my former guides,
               Have empty left their orbs, and shot their fires
               Into th' abysm of hell.

Compare Rev. 9.1: "I sawe a starre fal from heauen vnto the earth, and to him [the fifth angel] was giuen the key of the bottomles pit."

While all Protestant English Tudor Bibles have "bottomles pit" (the Rheims has "the pitte of bottomles depth"), the Greek word so translated is *abussos*, "abyss."

Compare also Rev. 6.13: "And the starres of heauen fell vnto the earth."

3.13.159–61:   Let heaven engender hail,
               And poison it in the source, and the first stone
               Drop in my neck.

In this passage Shakespeare appears to echo both the Exodus account of the seventh plague on Egypt, the plague of hail, and the Revelation account of hail "out of heauen." No parallel passage can be found in any of Shakespeare's other sources.

Ex. 9.23–24: "The Lorde sent thunder and haile, and lightening vpon the grounde: and the Lord caused haile to rayne vpon the Land of Egypt."

Rev. 16.21: "And there fel a great haile, like talents, out of heauen vpon the men."

3.13.162–66:   The next Caesarion smite,
Till by degrees the memory of my womb,
Together with my brave Egyptians all,
By the discandying of this pelleted storm,
Lie graveless."

A clearer reference than the preceding passage to the ten plagues on Egypt. The tenth plague was the death of Egypt's firstborn. After Cleopatra says to Antony that, if she is cold-hearted toward him, may the first hail-stone slay her, she asks that the next hailstone smite her firstborn son, Caesarion, and that the hail may then smite the rest of Egypt's inhabitants.

Ex. 9.25: "The haile smote throughout al the land of Egypt all that was in the fielde, both man and beast: also the haile smote al the herbes of the fielde."

The First Folio, the only authority for the play, has "smile" in line 162. Rowe emends this to "smite" and most editors follow Rowe. Justification for Rowe's emendation comes from the fact that the words "smite," "smote," and "smitten" are repeatedly used in the Exodus account of the ten plagues, and Shakespeare appears to have had the account of the Ten Plagues in mind in this passage.

For "lie graveless," compare Rev. 11.8–9: "Their corpses shall lie in the streetes of the great city, which spiritually is called Sodom and Egypt.... And shall not suffer their carkeises to be put in graues."

3.13.166–67:   Till the flies and gnats of Nile
Have buried them for prey!

The fourth plague was the plague of flies. Ex. 8.24: "There came great swarmes of flies into the house of Pharaoh, and into his seruants houses, so that through all the land of Egypt, the earth was corrupt by the swarmes of flies."

[3.13.173–75: Isa. 63.1–3.]

4.6.11–14:   Alexas did revolt, and went to Jewry on
Affairs of Antony, there did dissuade

Great Herod to incline himself to Caesar,
And leave his master Antony.

Shakespeare's source is not Scripture, but North's translation of Plutarch, which he follows closely (5.306). However, many in Shakespeare's audience, perhaps the majority, would have been reminded of Herod the Great of Scripture.
See 3.6.73 above.

4.8.16: Lord of lords!

Rev. 17.14: "For he is Lord of Lordes, and King of Kings."
See also Rev. 19.16 and 3.6.13 above.

4.12.47: The witch shall die.

Compare Ex. 22.18: "Thou shalt not suffer a witch to liue."
At best an analogy rather than a reference.

4.14.26: Shall die the death.

A common expression, frequently found in most Tudor versions of the Bible, that translates the Hebrew phrase *mōt tamūt*, "dying thou shalt die."
Gen. 2.17: "Thou shalt die the death."
See also Gen. 20.7; 1 Sam. 14.39, 44; 1 Kings 2.37, 42; 2 Kings 1.4, 6, 16; Jer. 26.8; Ezek. 33.8, 14.

[4.14.36: Job 7.21.]

4.14.106–107, 133: 2. *Guard.* The star is fall'n.
1. *Guard.* And time is at his period.
All. Alas, and woe!
. . . .
1. *Guard.* Woe, woe are we, sir.

Compare the following passages in Revelation, which Shakespeare appears to echo:
Rev. 8.10: "There fel a great starre from heauen."
Rev. 10.6: "Time should be no more."
Rev. 8.13: "Wo, wo, wo to the inhabitants of the earth."

4.15.33:   Our strength is all gone into heaviness.

Compare Ecclus. 38.18: "The heauines of the heart breaketh the strength." When Cleopatra and her attendants are unable at first to hoist Antony up into the monument, Cleopatra attributes their lack of strength to sorrow. That is also the sense of the text in Ecclesiasticus.

North: "Cleopatra stowping downe with her head, putting to all her strength to her uttermost power, did lift him up with much a doe" (5.310).

4.15.85:   Our lamp is spent, it's out.

With overtones of the parable of the ten virgins.

Matt. 25.8: "Our lampes are out."

Compare Samuel Daniel's play *The Tragedie of Cleopatra*: "Like as a burning Lampe, whose liquor spent" (5.415.315).

In Daniel, however, the simile is applied to Cleopatra's death, rather than Antony's. If Shakespeare had in mind the parable of the foolish virgins whose lamps went out, Daniel's lamp image may have suggested it to him.

5.1.15–17:   The round world
              Should have shook lions into civil streets,
              And citizens to their dens.

Compare Ps. 93.2: "He hath made the rounde world so sure: that it can not be moued."

Evidently a reference to the Psalter. The Geneva (93.1) omits "rounde": "The world also shall be established, that it cannot be mooued."

See *Macbeth* 2.1.56, where the reference to Ps. 93.2 according to the Psalter is clearer.

With reference also to the tradition that prodigious signs accompany the deaths of great persons. See *Julius Caesar* 2.2.18; *Hamlet* 1.1.114–16; *Othello* 5.2.99–101 and the comments thereon.

[5.2.20: 1 Chron. 29.14.]

[5.2.51: 2 Cor. 5.1.]

5.2.79–86:   His face was as the heav'ns, and therein stuck
              A sun and moon, which kept their course, and lighted
              The little O, th' earth.

. . . .
His legs bestrid the ocean, his rear'd arm
Crested the world, his voice was propertied
As all the tuned spheres, and that to friends;
But when he meant to quail and shake the orb,
He was as rattling thunder.

Compare Rev. 10.1–5: "And I sawe another mightie Angel come downe from heauen, clothed with a cloude, and the rainebowe vpon his head, and his face was as the sunne, and his feete as pillers of fire. And he had in his hand a litle booke open, and he put his right foote vpon the sea, and his left on the earth, and cryed with a loud voyce, as when a lyon roareth: and when he had cryed, seuen thunders vttered their voyces. And when the seuen thunders had vttered their voyces, I was about to write.... And the Angel which I sawe stand vpon the sea and vpon the earth, lift vp his hand to heauen."

Compare Shakespeare's use of Revelation in this passage with that at 3.6.66–68; 3.13.145–47; and 4.14.106–107, where the echoes of Revelation are clearer. Some of the correspondences between Shakespeare's play and the book of Revelation may be accidental, but it is unlikely that all of them are.

The closest parallel in Shakespeare's secular sources occurs in Mary Sidney's translation of Robert Garnier's *The Tragedie of Antonie*: "Thy eies, two Sunnes, the lodging place of love" (5.405.1941).

5.2.86–88:   For his bounty,
             There was no winter in't; an autumn it was
             That grew the more by reaping.

Compare Rev. 14.15–16: "Thrust in thy sickle and reape: for the time is come to reape: for the haruest of the earth is ripe.... The earth was reaped."

By itself, this passage hardly appears to be a valid reference to Rev. 14.15–16. But in view of Shakespeare's frequent use of Revelation elsewhere in the play and a more certain reference to the Apocalypse in the lines immediately preceding this passage, it becomes more plausible that the image of reaping in these lines may also have been suggested by Rev. 14.

5.2.138–50.   These lines, wherein Cleopatra pretends to have given Caesar
              an honest account of her valuables but has kept back an equal
              amount, have overtones of the parable of the Unjust Steward
              at Luke 16. Compare especially Caesar's words, "Nay, blush
              not, Cleopatra, I approve / Your wisdom in the deed" (149–

50), with Luke 16.8: "And the Lorde commended the vniust stewarde, because hee had done wisely." Caesar's words to Cleopatra, "I approve / Your wisdom in the deed," do not occur in any of Shakespeare's other sources (5.314; 5.424).

5.2.193–94:   Finish, good lady, the bright day is done,
              And we are for the dark.

Compare Job 10.21–22: "Before I goe and shall not returne, euen to the lande of darkenesse and shadowe of death:... darke as darkenes it selfe,... the light is there as darkenes."

[5.2.306: Gen.3.1, ff.]

[5.2.308: Rev. 2.28.]

Coriolanus

Coriolanus, the last of Shakespeare's Roman plays, is based primarily on North's translation of Plutarch's "Life of Coriolanus." Although Shakespeare followed North's text closely and some of the outstanding passages in the play are heavily indebted to North, North did not influence Shakespeare's biblical references. Only one biblical reference occurs in North's text. North borrowed the phrase "bottomles pyt" (5.517) from Revelation 20 to translate Amyot's *un abîme de malédiction* (Plutarch, *bárathron*). Shakespeare did not use that reference in his play.

Next in importance as a source for Shakespeare was Livy's *Romane Historie* which Shakespeare would have known from his schooldays. He also knew Philemon Holland's English translation of Livy, published in 1600. The history of Rome by Lucius Florus may also have been used by Shakespeare. If so, Shakespeare would have read Florus in Latin, since Florus's *Roman Histories* (an epitome of Livy) was not translated into English until 1619. Like Plutarch, both Livy and Florus were "pagan" historians, and no biblical references occur in their writings. Nor did the English translators of Livy and Florus use any biblical expressions in those portions of their translations that deal with the life of Coriolanus.

Were it not for Menenius's fable of the belly in *Coriolanus* (1.1.96–154), there would be little reason to suspect that Shakespeare used any other source. But that fable can be found not only in Plutarch and Livy, but also in Erasmus's *Copia*, Aesop's *Fables*, Caxton's collection of fables, Sidney's *Defence*, Camden's *Remaines*, and, most of all, in William Averell's *A Meruailous Combat of Contrarieties. Malignantlie Striuing in the Members of Mans Bodie*, which was published in 1588. Averell greatly expanded the fable and made it the centerpiece of his work. Linguistic similarities indicate that Shakespeare read the fable in most, if not all, of these secondary sources; he appears to have borrowed specific words from at least three of them. But except for Averell, none of the works in which the fable appears had any influence on Shakespeare's biblical references. Averell's treatise, however, contributed to *Coriolanus* not only many words—including "contrariety" and "malignantly" from its title page—but also gave Shakespeare at least one and possibly two biblical references, those at 2.1.257–58 and 2.3.115.

Although the fable of the belly is similar to Paul's illustration at 1 Corinthians 12 about the need for cooperation among the members of the body,

Shakespeare's source for the fable was not 1 Corinthians. A reading of the many non-biblical versions of the fable available to Shakespeare makes it clear that he drew on them for Menenius's allegory.

Just before Shakespeare wrote his play, several works were published which used the story of Coriolanus to promulgate certain political ideas. Among these works were William Fulbecke's *The Pandectes of the Law of Nations* (1602), Thomas Digges's *Foure Paradoxes, or Politique Discourses* (1604), and similar works by Richard Knolles, Edward Forset, and others. These works were written to warn of the dangers of democracy, the ingratitude of the people, and how unwise it is for magistrates to be chosen by the multitude. They stress the duties of subjects toward their rulers and praise the noble soldier. Most of them cite the banishment of Coriolanus as a prime example of the evils of democracy. Thus Shakespeare wrote within a definite tradition, a tradition that contributed to the atmosphere of the play: he minimizes the grievances and injustices suffered by the commoners, and emphasizes their ingratitude and rebellious nature.

It is not certain if Shakespeare read any of these works. He may have read Digges, and perhaps Forset. But there is no evidence that any of these works influenced his biblical references in *Coriolanus*.

In the list that follows, page numbers preceded by the number 5, as in (5.514), refer to volume 5 of Bullough.

[1.1.96–154: 1 Cor. 12.14–26.]

[1.1.205: Matt. 25.35.]

1.1.206:   That dogs must eat.

Compare Matt. 15.27, Bishops': "The litle dogges also eate of the crummes whiche fal from their maisters table."

The Taverner and Great Bibles are parallel to the Bishops'. All other versions—Tyndale, Coverdale, Matthew, Geneva, Rheims—have "whelpes" rather than "dogges" at Matt. 15.27.

Shakespeare, however, may have had a proverb in mind, since the citizens are said to be quoting proverbs. If so, the closest proverbs would be:

"It is an ill dog that deserves not a crust" (Tilley, D 487).

"Hungry dogs will eat dirty puddings" (Tilley, D 538).

Digna canis pabulo, "A dog is worthy of his food." (John Baret, *An Aluearie or Quadruple Dictionarie,* 1580 (*STC* 1411)).

1.3.6:   The only son of my womb.

Compare Prov. 31.2: "The sonne of my wombe."

1.3.15–16:   I sprang not more in joy at first hearing he was a man-child.

Compare Luke 1.44: "Assone as the voice of thy salutation sounded in myne eares, the babe sprang in my belly for ioy."

[1.3.47: Josh. 10.24.]

1.9.32–34:   Of all
The treasure in this field achiev'd and city,
We render you the tenth.

According to North's translation of Plutarch, Coriolanus was not offered a tenth of the spoils of war for capturing the city of Corioles, but was told to "choose out of all the horses they had taken of their enemies, and of all the goodes they had wonne (whereof there was great store) tenne of every sorte which he liked best, before any distribution should be made to other" (5.514).

But North's marginal caption on this passage is, "The tenth parte of the enemies goods offered Martius for rewarde of his service," and Shakespeare followed that caption. Both North and Shakespeare were no doubt influenced by the biblical tithe, first mentioned in Genesis. After Abraham returned "from the slaughter ... of the Kings" with much booty and was blessed by Melchizedek, Abraham "gaue him tythe of all" (Genesis 14.17–20). The Pentateuch sets forth an elaborate code for tithing, and this became the standard in Christianity

[2.1.6: Isa. 1.3, Noble.]

2.1.6–9:   *Sic.* Nature teaches beasts to know their friends.
Men. Pray you, who does the wolf love?
Sic. The lamb.
Men. Ay, to devour him.

Compare Ecclus. 13.16, 18 (13.15, 17, AV): "Euerie beast loueth his like.... How can the wolfe agree with the lambe?"
Compare also Isa. 11.6; 65.25.

[2.1.67: John 8.19.]

2.1.114–15:   It gives me an estate of seven years' health.

The idea of "seven years' health" may have been inspired by the seven years of plenty of Gen. 41.29. "Beholde, there come seuen yeeres of great plentie in all the land." No parallel expression occurs in North's translation of Plutarch.

2.1.191:   The faults of fools but folly.

Compare Prov. 14.24: "The folie of fooles is foolishnes."
The Authorized Version, not yet published when *Coriolanus* was written, has: "The foolishnes of fooles is folly."

2.1.257–58:   Will be his fire
                      To kindle their dry stubble.

A common biblical image. Compare Isa. 5.24: "As the flame of fire deuoureth the stubble, and as the chaffe is consumed of the flame."
Compare Isa. 47.14: "They shalbe as stubble: the fyre shall burne them."
Compare also Obadiah 18; Joel 2.5; Mal. 4.1; 1 Cor. 3.12–15.
Shakespeare probably borrowed this reference from William Averell. In *A Meruailous Combat of Contrarieties* (*STC* 981), which Shakespeare gives clear evidence of having read prior to writing *Coriolanus*, Averell urges his countrymen to unite against the enemy in a time of crisis (1588) by means of love, "diuine loue, being a fire to burne vp the stubble of dissention" (sig. D4r, Averell's final exhortation "to all trve English heartes that loue God").

2.1.262–63:   I have seen the dumb men throng to see him, and
                      The blind to hear him speak.

Strongly reminiscent of the crowds of dumb and blind that came to Jesus.
Compare Matt. 15.30: "And great multitudes came vnto him, hauing with them, halt, blinde, domme, ... and cast them downe at Iesus feete."
Compare also Matt. 11.5: "The blind receiue sight ... and the deafe heare."
See also Luke 7.22.
There is no equivalent passage in Shakespeare's sources.

2.2.124–26:   Our spoils he kick'd at,
                    And look'd upon things precious as they were
                    The common muck of the world.

    Compare Phil. 3.7–8: "I have counted all things losse, and do iudge them to be dongue, that I might winne Christ."

2.3.33:   For conscience' sake.

    Compare 1 Cor. 10.25: "For conscience sake."
    Comparc Rom. 13.5: "For conscience sake."

2.3.54–56:   O me, the gods!
                    You must not speak of that. You must desire them
                    To think upon you.

    Compare Jonah 1.6: "Call vpon thy God, if so be that God will thinke vpon vs."

2.3.91–92:   You have been a scourge to her enemies, you have been a rod to
                    her friends.

    Compare 1 Kings 12.11: "My father hath chastised you with rods, but I will correct you with scourges."
    Compare Ps. 89.32: "I wyl visite their offenses with the rodde, and their sinne with scourges."

2.3.115:   Why in this woolvish toge should I stand here.

    Compare Matt. 7.15: "Beware of false Prophets, which come to you in sheepes clothing, but inwardely they are rauening wolues."
    Some authorities suggest that "woolvish" may be a variant of or a misprint for "woolish." But "woolvish" seems to be the correct reading, and the *Oxford English Dictionary* gives "wooluish" as a variant of "wolvish."
    If Shakespeare had Matt. 7.15 in mind when he penned this line, his reference to Matthew could have been suggested to him by Averell, who wrote of England's enemies: "They would be sheepe, but they are wolues couered in sheepes skinnes" (sig. E1r). See 2.1.257–58 above.

3.1.69–72:   We nourish 'gainst our Senate
               The cockle of rebellion, insolence, sedition,
               Which we ourselves have plough'd for, sow'd, and scatter'd,
               By mingling them with us.

Compare Matt. 13.24–25, Rheims: "The kingdom of heauen is resembled to a man that sowed good seede in his field. But when men were a sleepe, his enemy came and ouersowed cockle among the wheate."

Compare Hosea 10.13: "You haue plowed wickednes: ye haue reaped iniquitie."

Only the Rheims has "cockle" at Matt. 13; all other versions have "tares." Catholic apologists cite this passage in *Coriolanus* as evidence of Shakespeare's use of the Rheims New Testament (Hugh Pope, *English Versions of the Bible*, 275, n. 12). But Shakespeare is not referring to Scripture in this passage. His source is North, which he follows closely: "Moreover he sayed they nourished against them selves, the naughty seede and cockle, of insolencie and sedition, which had bene sowed and scattered abroade emongest the people.... Dyd but only nourishe their disobedience" (5.520).

Amyot simply has "the bad seeds of audacity and insolence": "Et disant qu'ils nourrissaient et couvaient à l'encontre d'eux-mêmes, de mauvaises semences d'audace et d'insolence, qui déjà avaient été jetés parmi le peuple." North added "cockle" when translating Amyot, since cockle had become proverbial as a weed in grain fields. Tilley records the following proverbs current in Shakespeare's day:

"Cockle and corn grow in the same field" (C 497).

"In much corn is some cockle" (C 659).

In *Love's Labor's Lost* Shakespeare has, "Sow'd cockle reap'd no corn" (4.3.380).

The Geneva has "cokle" at Job 31.41: "Let thistles growe in steade of wheate, and cockle in stead of barly," but, again, Shakespeare's use of the word "cockle" is from North, not Scripture.

For a more complete discussion of this passage, see my note, "Shakespeare and the Rheims New Testament," in *American Notes & Queries*, 22 (1984): 70–72.

3.1.82:   A man of their infirmity.

"Infirmity," in the sense of "human frailty," is probably biblical. Compare Rom. 6.19: "I speake after the maner of man, because of the infirmitie of your flesh."

Compare Heb. 4.15: "Which can not be touched with the feeling of our infirmities."

See also Acts 14.15.

[3.1.124: Compare *Richard II* 5.5.16–17; Matt. 19.24; Mark 10.25; Luke 18.25.]

[3.1.160–61: Rom. 7.19.]

3.1.256–57:   His heart's his mouth;
              What his breast forges, that his tongue must vent.

Ecclus. 21.26: "The heart of fooles is in their mouth: but the mouth of the wise is in their heart."

3.1.289–91:   Whose gratitude
              Towards her deserved children is enroll'd
              In Jove's own book.

Probably an echo of the biblical statement that the names of the faithful are written in the book of life.
Phil. 4.3: "Whose names are in the booke of life."
Rev. 21.27: "They which are written in the Lambes booke of life."
See also Rev. 3.5; 13.8; 17.8; 20.12, 15; 22.19; Mal. 3.16; Ex. 32.32.
The closest parallel in North occurs in a completely different context: "That all those which were of lawfull age to carie weapon, should come and enter their names into the muster masters booke, to goe to the warres" (5.509).
Compare 5.2.14–16 below.

3.2.138–41:   Arm yourself
              To answer mildly; for they are prepar'd
              With accusations, as I hear, more strong
              Than are upon you yet.

Compare Prov. 15.1: "A soft answere putteth away wrath: but grieuous wordes stirre vp anger."
At best an analogy, rather than a reference.

3.3.125–27:   Let every feeble rumor shake your hearts!
              Your enemies, with nodding of their plumes,
              Fan you into despair!

Compare Lev. 26.36: "I will send euen a faintnes into their hearts in the land of their enemies, and the sounde of a leafe shaken shall chase them, and they shall flee as fleeing from a sword, and they shall fall, no man pursuing them."

4.1.29–30:   Though I go alone,
              Like to a lonely dragon.

The image of a lonely dragon may have been inspired by Scripture. Job 30.29 compares a lonely person to dragons and ostriches: "I am a brother to the dragons, and a companion to the ostriches." The Geneva gloss on this text reads: "I am like the wilde beastes that desire most solitarie places."

Compare also Isa. 34.11–13 and 13.20–22, where dragons and wild beasts are said to inhabit lonely, desolate places.

Shakespeare's passage appears to echo a proverb, but Tilley records no comparable proverb in Shakespeare's day.

[4.5.117: Marriage Service, "Thy wedded wife."]

4.7.24–25:   Yet he hath left undone
              That which....

Compare the General Confession, Morning and Evening Prayer: "Wee haue left vndone those things which wee ought to haue done," based on Matt. 23.23, Bishops': "These ought ye to haue donne, and not to leaue the other vndonne."

See *Othello* 3.3.203–204; *Antony and Cleopatra* 3.1.14; *Julius Caesar* 4.2.8–9.

[5.1.25–28: Matt. 3.12.]

5.2.14–16:   I have been
              The book of his good acts, whence men have read
              His fame.

Compare Rev. 20.12: "The bookes were opened, ... and the dead were iudged of those things, which were written in the bookes, according to their workes."

At best an analogy, rather than a reference.

The closest parallel in Plutarch conveys just the opposite meaning. Coriolanus's mother tells him that if he destroys Rome, he would "be chronicled the plague and destroyer of thy countrie" (5.540). See 3.1.289–91 above.

5.3.27:   Those doves' eyes.

Compare Song of Sol. 4.1: "Thine eyes are like the dooues."
See also Song of Sol. 1.14 (1.15, AV).

5.3.46:   By the jealous queen of heaven.

Jer. 7.18: "The Queene of heauen."
See also Jer. 44.17, 18, 19, 25.

[5.3.139 ("all-hail"): Matt. 28.9 (all versions except Geneva).]

5.3.139–40:   Be blest
              For making up this peace!

Compare Matt. 5.9: "Blessed are the peacemakers."

5.3.183–4:   Behold, the heavens do ope,
             The gods look down.

Compare Acts 7.56: "Behold, I see the heauens open, and the Sonne of man standing at the right hand of God."

5.4.23–24:   He wants nothing of a god but eternity and a heaven to throne
             in.

A combination of Isa. 57.15 and 66.1.
Isa. 57.15: "Thus saith he, that is hie and excellent, he that inhabiteth the eternitie."
Isa. 66.1: "Thus saith the Lord, The heauen is my throne."
Shakespeare is considerably closer to the Geneva Bible in this passage. The Coverdale, Matthew, Taverner, Great, and Bishops' Bibles all read "he that dwelleth in euerlastyngnesse," in the former text, and "heauen is my seate" in the latter.

5.4.25:   Yes, mercy, if you report him truly.

In response to Menenius's statement that Coriolanus only lacks eternity and a throne in heaven to be accounted a god, Sicinius answers that Coriolanus also lacks godlike mercy. Many Scriptures speak of mercy as being one of God's outstanding attributes:
Ex. 34.6: "The Lorde, the Lord, strong, merciful, and gracious."
1 Chron. 16.34, 41: "His mercie endureth for euer."
Also 2 Chron. 5.13; 7.3, 6; 20.21; Ps. 106.1; 107.1; 118.1; 136.1, and many other texts, especially in the Psalms.
God's mercy is frequently mentioned in the homilies and the Prayer Book.
Communion Service: "Thou art the same Lord, whose property is alwayes to haue mercy."

[5.4.46: Luke 24.18.]

5.4.49–50:   The trumpets, sackbuts, psalteries, and fifes,
Tabors and cymbals.

Dan. 3.5, 7: "The cornet, trumpet, harpe, sackebut, psalterie, dulcimer, and all instruments of musike."
Compare 1 Chron. 13.8: "With timbrels and with cymbales and with trumpets."
Shakespeare is closer to the Geneva Bible in Daniel 3. Only the Geneva has "sackebut." All other versions have "shawme."

5.6.150–51:   Though in this city he
Hath widowed and unchilded many a one.

Compare Isa. 47.9: "These two things shall come to thee suddenly on one day, the losse of children and widowehoode."

Timon of Athens

Timon of Athens is the only known play by Shakespeare that was never finished and apparently never acted. Why Shakespeare abandoned the work at so late a stage of the composition is unknown, but the play provides rare insights into his manner of composition and has several biblical references that are of considerable interest.

Shakespeare's main sources for the play were Plutarch, Lucian, and an anonymous university play called *Timon*. The idea for the play came from a brief episode in Plutarch's "Life of Antony," which relates that after his defeat at Actium, Antony sought to become a recluse like Timon, the hater of mankind. Lucian's dialogue, *Timon, or the Misanthrope*, gave Shakespeare what he needed to fill out that brief passage and the few other details that he borrowed from Plutarch. Lucian was available to Shakespeare in Latin, French, and Italian; the French translation of Filbert Bretin, 1582, was his most likely source. Finally, Shakespeare must have seen or known the academic play *Timon*, which was not published till 1842. The correspondences between that play and Shakespeare's are too striking to be coincidental.

None of these sources provided Shakespeare with any of his biblical references. No biblical references can be expected from non-Christian writers like Plutarch or Lucian, or from close translations of their works. The anonymous university play contains at most some six biblical references and ten possible echoes of Scripture, but Shakespeare borrowed none of them. If Shakespeare's passage at 1.2.10–11 can be considered a *bona fide* biblical reference, then it might have been inspired by the university play, but the passage in question is ascribed to Plato in the academic play rather than to Scripture.

Secondary sources for Shakespeare include Painter's *Palace of Pleasure*, Lyly's *Campaspe*, and Montaigne's essay "Of Democritus and Heraclitus," but the portions of these works that are relevant to Shakespeare's play contain no biblical references or even remote biblical echoes. Shakespeare's references throughout the play are his own.

The biblical references in the play which have elicited the most comment are those which compare Timon's betrayal by his erstwhile friends to Judas's betrayal of Christ:

It grieves me to see so many dip their meat in one man's blood.

(1.2.40–41)

The fellow that sits next him, now parts bread with him, ... is the readiest man to kill him.

(1.2.46–49)

Who can call him
His friend that dips in the same dish?

(3.2.65–66)

These passages have caused some to compare Timon's two banquets to the Last Supper, but the comparisons are unconvincing. The first banquet is one of notorious indulgence and riotous feasting, highlighted by Cupid's sensuous Masque of Amazons. At the second banquet, Timon tricks his betrayers into coming; utters a prayer that mocks and curses them; serves them nothing but warm water, which he throws in their faces; and drives out his false friends in a fury, throwing the dishes after them. These incidents hardly suggest the Last Supper! As is Shakespeare's custom throughout his plays, his use of Scripture in *Timon* is primarily intended to serve dramatic ends rather than to have theological significance.

In the list that follows, page numbers preceded by the number 6, as in (6.274), refer to volume 6 of Bullough.

1.1.48–50:   The course I hold,
              ... flies an eagle flight, bold, and forth on,
              Leaving no tract behind.

Compare Wisdom 5.10–11: "As a shippe that passeth ouer the waues of the water, which when it is gone by, the trace thereof cannot be found, ... Or as a bird that flyeth thorow in the aire, and no man can see any token of her passage, but onely heare the noise of her winges, ... wheras afterward no token of her way can be found,..."

1.2.6–7:   I do return those talents,
            Doubled with thanks and service.

With clear overtones of the parable of the talents.
Matt. 25.20–22: "Master, thou deliueredst vnto mee fiue talents: beholde, I haue gained with them other fiue talents. ... Master, thou deliueredst vnto

me two talents: beholde, I haue gained two other talents with them."

Shakespeare's use of "talent" as a monetary unit originates with Lucian, who used the Greek word *tálanton*, a word carried over into other languages. Lucian's dialogue *Timon* relates how Timon paid sixteen talents to have the orator Demea released from prison; the anonymous play *Timon*, based on Lucian, has Timon pay sixteen talents to keep Demeas from being imprisoned (6.274, 309).

The word "talent" in Shakespeare's sources apparently reminded him of Jesus' parable of the talents. Ventidius's offer at 1.2.6–7 to return ten talents to Timon for the five talents that Timon paid to have him released from prison seems to have been influenced by the account at Matthew 25. There is no offer to repay or to render an account in any of Shakespeare's nonbiblical sources.

1.2.10–11: There's none
Can truly say he gives if he receives.

Compare Luke 6.34: "If yee lend to them of whome yee hope to receiue, what thank shall ye haue?"
Compare Acts 20.35: "It is a blessed thing to giue, rather then to receiue."
The closest parallel in Shakespeare's sources occurs in the anonymous university play *Timon*: "Plato in his Acrostikes saith, it is better to give than receave.... Wilt thou give? so thou shalt receave: wilt thou receave? then give" (6.337–38). These words are not spoken by Timon, however, but by the lying philosopher Stilpo in the last scene of the play, as he tries to beguile Timon of his newly-found gold.
Compare also Plutarch's "Life of Antony": Antony held that "the greatnes and magnificence of the Empire of Rome appeared most, not where the Romanes tooke, but where they gave much" (5.283).

1.2.40–41: It grieves me to see so many dip their meat in one man's blood.

1.2.46–49: There's much example for't: the fellow that sits next him, now parts bread with him, pledges the breath of him in a divided draught, is the readiest man to kill him.

The outstanding "example for't" is that of Judas Iscariot.
Matt. 26.23: "Hee that dippeth his hand with me in the dish, he shall betray me."
John 13.18: "He that eateth bread with me, hath lift vp his heele against me."

Ps. 41.9: "Yea, euen mine owne familier freende whom I trusted: whiche did also eate of my bread, hath laid great wayte for me."
See also Mark 14.18; Luke 22.21.

[1.2.201–202: Luke 16.4.]

1.2.224–25:   All the lands thou hast
              Lie in a pitch'd field.
              Alcib. Ay, defil'd land, my lord.

Compare Ecclus. 13.1: "He that toucheth pitche, shalbe defiled with it."
See *1 Henry IV* 2.4.410–13.

2.2.73–74:   *Page. [To the Fool.]* Why, how now, captain? what do you in this wise company?

Compare Prov. 13.20: "He that walketh with the wise, shall be wise: but a companion of fooles shalbe afflicted."

2.2.76–77:   Would I had a rod in my mouth, that I might answer thee pro-fitably.

Compare Prov. 26.3–4: "Vnto the horse belongeth a whip, to the asse a bridle, and a rodde to the fooles backe. Answere not a foole according to his foolishnes, least thou also be like him."
Compare Isa. 11.4: "The rod of his mouth."
Compare Rev. 19.15: "Out of his mouth went out a sharpe sworde, ... for he shall rule them with a rod of yron."
See also Rev. 1.16; 2.16.
Shakespeare combines Prov. 26 with the biblical expression "rod of his mouth," variations of which appear several times in Scripture

[2.2.155–57: Luke 16.1–2.]

[2.2.169–70: Prov. 19.4; 19.6–7; 14.20.]

2.2.176:   To think I shall lack friends.

Timon's words to his weeping steward, assuring him that his friends would not fail him in his time of need, seem to echo the parable of the Unjust Steward: "Make you friendes with the riches of iniquitie, that when ye shall want, they may receiue you into euerlasting habitations" (Luke 16.9).

Overtones of the same parable can also be found at 2.2.155–57, and especially at 4.3.497–98, 502–506.

3.2.65–66:   Who can call him
                 His friend that dips in the same dish?

Matt. 26.23: "Hee that dippeth his hand with me in the dish."
See 1.2.40–41 above.

[3.5.39: Rom. 12.19.]

3.5.56–57:   To be in anger is impiety;
                 But who is man that is not angry?

Compare Matt. 5.22: "Whosoeuer is angrie with his brother ... shall be culpable of iudgment."
Compare the more certain reference to Matthew chapter 5 at 4.3.466.

3.5.86–87:   Friend, or brother,
                 He forfeits his own blood that spills another.

Gen. 9.5–6: "For surely I wil require your blood, ... at the hand of a mans brother will I require the life of man. Whoso sheadeth mans blood, by man shal his blood be shed."

3.5.109–110:   Is this the balsom that the usuring Senate
                   Pours into captains' wounds?

Compare Luke 10.34: "And went to him, and bounde vp his woundes, and powred in oyle and wine."
Closest parallel in Lucian: "Heal this wound by scattering a little gold on it, for gold is a medicine that staunches blood very well" (6.273).
The passage in Lucian is from an altogether different context; Shakespeare is considerably closer to Luke.

3.6.9–14:   *1. Lord....* He hath sent me an earnest inviting, which many my
near occasions did urge me to put off; but he hath conjur'd me
beyond them, and I must needs appear.
2. Lord. In like manner was I in debt to my importunate business, but he would not hear my excuse.

With distinct overtones of the parable of the wedding invitation at Matt.
22.3–4 and Luke 14.16–19, 23. Compare especially the second Lord's
words, "he would not hear my excuse," with Luke 14.18, "they all with one
mynde began to make excuse," and the repeated phrase, "I pray thee, haue
me excused" (verses 18–19). In none of Shakespeare's nonbiblical sources
did those invited attempt to excuse themselves from Timon's feast.

3.6.61:   This is the old man still.

Compare the Baptism Service in the Prayer Book: "That he ... may cru-
cifie the olde man," based on Eph. 4.22: "That yee cast of [off] ... the olde
man," and Rom. 6.6: "Knowing this, that our olde man is crucified with
him."

[3.6.120: Matt. 7.9. But Shakespeare is probably indebted to the university play (6.328–29).]

4.1.25–28:   Lust, and liberty,
Creep in the minds and marrows of our youth,
That 'gainst the stream of virtue they may strive,
And drown themselves in riot!

Ecclus. 4.28, Bishops': "And striue thou not agaynst the streame: But for
ryghteousnesse take paynes with al thy soule, and for the trueth, striue thou
vnto death."
The Coverdale, Matthew, Taverner, and Great Bibles all have "stryue
thou not againste the streame," which only the Geneva lacks.
The Geneva reads: 'Striue for the trueth vnto death, (and defende iustice
for thy life)."
In this passage, Shakespeare's reference is to the traditional versions of his
day rather than to the Geneva.

[4.2.10–15: Prov. 19.4, 7; Ecclus. 13.22.]

4.3.64:   For all her cherubin look.

Derived ultimately from Scripture. See the reference at *Macbeth* 1.7.22 for a discussion of this reference.

4.3.172–73:   *Alcib.* I never did thee harm.
             Tim. Yes, thou spok'st well of me.
             Alcib. Call'st thou that harm?

Compare Luke 6.26: "Wo be to you when all men speake well of you."
If Shakespeare had Luke 6.26 in mind in this passage, then he was considerably closer to the Geneva Bible. All other Protestant English Bibles (Tyndale, Coverdale, Matthew, Taverner, Great, Bishops') read parallel to the Bishops' Bible: "Wo vnto you when menne shal praise you." The Rheims has: "Wo, when al men shal blesse you."

[4.3.191: John 14.2, Tyndale, Matthew, Great. See also 5.1.215–16.]

[4.3.245–47: 1 Tim. 6.6–8.]

4.3.466:   When man was wish'd to love his enemies!

Matt. 5.44: "I say vnto you, Loue your enemies: blesse them that curse you."

4.3.493–94:   Surely, this man
              Was born of woman.

Compare Job 14.1: "Man that is borne of woman."
Compare also the Burial Service: "Man that is borne of a woman."

4.3.497–98, 502–506:   One honest man ...
                       ... and he's a steward.
                       Methinks thou art more honest now than wise;
                       For, by oppressing and betraying me,
                       Thou mightst have sooner got another service;
                       For many so arrive at second masters,
                       Upon their first lord's neck.

With clear overtones of the parable of the Unjust Steward at Luke 16.1–9. Compare especially verse 8: "The Lorde commended the vniust stewarde, because hee had done wisely. Wherefore the children of this world are ... wiser then the children of light."

Flavius is more honest than wise; the Unjust Steward was more wise than honest.

Compare *Othello* 3.3.381–83.

5.1.10–11:   You shall see him a palm in Athens again, and flourish
             With the highest.

Ps. 92.11 (92.12, Geneva): "The ryghteous shal florishe lyke a palme tree."

See also *Hamlet* 5.2.40.

Shakespeare's debt to Ps. 92 is obvious. The palm tree is not native to England. Compare also Ps. 1.3–4.

[5.1.44–45: John 9.4. Most likely an analogy rather than a reference. John 9.4, however, occurs in the Commination Service in the Prayer Book.]

5.1.165–66:   Who, like a boar too savage, doth root up
              His country's peace.

Ps. 80.13: "The wilde boare out of the wood dooth roote it vp."
The Geneva has "hath destroyed it" in place of "dooth roote it vp."

5.1.215–16:   Timon hath made his everlasting mansion
              Upon the beached verge.

Most likely an echo of John 14.2 (Tyndale, Matthew, Great, Rheims): "In my fathers house are many mansions.... I goe to prepare a place for you."

The Coverdale and Taverner Bibles have "dwellynges" rather than "mansions." The Geneva and the Bishops' have "dwelling places." In this instance Shakespeare's reference is neither to the most popular nor to the most available versions of his day.

See 4.3.191 above.

5.3.3:   Timon is dead, who hath outstretch'd his span.

Ps. 39.6 (39.5, Geneva): "Beholde, thou hast made my dayes as it were a spanne long."

A reference to the Psalter. The Geneva and even the Bishops' versions of the Psalms have "hand breadth" instead of "span."

Compare *Othello* 2.3.71–72.

[5.4.42–44: John 10.1–16.]

Appendix A
Index to Shakespeare's Biblical References

The following index to biblical references in Shakespeare's tragedies is arranged according to the books of the Bible from Genesis onward. To make the index as useful as possible, I have included not only the principal passages in Scripture to which Shakespeare refers, but also a large number of the secondary texts that parallel them. These secondary passages are sufficiently similar to Shakespeare's principal references to warrant their inclusion in this appendix. None of the items cited throughout the text in small type within brackets, however, are included in the appendix.

Whenever the chapter and verse numbers in the Geneva Bible and the Psalter differ from those in the Authorized Version, the numberings of the Authorized Version are given in parenthesis.

The Old Testament

Genesis

2.8, 15	*Ham.* 5.1.30–31, 36–37
2.17	*Ant.* 4.14.26
2.24	*Rom.* 2.6.37; *JC* 2.1.272–73; *Ham.* 4.3.52
3.14	*Oth.* 4.2.15–16
3.19	*Ham.* 2.2.308; 4.2.5–6; 5.1.209–10; *Mac.* 5.5.23
3.23	*Ham.* 5.1.30–31, 36–37
3.24	*Ham.* 4.3.48; *Tro.* 3.2.69; *Oth.* 4.2.63; *Mac.* 1.7.22; *Timon* 4.3.64
4.8	*Ham.* 5.1.76–77
4.10–11	*Ham.* 3.3.36–38; *Mac.* 3.4.121
4.11	*Timon* 3.1.16, 22; 5.2.183
Chap 6–8	*JC* 1.2.152–53
9.5–6	*Timon* 3.5.86–87
9.6	*Mac.* 3.4.121
10.8–9	*JC* 1.2.152–53
14.17–20	*Cor.* 1.9.32–34

18.16	*Oth.* 3.4.197
31.49–50	*Mac.* 4.3.120–21
41.1–36	*Lear* 5.3.24–25
41.5–7, 22–24	*Ham.* 3.4.64–65
41.29	*Cor.* 2.1.114–15
47.6	*Oth.* 1.1.70–71
49.4	*Oth.* 5.2.134
49.9	*Ant.* 3.13.94

Exodus

3.14	*Oth.* 1.1.65; 4.1.270
7.12	*Tro.* 5.4.33–35
8.21–23	*Oth.* 1.1.70–71
8.24	*Ant.* 3.13.166–67
9.23–24	*Ant.* 3.13.159–61
9.25	*Ant.* 3.13.162–66
20.12	*Lear* 1.1.96–98; 3.4.80–83
20.13	*Ham.* 1.2.131–32
20.14	*Lear* 3.4.80–83
21.23–25	*Oth.* 2.1.299
22.18	*Ant.* 4.12.47
34.6	*Cor.* 5.4.25

Leviticus

18.16	*Ham.* 3.4.15
20.10	*Lear* 4.6.109–11
20.21	*Ham.* 3.4.15
24.20	*Oth.* 2.1.299
26.36	*Cor.* 3.3.125–27

Numbers

5.11–31	*Oth.* 4.2.103–104

Deuteronomy

5.16	*Lear* 1.1.96–98; 3.4.80–83
6.5	*Rom.* 3.5.226–27
6.16	*Oth.* 4.1.8
19.21	*Oth.* 2.1.299
21.6–7	*Mac.* 2.2.64
21.8	*Mac.* 5.8.5–6
22.6	*Mac.* 4.3.218–19

22.21	*Oth.* 5.2.132
22.22	*Lear* 4.6.109–111
25.5–10	*Ham.* 3.4.15

Judges

| 11.30–40 | *Ham.* 2.2.403–12 |
| 15.4–5 | *Lear* 5.3.22–23 |

1 Samuel

2.33	*Mac.* 4.1.110
17.7	*Tro.* 5.5.9
17.26	*Tro.* 4.5.65–66
17.35	*Oth.* 5.2.355–56
18.6–7	*Tro.* 3.3.211–13
20.23	*Mac.* 4.3.120–21
21.5	*Oth.* 4.2.82–85
24.16 (24.15)	*Mac.* 4.3.120–21
25.41	*Timon* 1.1.331–32
26.9	*Lear* 3.7.58; *Mac.* 2.3.68
28.14	*Ham.* 2.2.598–600
28.21–25	*Mac.* 4.1.125–28

2 Samuel

1.14	*Lear* 3.7.58
12.7	*Lear* 3.7.58
14.25	*Lear* 5.3.137–38
17.8	*Titus* 4.1.96–97
22.11	*Mac.* 1.7.22–23

1 Kings

2.32–33	*Rom.* 5.3.62; *Oth.* 1.3.177
2.37	*Rom.* 5.3.62
12.11	*Cor.* 2.3.91–92
21.23	*Titus* 5.3.197–99
22.19	*Ham.* 1.5.92

2 Kings

| 9.36–37 | *Titus* 5.3.197–99 |
| 18.21 | *Ant.* 3.13.67–69 |

1 Chronicles

13.8	*Cor.* 5.4.49–50
16.34, 41	*Cor.* 5.4.25

2 Chronicles

9.8	*Ant.* 3.6.87–89
13.15	*JC* 5.2.5

Esther

6.6	*Tro.* 4.5.65–66
8.8	*Lear* 3.6.79–81

Job

2.7–10	*Oth.* 4.2.47–53
3.1–8	*Mac.* 4.1.133–34
3.17	*JC* 5.5.41–42
3.17–18	*Titus* 1.1.150–56
6.2	*Titus* 1.1.55
7.9–10	*Ham.* 3.1.77–79; *Lear* 5.3.308
7.21	*Rom.* 3.1.97–98; *Ham.* 1.2.70–71
8.9	*Mac.* 5.5.24
10.21–22	*Ham.* 3.1.77–79; *Ant.* 5.2.193–94
14.1	*Mac.* 5.3.6; 5.7.11; *Timon* 4.3.493–94
14.1–2	*Mac.* 5.5.24
16.22	*Ham.* 3.1.77–79
17.14	*Lear* 4.1.33
18.6	*Mac.* 5.5.23
21.17	*Mac.* 5.5.23
25.6	*Lear* 4.1.33
30.29	*Cor.* 4.1.29–30
31.6	*Titus* 1.1.55
31.41	*Cor.* 3.1.69–72
37.9	*Oth.* 5.2.220
40.20–21 (41.1–2)	*Ant.* 2.5.10–13

Psalms

1.3	*Mac.* 1.4.28–29; *Timon* 5.1.10–11
2.2	*Ant.* 3.6.66–68
7.17 (7.16)	*Titus* 3.1.273–74; *Ham.* 5.2.385
8.4–6	*Ham.* 2.2.303–307; *Lear* 3.4.102–103

18.4	*Tro.* 4.1.58; *Oth.* 1.1.154
18.10	*Mac.* 1.7.22–23
19.5	*Tro.* 4.4.145
22.6	*Lear* 4.1.33
22.12	*Ant.* 3.13.126–28
22.15	*Mac.* 5.5.23
28.3	*JC* 4.1.50–51
30.5–6	*Rom.* 4.5.126–28
39.6 (39.5)	*Oth.* 2.3.71–72; *Timon* 5.3.3
39.7 (39.6)	*Mac.* 5.5.24
41.9	*Timon* 1.2.40–41, 46–49
45.11 (45.10)	*Tro.* 4.2.96
46.2–3	*Lear* 3.1.5–6
51.3	*Rom.* 3.2.109–111
51.7	*Ham.* 3.3.45–46
58.4–5	*Tro.* 2.2.172–73
68.15	*Ant.* 3.13.126–28
80.5	*Titus* 3.2.37–38
80.13	*Timon* 5.1.165–66
83.10	*Ant.* 1.1.35
84.1, 3	*Mac.* 1.6.1–10
89.32	*Cor.* 2.3.91–92
90.9	*Rom.* 5.3.229–30; *Mac.* 5.5.26–27
92.11 (92.12)	*Ham.* 5.2.40; *Mac.* 1.4.28–29; *Timon* 5.1.10–11
93.2 (93.1)	*Mac.* 2.1.56; *Ant.* 5.1.15–17
101.5 (101.4)	*Lear* 3.4.85
101.7 (101.5)	*Lear* 3.4.85
102.25–27	*Oth.* 2.1.64–65
104.4	*Ham.* 1.4.39
104.5	*Mac.* 2.1.56
107.23–26	*Oth.* 2.1.187–89
107.27	*Rom.* 2.3.3
115.7–8	*JC* 1.1.35
115.17	*Titus* 1.1.150–56; *Ham.* 5.2.358
116.3	*Tro.* 4.1.58; *Oth.* 1.1.154
127, Superscription	*Mac.* 5.5.49
140.3	*Lear* 1.4.288
144.1	*Tro.* 2.3.244
144.4	*Ham.* 4.2.28–30; *Mac.* 5.5.24
148.12	*Tro.* 2.2.104

Proverbs

5.15–18	*Oth.* 4.2.57–62
6.6, 8	*Lear* 2.4.67–68
13.20	*Lear* 1.4.15–16; *Timon* 2.2.73–74

14.24	*Cor.* 2.1.191
15.1	*Cor.* 3.2.138–41
16.5	*Lear* 3.4.85
17.12	*Titus* 4.1.96–97
17.22	*Ant.* 1.4.27
17.27–28	*Lear* 1.4.15–16
20.14	*Tro.* 4.1.76–77
21.4	*Lear* 3.4.85
22.1	*Oth.* 3.3.155–59
25.16	*Rom.* 2.6.11–14
26.3–4	*Timon* 2.2.76–77
27.2	*Tro.* 1.3.240–42
28.13	*Lear* 1.1.281–82
28.25	*Lear* 3.4.85
30.25	*Lear* 2.4.67–68
31.2	*Cor.* 1.3.6

Ecclesiastes

1.14	*Ham.* 1.2.133–34
3.1–2	*Mac.* 5.5.17–18
3.1, 4	*Titus* 3.1.263–65
3.20	*Ham.* 2.2.308; 4.2.5–6; 5.1.209–10
7.3 (7.1)	*Oth.* 3.3.155–59
7.30 (7.28)	*Ham.* 2.2.178–79
9.6	*Titus* 1.1.150–56
9.11	*Titus* 1.1.150–56
12.6 (12.5)	*Titus* 1.1.83

Song of Solomon

1.14 (1.15)	*Cor.* 5.3.27
4.1	*Cor.* 5.3.27

Isaiah

1.18	*Ham.* 3.3.45–56
5.14	*Ham.* 1.2.244
5.24	*Cor.* 2.1.257–58
11.4	*Timon* 2.2.76–77
11.6	*Cor.* 2.1.6–9
14.12	*Mac.* 4.3.22
24.20	*Rom.* 2.3.3
34.4	*Ham.* 1.5.92
34.11–13	*Cor.* 4.1.29–30
36.6	*Ant.* 3.13.67–69

40.2–3	*Ham.* 1.3.53
47.9	*Cor.* 5.6.150–51
47.14	*Cor.* 2.1.257–58
55.2	*Oth.* 3.3.322
57.15	*Cor.* 5.4.23–24
65.17	*Ant.* 1.1.17
65.25	*Cor.* 2.1.6–9
66.1	*Cor.* 5.4.23–24

Jeremiah

7.18	*Cor.* 5.3.46
8.2	*Ant.* 1.1.35
12.2	*Mac.* 1.4.28–29
16.4	*Ant.* 1.1.35
30.7	*Oth.* 4.2.42, 124
44.17–19, 25	*Cor.* 5.3.46

Lamentations

1.12	*Titus* 3.1.216
1.18	*Titus* 3.1.216
1.20	*Titus* 3.1.230
2.11	*Titus* 3.1.230
2.19	*Titus* 3.1.206

Ezekiel

1.4	*Oth.* 5.2.220
9.10	*Oth.* 1.3.177
16.30	*JC* 2.4.39–40
16.49	*Ham.* 3.3.80
29.6–7	*Ant.* 3.13.67–69
37.11	*Ant.* 1.4.27

Daniel

2.42	*Ant.* 1.1.35
3.5, 7	*Cor.* 5.4.49–50
5.27	*Titus* 1.1.55
6.8, 12, 15	*Lear* 3.6.79–81
12.7	*Titus* 3.1.206

Hosea

10.13	*Cor.* 3.1.69–72
13.8	*Titus* 4.1.96–97

Joel

1.15	*Oth.* 4.2.42, 124
2.13	*Ham.* 3.4.34–35
2.28	*Tro.* 5.3.63

Jonah

1.6	*Cor.* 2.3.54–56

Micah

1.7	*Ham.* 4.2.28–30

Nahum

3.12	*Mac.* 4.3.237–38

The Apocrypha

1 Esdras

4.21	*Tro.* 4.2.96

2 Esdras

7.32	*Ham.* 5.2.358

Wisdom

2.1	*Ham.* 3.1.77–79
2.5	*Mac.* 5.5.24
2.7–8	*Ham.* 1.3.47–50; *Mac* 2.3.18–19
5.10–11	*Timon* 1.1.48–50

5.13	*Rom.* 3.4.4
7.3	*Lear* 4.6.178–83
7.6	*Lear* 4.6.178–83

Ecclesiasticus

4.28	*Timon* 4.1.25–28
7.3 (7.1)	*Oth.* 3.3.155–59
9.17	*Lear* 1.4.15–16
13.1	*Oth.* 2.3.360; *Timon* 1.2.224–25
13.16, 18 (13.15, 17)	*Cor.* 2.1.6–9
21.26	*Lear* 1.1.91–92; *Cor.* 3.1.256–57
22.10	*Ham.* 4.2.22–24
26.9	*Oth.* 4.2.25–26
26.15	*Ham.* 1.3.53
31.27–28	*Oth.* 2.3.309–10
38.17, 23	*Ham.* 1.2.92–102
38.18	*Ant.* 4.15.33
40.18	*Mac.* 3.2.4–5
41.4	*Ham.* 1.2.92–102
41.12	*Oth.* 3.3.155–59

Baruch

| 4.14, 20; 5.2 | *Ham.* 1.2.131 |

1 Maccabees

| 6.46 | *Ham.* 1.2.131–32 |

2 Maccabees

| 14.41 | *Ham.* 1.2.131–32 |

The New Testament

Matthew

2.1–20	*Ham.* 3.2.13–14
2.2, 9	*Timon* 4.2.32–33
2.7–8	*Ant.* 1.2.28–29; 3.3.2–5; 3.6.73

2.22	*Ant.* 3.6.73
3.4	*Oth.* 1.3.347–49
3.7	*Tro.* 3.1.133
3.9	*Ham.* 3.4.126–27
4.1–10	*Oth.* 2.3.351–53; *Mac.* 1.3.123–25
4.7	*Oth.* 4.1.8
4.8–9	*Oth.* 4.3.64, 68–70
4.10	*Oth.* 1.1.108–109
5.9	*Cor.* 5.3.139–40
5.22	*Timon* 3.5.56–57
5.29	*Lear* 1.4.301–303; *Mac.* 2.2.56
5.33–34	*Lear* 3.4.80–83
5.34	*Rom.* 2.2.112; *Tro.* 1.3.31
5.37	*Lear* 4.6.98–100
5.39	*Lear* 4.2.51
5.44	*Ham.* 5.1.259; *Mac.* 2.4.40–41; 3.1.87–88;
	Timon 4.3.466
6.12	*Oth.* 2.3.111–12
6.26	*Mac.* 4.2.31–32
7.3	*Ham.* 1.1.112
7.13–14	*Ham.* 1.3.47–50; *Tro.* 3.3.154–55; *Mac.* 2.3.18–19
7.15	*Rom.* 3.2.76; *Cor.* 2.3.115
8.12	*Ham.* 5.1.240–42
8.16	*Ham.* 3.4.169–70
9.22	*JC* 2.1.327–28
9.33	*Ham.* 3.4.169–70
10.4	*Oth.* 5.2.348
10.21	*Lear* 1.2.106–12, 144–46
10.28	*Oth.* 5.2.32
10.29	*Ham.* 5.2.219–20; *Tro.* 2.1.70–71
11.5	*Cor.* 2.1.262–63
12.24–27	*Mac.* 2.3.4
12.34	*Tro.* 3.1.133
13.24–25	*Cor.* 3.1.69–72
13.45–46	*Tro.* 2.2.81–83; *Oth.* 5.2.347–48; *Mac.* 3.1.67–68
14.6, 8	*Ant.* 3.3.2–5
15.27	*Cor.* 1.1.206
15.30	*Cor.* 2.1.262–63
16.17	*Ham.* 1.5.22
16.18–19	*Oth.* 4.2.90–92
16.26	*Oth.* 4.3.64, 68–70
16.28	*JC* 2.2.33
18.8	*Mac.* 2.3.18–19
18.9	*Mac.* 2.2.56
18.10	*JC* 3.2.181
19.5	*Tro.* 4.2.96

19.5–6	*Rom.* 2.6.37; *JC* 2.1.272–73; *Ham.* 4.3.52; *Tro.* 3.1.101–102
19.16	*Rom.* 4.1.55
19.24	*Tro.* 2.1.80
22.3–4	*Timon* 3.6.9–14
22.37	*Rom.* 3.5.226–27
23.17, 19	*Tro.* 2.2.56–57
23.22	*Tro.* 1.3.31
23.23	*JC* 4.2.8–9; *Oth.* 3.3.203–204; *Ant.* 3.1.14; *Cor.* 4.7.24–25
23.27	*Timon* 4.2.98
23.33	*Tro.* 3.1.133
24.3, 6, 7–14	*Lear* 5.3.264–65
24.12	*Lear* 1.2.106–12, 144–46
24.29	*Ham.* 1.1.117–24
24.31	*Rom.* 3.2.67; *Mac.* 1.7.19
25.6	*Rom.* 4.4.27–28
25.8	*Ant.* 4.15.85
25.15	*Mac.* 3.1.96–99
25.20–22	*Timon* 1.2.6–7
25.41	*Titus* 5.1.147–50
26.14–16	*Oth.* 5.2.347
26.20–29	*JC* 2.2.126
26.23	*Timon* 1.2.40–41, 46–49; 3.2.65–66
26.24	*Tro.* 4.2.85–86; *Oth.* 4.2.69
26.47, 52	*Oth.* 1.2.59
26.48–49	*Oth.* 5.2.358–59
27.4–5	*Oth.* 5.2.358–59
27.24	*Mac.* 2.2.64
27.33	*Mac.* 1.2.40
27.45, 51–53	*Oth.* 5.2.99–101; *Mac.* 2.4.6–10
27.52	*JC* 2.2.18; *Ham.* 1.1.114–16

Mark

1.6	*Oth.* 1.3.347–49
3.15	*Ham.* 3.4.169–70
3.22	*Mac.* 2.3.4
4.39	*Oth.* 5.2.46
5.9	*Mac.* 4.3.55–56
5.30	*JC* 1.2.15
8.36	*Mac.* 3.1.67–68
9.47	*Mac.* 2.2.56
10.7–8	*Rom.* 2.6.37; *Ham.* 4.3.52
10.25	*Tro.* 2.1.80
10.49	*JC* 1.2.20–21

12.30	*Rom.* 3.5.226–27
14.21	*Oth.* 4.2.69
15.22	*Mac.* 1.2.40
15.33	*Oth.* 5.2.99–101; *Mac.* 2.4.6–10.

Luke

1.7, 57	*Ant.* 1.2.28–29
1.44	*Cor.* 1.3.15–16
2.49	*Lear* 4.4.23–24
3.7	*Tro.* 3.1.133
4.1–12	*Oth.* 2.3.351–53; *Mac.* 1.3.123–25
4.12	*Oth.* 4.1.8
5.31	*JC* 2.1.327–28
6.26	*Timon* 4.3.172–73
6.27–28	*Mac.* 3.1.87–88
6.29	*Lear* 4.2.51
6.34	*Timon* 1.2.10–11
6.42	*Ham.* 1.1.112
8.25	*Tro.* 5.2.67
8.30	*Mac.* 4.3.55–56
10.18	*Mac.* 4.3.22
10.34	*Timon* 3.5.109–10
10.39–40	*Oth.* 1.3.147–50
11.4	*Oth.* 2.3.111–12
11.15–19	*Mac.* 2.3.4
11.27	*Tro.* 2.3.241
12.6	*Tro.* 2.1.70–71
14.15–16	*Ham.* 4.3.16–18, 33
14.16–19, 23	*Timon* 3.6.9–14
15.15–16	*Lear* 4.7.38
16.1–9	*Timon* 4.3.497–98, 502–506
16.8	*Oth.* 3.3.381–83; *Ant.* 5.2.138–50
16.9	*Timon* 2.2.176
16.20	*Ham.* 1.5.72–73; *Tro.* 2.3.33; 5.1.65
16.22	*Ham.* 5.2.359–60
17.10	*Mac.* 1.4.23–26
17.29	*Oth.* 4.1.234
18.7–8	*Lear* 4.2.78–80
18.25	*Tro.* 2.1.80
19.40	*JC* 3.2.229–30; *Ham.* 3.4.126–27; *Mac.* 2.1.58; 3.4.122
22.44	*JC* 5.1.48–49
23.34	*Rom.* 1.1.65
23.44–45	*Oth.* 5.2.99–101; *Mac.* 2.4.6–10

John

1.16	*Rom.* 2.3.86
2.4	*JC* 5.5.20
5.28–29	*Mac.* 2.3.77–79
8.4–5	*Lear* 4.6.109–111
8.44	*Mac.* 1.3.107; 5.5.42–43
13.18	*Timon* 1.2.40–41, 46–49
13.27	*Mac.* 1.7.1–2
14.2	*Timon* 5.1.215–16
15.6	*Lear* 4.2.34–36
18.11	*Oth.* 1.2.59
19.17	*Mac.* 1.2.40
21.15–17	*Oth.* 3.3.117

Acts

1.9–11	*Rom.* 2.2.28–32
2.17	*Tro.* 5.3.63
2.19–20	*Ham.* 1.1.117–24
2.38	*Oth.* 2.3.342–44
7.42	*Ham.* 1.5.92
7.56	*Cor.* 5.3.183–84
10.42	*Ham.* 5.1.126, 251
12.15	*JC* 3.2.181
20.35	*Timon* 1.2.10–11
23.3	*Titus* 4.2.98

Romans

4.3	*Ham.* 5.1.35–36
6.6	*Timon* 3.6.61
6.12–13, 21	*Rom.* 2.3.27–30
6.19	*Cor.* 3.1.82
7.18–24	*Rom.* 2.3.27–30
8.24	*Oth.* 2.3.106–107
9.18–23	*Oth.* 2.3.102–104
11.5	*Ham.* 3.2.63–65
11.28	*Ham.* 3.2.63–65
12.15	*Titus* 3.1.244
12.17, 20–21	*Mac.* 2.4.40–41
12.19	*Titus* 4.1.128–29
13.4	*Ham.* 3.4.173–75; *Ant.* 3.6.87–89
13.5	*Cor.* 2.3.33
13.8	*Oth.* 5.2.59–61
13.9–10	*Titus* 4.2.41–43

13.12–14	*Lear* 3.4.87–90
15.1	*JC* 4.3.86

1 Corinthians

3.12–15	*Cor.* 2.1.257–58
7.14	*Oth.* 2.3.342–44
10.25	*Cor.* 2.3.33
12.25–26	*Oth.* 3.4.146–48
13.2	*Mac.* 4.3.157
15.10	*Oth.* 1.1.65
15.31	*Mac.* 4.3.109–111
15.52	*Rom.* 3.2.67; *Ham.* 5.1.229–30; *Mac.* 2.3.82–83
15.55	*Ham.* 3.4.81; *Tro.* 5.2.67

2 Corinthians

1.18–19	*Lear* 4.6.98–100
1.22	*Ham.* 3.2.63–65; *Oth.* 2.3.342–44
5.20	*Oth.* 5.2.26–27
6.10	*Lear* 1.1.250
8.9	*Lear* 1.1.250
11.2	*Tro.* 4.4.80
11.6	*Oth.* 1.3.81
11.14	*Ham.* 2.2.598–600; *Oth.* 2.3.351–53; *Mac.* 1.3.123–25
12.10	*JC* 1.3.91

Galatians

4.21–30	*Ham.* 5.1.35–36
5.17	*Rom.* 2.3.27–30

Ephesians

1.13–14	*Oth.* 2.3.342–44
2.5, 8	*Tro.* 3.1.15
4.2	*Oth.* 1.2.9–10
4.7	*Mac.* 3.1.96–99
4.22	*Timon* 3.6.61
4.27	*Oth.* 2.3.296–97
4.30	*Ham.* 3.2.63–65; *Oth.* 2.3.342–44
5.22	*Oth.* 5.2.196
5.31	*JC* 2.1.272–73; *Ham.* 4.3.52
6.1–2	*Lear* 1.1.96–98; 3.4.80–83
6.12	*Ham.* 1.5.22

Philippians

3.7–8	*Cor.* 2.2.124–26
4.3	*Cor.* 3.1.289–91

Colossians

3.13	*Oth.* 1.2.9–10

1 Thessalonians

1.4	*Ham.* 3.2.63–65
4.3–4	*Oth.* 4.2.82–85
4.9	*Oth.* 5.2.59–61
4.16	*Ham.* 5.1.229–30; *Mac.* 2.3.82–83

1 Timothy

2.9	*Lear* 3.4.80–83
6.6	*Mac.* 3.2.4–5
6.6–8	*Oth.* 3.3.172–73
6.7	*Ham.* 5.2.219–24

2 Timothy

4.1	*Ham.* 5.1.126, 251

Titus

2.9–10	*Ham.* 3.2.336
2.11	*Tro.* 3.1.15

Hebrews

1.8	*Tro.* 1.3.31
1.14	*Ham.* 1.4.39; 5.1.240–42
2.6	*Lear* 3.4.102–103
2.9	*JC* 2.2.33
4.15	*Cor.* 3.1.82
6.7	*Titus* 3.1.16, 22
6.13	*Rom.* 2.2.113–14
9.27	*JC* 4.3.191
12.6	*Oth.* 5.2.21–22
13.2	*Ham.* 1.5.165

James

5.11	*Oth.* 4.2.47–53
5.12	*Lear* 4.6.98–100

1 Peter

3.4–5	*Oth.* 1.3.94–95
3.5–6	*Oth.* 5.2.196
3.7	*Rom.* 1.1.15–16; *Ham.* 1.2.146
4.5	*Ham.* 5.1.126, 251
4.7	*Lear* 5.3.264–65
4.10	*Mac.* 3.1.96–99
5.8	*Mac.* 3.1.67–68

2 Peter

3.13	*Ant.* 1.1.17

1 John

3.2	*Ham.* 4.5.43–44
3.11	*Oth.* 5.2.59–61
4.18	*Mac.* 4.2.12

Revelation

3.20	*Ham.* 4.3.16–18, 33
6.13	*Mac.* 4.3.237–38; *Ant.* 3.13.145–47
7.1	*Mac.* 4.1.52–55
Chap 8–11	*Mac.* 1.7.19
8.2, 6	*Mac.* 1.7.19
8.10, 13	*Ant.* 4.14.106–107, 133
9.1	*Ham.* 4.5.132–34; *Ant.* 3.13.145–47
10.1–5	*Ant.* 5.2.79–86
10.6	*Ant.* 4.14.106–107, 133
10.9–10	*Oth.* 1.3.347–49
11.7	*Ham.* 4.5.132–34
11.8–9	*Ant.* 3.13.162–66
11.19	*Mac.* 2.3.67–69
12.9	*Mac.* 3.1.67–68
14.10	*Ham.* 1.5.3; *Oth.* 4.1.234
14.15–16	*Ant.* 5.2.86–88
16.21	*Ant.* 3.13.159–61
17.1–2	*Ant.* 3.6.66–68

17.8	*Ham.* 4.5.132–34
17.14	*Ant.* 3.6.13; 4.8.16
19.9	*Ham.* 4.3.16–18, 33
19.15	*Timon* 2.2.76–77
19.16	*Ant.* 3.6.13; 4.8.16
19.19	*Ant.* 3.6.66–68
20.1	*Ham.* 4.5.132–34
20.10	*Titus* 3.1.242; 5.1.147–50; *Oth.* 4.1.234; *Mac.* 2.3.18–19
20.12	*Cor.* 5.2.14–16
20.12–13	*Mac.* 2.3.77–79
21.1	*Ant.* 1.1.17
21.8	*Oth.* 4.1.234; 5.2.129
21.27	*Cor.* 3.1.289–91

Appendix B
References to the Book of
Common Prayer

Morning Prayer: *Rom.* 3.2.109–111; *Ham.* 3.4.34–35; *Oth.* 2.3.111–112
    General Confession: *JC* 4.2.8–9; *Oth.* 3.3.203–204; *Ant.* 3.1.14; *Cor.*
        4.7.24–25
    Apostles' Creed: *Ham.* 5.1.126, 251
(All the above passages to which Shakespeare refers were also recited at
Evening Prayer.)

The Litany: *Titus* 1.1.117–18

Communion Service: *Titus* 1.1.117–18; *Cor.* 5.4.25
    Nicene Creed: *Ham.* 5.1.126, 251; *Mac.* 1.7.7
    Exhortation: *Ham.* 3.4.149; *Oth.* 4.2.152–53
    General Confession: *Rom.* 3.2.109–111; *Oth.* 4.2.152–53

Baptism: *Timon* 3.6.61

The Catechism: *Ham.* 3.2.336; *Lear* 1.1.96–98; 3.4.80–83

Matrimony: *Rom.* 2.6.37; 3.3.129; 4.1.12–14; 4.1.55; *JC* 2.1.272–73;
        Ham. 1.5.49–50; 3.2.251–52; 4.3.52; *Oth.* 5.2.196; *Ant.*
        2.2.143–45

Burial Service: *Ham.* 2.2.308; 3.4.81; 4.2.5–6; 5.1.209–10; 5.1.251; 5.2.219–
        24; 5.2.347; *Mac.* 5.3.6; 5.5.23; 5.5.24; *Timon* 4.3.493–94

Appendix C
References to the Homilies

Of the Misery of All Mankinde: *Lear* 4.4.3–5; *Mac.* 5.5.23

Against Swearing and Periury: *Rom.* 2.2.112; *Ham.* 2.2.403–12

Against the Feare of Death: *Ham.* 5.2.359–60

Concerning Good Order, and Obedience to Rulers and Magistrates: *Ham.* 1.3.20–24; 3.3.8–10; 3.4.173–75; *Tro.* 1.3.78–137; *Ant.* 3.6.87–89

Against Whoredome and Vncleannesse (Against Adultery): *Oth.* 3.3.155–59; *Lear* 3.4.87–90

Against Contention: *Oth.* 3.3.155–59

Against Excess of Apparell: *Ham.* 3.1.142–46

Of the State of Matrimonie: *Rom.* 2.6.37; *Ham.* 1.2.135; 1.2.146; 3.1.58; *Oth.* 5.2.196

Against Idlenesse: *Oth.* 4.2.57–62

Against Disobedience and Wilfull Rebellion: *Ham.* 3.4.173–75; *Tro.* 1.3.78–137; *Lear* 1.2.106–12, 144–46; *Mac.* 1.7.20; 2.3.64–65; 2.3.68; 4.3.22; *Ant.* 3.6.87–89

Bibliography

Works actually consulted or cited. Titles listed in the introductory comments on each play that are not included in this bibliography are those sources used by Shakespeare that can be found in Geoffrey Bullough's *Narrative and Dramatic Sources of Shakespeare*, 8 vols.

Works by Shakespeare

The Riverside Shakespeare. Edited by G. Blakemore Evans, et al. Boston: Houghton Mifflin, 1974.

Antony and Cleopatra. Edited by Horace Howard Furness. A New Variorum Shakespeare. Philadelphia: J. B. Lippincott Co., 1907.

Antony and Cleopatra. Edited by M. R. Ridley. The Arden Shakespeare. London: Methuen, 1954.

Antony and Cleopatra. Edited by John Dover Wilson. The New Shakespeare. Cambridge: Cambridge University Press, 1950.

Coriolanus. Edited by Philip Brockbank. The Arden Shakespeare. London: Methuen, 1976.

Coriolanus. Edited by Horace Howard Furness, Jr. A New Variorum Shakespeare. Philadelphia: J. B. Lippincott Co., 1928.

Coriolanus. Edited by John Dover Wilson. The New Shakespeare. Cambridge: Cambridge University Press, 1960.

The Tragedy of Hamlet. Edited by Edward Dowden. 6th ed. The Arden Shakespeare. London: Methuen, 1928.

Hamlet. Edited by Harold Jenkins. The Arden Shakespeare. London: Methuen, 1982.

Hamlet. Edited by Horace Howard Furness. 2 vols. 1877. Reprint. A New Variorum Shakespeare. New York: American Scholar Publications, 1965.

Hamlet. Edited by John Dover Wilson. The New Shakespeare. Cambridge: Cambridge University Press, 1936.

Die Tragische Geschichte von Hamlet Prinzen von Daenemark ... Begleitet von Auszugen die den Geschichten von Saxo Grammaticus und Francois de Belleforest. Weimar: Cranach Presse, 1928.

Hamlet: First Quarto, 1603. Shakespeare Quarto Facsimiles, no. 7. Oxford: Clarendon Press, 1965.

Shakespeare's Hamlet: The Second Quarto, 1604. San Marino, Calif., 1964.

Julius Caesar. Edited by T. S. Dorsch. The Arden Shakespeare. London: Methuen, 1955.

Julius Caesar. Edited by Horace Howard Furness, Jr. A New Variorum Shakespeare. Philadelphia: J. B. Lippincott Co., 1913.

Julius Caesar. Edited by John Dover Wilson. The New Shakespeare. Cambridge: Cambridge University Press, 1949.

King Lear. Edited by George Ian Duthie and John Dover Wilson. The New Shakespeare. Cambridge: Cambridge University Press, 1960.

King Lear. Edited by Horace Howard Furness. 1880. Reprint. A New Variorum Shakespeare. New York: American Scholar Publications, 1965.

King Lear. Edited by Kenneth Muir. The Arden Shakespeare. London: Methuen, 1952.

Macbeth. Edited by Horace Howard Furness. 1873. Reprint. A New Variorum Shakespeare. New York: American Scholar Publications, 1963.

Macbeth. Edited by Kenneth Muir. The Arden Shakespeare. London: Methuen, 1962.

Macbeth. Edited by John Dover Wilson. The New Shakespeare. London: Cambridge University Press, 1947.

Othello. Edited by Horace Howard Furness. 1886. Reprint. A New Variorum Shakespeare. New York: American Scholar Publications, 1965.

Othello. Edited by M. R. Ridley. The Arden Shakespeare. London: Methuen, 1962.

The Tragedy of Othello. Edited by Lawrence J. Ross. Indianapolis: Bobbs-Merrill, 1974.

Othello. Edited by Alice Walker and John Dover Wilson. The New Shakespeare. Cambridge: Cambridge University Press, 1957.

Romeo and Juliet. Edited by Horace Howard Furness. 1871. Reprint. A New Variorum Shakespeare. New York: American Scholar Publications, 1963.

Romeo and Juliet. Edited by Brian Gibbons. The Arden Shakespeare. London: Methuen, 1980.

Romeo and Juliet. Edited by John Dover Wilson and George Ian Duthie. The New Shakespeare. Cambridge: Cambridge University Press, 1955.

Timon of Athens. Edited by J. C. Maxwell. The New Shakespeare. Cambridge: Cambridge University Press, 1957.

Timon of Athens. Edited by H. J. Oliver. The Arden Shakespeare. London: Methuen, 1959.

Titus Andronicus. Edited by J. C. Maxwell. The Arden Shakespeare. London: Methuen, 1961.

Titus Andronicus. Edited by John Dover Wilson. The New Shakespeare. Cambridge: Cambridge University Press, 1948.

Troilus and Cressida. Edited by K. Deighton. The Arden Shakespeare. Indianapolis: Bobbs-Merrill, 1906.

Troilus and Cressida. Edited by Harold N. Hillebrand. A New Variorum Shakespeare. Philadelphia: J. B. Lippincott Co., 1953.

Troilus and Cressida. Edited by Kenneth Palmer. The Arden Shakespeare. London: Methuen, 1982.

Troilus and Cressida. Edited by Alice Walker. The New Shakespeare. Cambridge: Cambridge University Press, 1957.

Other Works Cited

Ackermann, Carl. *The Bible in Shakespeare.* N.d. Reprint. Folcroft, Pa.: Folcroft Press, 1971.

Adams, Joseph Quincy, Jr. "The Authorship of *A Warning for Fair Women.*" *PMLA* 28 (1913): 594–620.

———, ed. *Chief Pre-Shakespearean Dramas.* Cambridge, Mass.: Houghton Mifflin, 1924.

Aeschylus. *The Persians.* Loeb Classical Library. Cambridge, Mass.: Harvard University Press, 1956.

Anders, Henry R. D. "The Elizabethan ABC with the Catechism." *The Library* 16 (1935): 32–48.

———. *Shakespeare's Books.* 1904. Reprint. New York: AMS Press, 1965.

Anderson, M. D. *Drama and Imagery in English Medieval Churches.* Cambridge: Cambridge University Press, 1963.

Appian. *An Avncient Historie and Exquisite Chronicle of the Romanes Warres, both Ciuile and Foren. Written in Greeke by ... Appian of Alexandria.* London, 1578.

Arden of Feversham. The Tragedy of Master Arden of Faversham. Edited by M. L. Wine. London: Methuen, 1973.

Averell, William. *A Meruailous Combat of Contrarieties. Malignantlie Striuing in the Members of Mans Bodie.* [London], 1588.

Baikie, James. *The English Bible and Its Story.* London: Seeley, Service & Co., 1928.

Baldwin, Thomas W. *William Shakspere's Petty School.* Urbana: University of Illinois Press, 1943.

———. *William Shakspere's Small Latine & Lesse Greeke.* 2 vols. Urbana: University of Illinois Press, 1944.

Bandello, Matteo. *Matteo Bandello: Twelve Stories Selected and done into English ... by Percy Pinkerton.* London: John C. Nimmo, 1895.

Barb, A. A. "Cain's Murder-Weapon and Samson's Jawbone of an Ass." *Journal of the Warburg and Courtauld Institutes* 35 (1972): 386–89.

Battenhouse, Roy W. *Shakespearean Tragedy: Its Art and Its Christian Premises*. Bloomington: Indiana University Press, 1969.

Bayne, The Rev. Ronald. "Religion." In *Shakespeare's England: An Account of the Life and Manners of his Age*. Vol. 1. Oxford: Clarendon Press, 1916, 48–78.

Berry, Lloyd E. "Introduction to the Facsmilie Edition." In *The Geneva Bible: A facsimile of the 1560 edition*. Madison: University of Wisconsin Press, 1969.

Bethell, S. L. "Shakespeare's Imagery: The Diabolic Images in *Othello*." *Shakespeare Survey* 5 (1952): 62–80.

Bevington, David, ed. *Medieval Drama*. Boston: Houghton Mifflin, 1975.

The Bible. (The Geneva Bible.) Geneva, 1560.

The Bible. (The Geneva Bible.) London, 1576, 1578, 1582, 1589, 1598, 1599 (3 eds.), 1600, 1603, 1607, 1608, 1610, 1615.

The holie Bible. (The Bishops' Bible.) London, 1568, 1572, 1584.

The Byble. (The Great Bible.) London, 1553.

The Byble. (Matthew's Bible.) London, August, 1549.

The whole Byble. (The Coverdale Bible.) London, 1553.

Biblia. The Byble. (The Coverdale Bible.) 1535. Reprint. Folkestone, England: Wm. Dawson & Sons, 1975.

The Holy Bible ... Made from the Latin Vulgate by John Wycliffe and His Followers. Edited by Josiah Forshall and Sir Frederic Madden. 4 vols. Oxford: Oxford University Press, 1850.

The Holy Bible. (Authorized King James Bible.) London, 1613, 1648; Cambridge, 1630.

The Holie Bible. (Roman Catholic Douay Old Testament.) 2 vols. Doway, 1609–10.

The Bible. *The New Testament. Translated out of the Latin Vulgat by John Wiclif ... about 1378*. London, 1731.

The Bible. New Testament. (Tyndale's New Testament.) 1526. Reprint. London: Paradine, 1976.

The Bible. *The New Testament translated by William Tyndale ... 1534*. Cambridge: Cambridge University Press, 1939.

The Bible. *The Nevv Testament*. (Roman Catholic Rheims New Testament.) Rhemes, 1582, 1633.

The Bible. *The Paraphrase of Erasmus vpon the Newe Testamente*. 2 vols. (Great Bible New Testament with Erasmus's verse by verse commentary on the text.) London, 1548–49.

The Bible. *The Newe Testament*. (Tomson's New Testament.) London, 1583, 1596, 1597, 1599, 1601, 1607, 1610.

The Bible. *The New Testament Octapla: Eight English Versions of the New*

Testament in the Tyndale-King James Tradition. Edited by Luther A. Weigle. New York: Nelson, 1962.

The Bible. *The Revelation of Saint Iohn the Apostle.* London, 1599, 1600, 1607. (Junius's edition of Revelation.)

The Bible. *The Whole Booke of Psalmes. Collected into English Meetre, by Thomas Sternhold, John Hopkins, and others.* London, 1583, 1591, 1599, 1600, 1604, 1607, 1609, 1613, 1615, 1616, 1632, 1634, 1635, 1648.

The Bible. *The Genesis Octapla: Eight English Versions of the Book of Genesis in the Tyndale-King James Tradition.* Edited by Luther A. Weigle. New York: Nelson, 1965.

The Bible. *Biblia Sacra.* (Latin Vulgate Bible.) Rome: Vatican Press, 1598.

The Bible. *Biblia Sacra.* 2 vols. (Henry Middleton's 3d ed. of the Latin Bible of Tremellius and Junius.) London, 1585.

The Bible. New Testament. *Novvm Testamentvm. Omne, Tertio Iam Ac Diligentius ab Erasmo Roterdamo.* (Greek and Latin texts in parallel columns.) Basle, Switzerland: J. Froben, March, 1519; 1535.

The Bible. New Testament. (Greek and Latin texts in parallel columns.) *Novvm Testamentvm Graece & Latine ... D. Erasmi Roterod.* Paris, 1543.

Birch, William John. *An Inquiry into the Philosophy and Religion of Shakspere.* N.d. Reprint. New York: Haskell House, 1972.

Birchenough, Edwyn. "The Prymer in English." *The Library* 18 (1937): 177–94.

Blench, J. W. *Preaching in England in the Late Fifteenth and Sixteenth Centuries.* New York: Barnes & Noble, 1964.

Bodin, Jean. *The Six Bookes of a Commonweale: A Facsimile reprint of the English translation of 1606.* Edited by Kenneth D. McRae. Cambridge, Mass.: Harvard University Press, 1962.

Boecker, Alexander. *A Probable Italian Source of Shakespeare's "Julius Caesar."* 1913. Reprint. New York: AMS Press, 1971.

A Booke of Christian Prayers. London, 1590. ("Queen Elizabeth's Prayer Book.")

The Booke of Common Prayer. London, June 16, 1549; 1591, 1603?, 1605, 1607, 1613, 1616?, 1642, 1840.

The Book of Common Prayer, 1559. Edited by John E. Booty. Charlottesville, Va.: University Press of Virginia, 1976.

Bradbrook, Muriel C. "What Shakespeare Did to Chaucer's *Troilus and Criseyde.*" *Shakespeare Quarterly* 9 (1958): 311–19.

Bradley, A. C. *Shakespearean Tragedy.* London: Macmillan, 1904.

Bradner, Leicester. *The Life and Poems of Richard Edwards.* Yale Studies in English, no. 74. New Haven, Conn.: Yale University Press, 1927.

Bright, Timothy. *A Treatise of Melancholie.* London, 1586. Reprint. New

York: Da Capo Press, 1969.

Brook, Stella. *The Language of The Book of Common Prayer*. New York: Oxford University Press, 1965.

Brooke, Arthur. *Brooke's 'Romeus and Juliet': Being the Original of Shakespeare's 'Romeo and Juliet' Newly Edited by J. J. Munro*. 1908. Reprint. New York: AMS Press, 1970.

———. *Romeus and Iuliet: 1562*. New York: Da Capo Press, 1969.

———. *Romeus and Iuliet*. In *Romeus and Iuliet* [by] *Arthur Brooke. Rhomeo and Iulietta* [by] *William Painter*, edited by P. A. Daniel. London: N. Trubner for the New Shakspere Society, 1875.

Brown, James Buchan. *Bible Truths with Shakespearian Parallels*. 1886. Reprint. New York: AMS Press, 1975.

Brown, John Howard. *Elizabethan Schooldays*. 1933. Reprint. New York: Benjamin Blom, 1972.

Bruce, Frederick F. *The English Bible: A History of Translations from the earliest English Versions to the New English Bible*. Rev. ed. New York: Oxford University Press, 1970.

Bryant, J. A., Jr. *Hippolyta's View: Some Christian Aspects of Shakespeare's Plays*. Lexington: University of Kentucky Press, 1961.

Bullen, A. H., ed. *A Collection of Old English Plays*. 4 vols. London: Wyman & Sons, 1885.

Bullough, Geoffrey. *Narrative and Dramatic Sources of Shakespeare*. 8 vols. New York: Columbia University Press, 1957–75.

Bulman, James C., Jr. "The Date and Production of 'Timon' Reconsidered." *Shakespeare Survey* 27 (1974): 111–127.

———. "Shakespeare's Use of the 'Timon' Comedy." *Shakespeare Survey* 29 (1976): 103–116.

Burgess, William. *The Bible in Shakespeare*. 1903. Reprint. New York: Haskell House, 1968.

Butterworth, Charles C. "Early Primers for the Use of Children." *Papers of the Bibliographical Society of America* 43 (1949): 374–82.

———. *The English Primers (1529–1545)*. 1953. Reprint. New York: Octagon Press, 1971.

———. *The Literary Lineage of the King James Bible 1340–1611*. Philadelphia: University of Pennsylvania Press, 1941.

Calvin, John. *The Institution of Christian Religion, written in Latine by M. John Caluine, and translated into English ... by Thomas Norton*. London, 1587.

The Cambridge History of the Bible. Edited by S. L. Greenslade. Cambridge: Cambridge University Press, 1963.

Carter, John, and Percy H. Muir. *Printing and the Mind of Man*. London: Cassell & Co., 1967.

Carter, Thomas. *Shakespeare and Holy Scripture.* 1905. Reprint. New York: AMS Press, 1970.

———. *Shakespeare, Puritan and Recusant.* 1897. Reprint. New York: AMS Press, 1970.

Cavendish, George. *The Life and Death of Cardinal Wolsey.* Edited by Richard S. Sylvester. London: Early English Text Society, 1959.

Caxton, William. *Caxton's Aesop.* Edited by R. T. Lenaghan. Cambridge, Mass.: Harvard University Press, 1967.

Chambers, Edmund K. *The Elizabethan Stage.* 4 vols. 1923. Reprint. Oxford: Clarendon Press, 1965.

———. *William Shakespeare: A Study of Facts and Problems.* 2 vols. Oxford: Clarendon Press, 1930.

Charlton, Kenneth. *Education in Renaissance England.* London: Routledge and Kegan Paul, 1965.

Chaucer, Geoffrey. *The Works of Geoffrey Chaucer.* 2d ed. Edited by F. N. Robinson. Boston: Houghton Mifflin, 1957.

The Church and the Law of Nullity of Marriage: The Report of a Commission appointed by the Archbishops of Canterbury and York in 1949 at the request of the Convocations. London: Society for Promoting Christian Knowledge, 1955.

Cicero, Marcus Tullius. *Cicero: The Speeches.* Edited and translated by N. H. Watts. Loeb Classical Library. London: William Heinemann, 1931.

———. *Orationes.* Edited by Albert Curtis Clark. Oxford Classical Texts Series. Oxford: Oxford University Press, 1963.

Clemen, Wolfgang H. *The Development of Shakespeare's Imagery.* London: Methuen, 1951.

Colie, Rosalie L. "The Energies of Endurance: Biblical Echo in *King Lear.*" In *Some Facets of King Lear: Essays in Prismatic Criticism.* Edited by Rosalie L. Colie and F. T. Flahiff. Toronto: University of Toronto Press, 1974.

Constitvtions and Canons Ecclesiasticall. 1604. Reprint. Oxford: Clarendon Press, 1923.

Constitutions and Canons Ecclesiastical. In *The Book of Common Prayer.* 5th ed. Edited by Richard Mant, D. D. London, 1840.

Coursen, Herbert R., Jr. *Christian Ritual and the World of Shakespeare's Tragedies.* Lewisburg, Pa.: Bucknell University Press, 1976.

Craig, Hardin, ed. *Two Coventry Corpus Christi Plays.* 2d ed. Early English Text Society. London: Oxford University Press, 1967.

Cross, Claire. *The Royal Supremacy in the Elizabethan Church.* London: George Allen, 1969.

Cuming, G. J. *A History of Anglican Liturgy.* London: Macmillan, 1969.

Daniel, Samuel. *The Complete Works in Verse and Prose of Samuel Daniel.*

Edited by Alexander B. Grosart. 5 vols. 1885. Reprint. New York: Russell & Russell, 1963.

Darlow, T. H., and H. F. Moule. *Historical Catalogue of Printed Editions of the English Bible 1525–1961*. Revised by A. S. Herbert. London: British and Foreign Bible Society, 1968.

De Groot, John Henry. *The Shakespeares and "The Old Faith."* 1946. Reprint. Freeport, N. Y.: Books for Libraries, 1968.

Dictionary of National Biography. 22 vols. Oxford: Oxford University Press, 1921–22.

Digges, Thomas. *Foure Paradoxes, or Politique Discourses*. London, 1604.

Eaton, Thomas Ray. *Shakespeare and the Bible*. 1860. Reprint. New York: AMS Press, 1972.

Elton, William R. *King Lear and the Gods*. San Marino: Huntington Library, 1966.

Erasmus, Desiderius. *Collected Works of Erasmus: ... De Copia/De Ratione Studii*. Vol. 24. Edited by Craig R. Thompson. Toronto: University of Toronto Press, 1978.

Farnham, Willard. *Shakespeare's Tragic Frontier: The World of His Final Tragedies*. Berkeley: University of California Press, 1963.

The First and Second Prayer Books of Edward VI. Introduction by Bishop Gibson. London: J. M. Dent, 1952.

Florio, John. *Second Frvtes*. 1591. Reprint. Gainesville, Fla.: Scholars' Facsmilies & Reprints, 1953.

Foakes, R. A., and R. T. Rickert. *Henslowe's Diary*. Cambridge: Cambridge University Press, 1961.

———. "Suggestions for a New Approach to Shakespeare's Imagery." *Shakespeare Survey* 5 (1952): 81–92.

Forset, Edward. *A Comparative Discovrse of the Bodies Natvral and Politiqve*. London, 1606. Reprint. New York: Da Capo Press, 1973.

Fripp, Edgar I. *Shakespeare, Man and Artist*. 2 vols. London: Oxford University Press, 1938.

Frye, Roland Mushat. *The Renaissance HAMLET: Issues and Responses in 1600*. Princeton: Princeton University Press, 1984.

———. *Shakespeare and Christian Doctrine*. Princeton: Princeton University Press, 1963.

Fulbecke, William. *The Pandectes of the Law of Nations*. London, 1602.

Fulke, William. *The Text of the New Testament of Iesvs Christ, Translated ovt of the vulgar Latine by the Papists of the traiterous Seminarie at Rhemes.... Wherevnto Is added the Translation out of the Original Greeke, commonly vsed in the Church of England, With a Confvtation Of All Svch Arguments*. By W. Fvlke. London, 1589, 1617.

Gee, Henry. *The Elizabethan Prayer-Book and Ornaments.* London: Macmillan, 1902.

Glass, Henry Alexander. *The Story of the Psalters.* London: Kegan Paul, 1888.

Gollancz, Israel. *The Sources of Hamlet.* London: Oxford University Press, 1926.

Greenslade, S. L. *"Introduction" to The Coverdale Bible, 1535.* Folkestone, England: Wm. Dawson & Sons, 1975.

Greg, W. W. "The Date of *King Lear* and Shakespeare's Use of Earlier Versions of the Story." *The Library* 20 (1940): 377–400.

———. *The Shakespeare First Folio.* London: Oxford University Press, 1955.

Grimaldus, Goslicius Laurentius. *A Common-Wealth of Good Counsaile.* London, 1607.

———. *The Counsellor.* London, 1598.

Haller, William. *The Rise of Puritanism.* New York: Harper, 1957.

Harrison, William. *The Description of England.* Edited by Georges Edelen. Ithaca, N. Y.: Cornell University Press, 1968.

———. *Elizabethan England.* Edited by Lothrop Withington. London: Walter Scott Publishing Co., n.d.

Hart, Alfred. *Shakespeare and the Homilies.* 1934. Reprint. New York: Octagon Books, 1970.

Hassel, Rudolph Chris, Jr. *Renaissance Drama & the English Church Year.* Lincoln: University of Nebraska Press, 1979.

Haugaard, William P. *Elizabeth and the English Reformation.* Cambridge: Cambridge University Press, 1968.

Heilman, Robert B. *Magic in the Web: Action and Language in "Othello."* Lexington: University of Kentucky Press, 1956.

Herbert, A. S. (See Darlow and Moule.)

Herr, Alan Fager. *The Elizabethan Sermon: A Survey and a Bibliography.* 1940. Reprint. New York: Octagon Books, 1969.

Hinman, Charlton, ed. *The First Folio of Shakespeare: The Norton Facsimile.* New York: W. W. Norton & Co., 1968.

Histrio-Mastix. 1610. Reprint. [London?]: The Tudor Facsimile Texts, 1912.

Holinshed, Raphael. *The First and second volumes of Chronicles, ... First collected and published by Raphaell Holinshed, William Harrison, and others: Now newlie augmented ... to the year 1586.* [London, 1587?]

Holland, Philemon, trans. *The Historie of the World. Commonly called, The Natvrall Historie of C. Plinivs Secvndvs.* London, 1601.

Holmer, Joan Ozark. "Othello's Threnos: 'Arabian Trees' and 'Indian' versus 'Judean'." *Shakespeare Studies* 13 (1980): 145–67.

Homilies. *Certaine Sermons Or Homilies appointed to be read in Chvrches, In the time of the late Queene Elizabeth of famous memory.* London, 1623, 1676, 1824; Oxford, 1683.

Homilies. *The Seconde Tome of Homelyes, ... set out by the aucthoritie of the Quenes Maiestie.* London, 1563.

Honigmann, E. A. J. *Shakespeare: Seven Tragedies.* London: Macmillan, 1976.

———. "Timon of Athens." *Shakespeare Quarterly* 12 (1961): 3–20.

Hunter, Robert G. *Shakespeare and the Mystery of God's Judgments.* Athens: University of Georgia Press, 1976.

Ide, Richard S. "The Theatre of the Mind: An Essay on *Macbeth*." *ELH* 42 (1975): 338–61.

Jack, Jane H. "Macbeth, King James, and the Bible." *ELH* 22 (1955); 173–93.

James I. *Basilicon Doron.* Edinburgh, 1599. Reprint. Menston, England: Scolar Press, 1969.

———. *A Covnterblaste to Tobacco.* London, 1604. Reprint. New York: Da Capo Press, 1969.

———. *Daemonologie.* Edinburgh, 1597. Reprint. New York: Da Capo Press, 1969.

———. *A Fruitefull Meditation, ... in forme and maner of a Sermon.* London, 1603.

Jorgensen, Paul A. *Lear's Self-Discovery.* Berkeley: University of California Press, 1967.

———. *Our Naked Frailties: Sensational Art and Meaning in "Macbeth."* Berkeley: University of California Press, 1971.

———. *Redeeming Shakespeare's Words.* Berkeley: University of California Press, 1962.

Kaula, David. "'Let Us Be Sacrificers'; Religious Motifs in *Julius Caesar*." *Shakespeare Studies* 14 (1981): 197–214.

———. *Shakespeare and the Archpriest Controversy: A Study of Some New Sources.* The Hague: Mouton, 1975.

Kelly, Faye L. *Prayer in Sixteenth-Century England.* University of Florida Humanities Monograph 22. Gainesville: University of Florida Press, 1966.

Kindred and Affinity as Impediments to Marriage: Being the Report of a Commission appointed by His Grace the Archbishop of Canterbury. London: Society for Promoting Christian Knowledge, 1940.

Klein, Arthur J. *Intolerance in the Reign of Elizabeth.* 1917. Reprint. Port Washington, N.Y.: Kennikat Press, 1968.

Knappen, M. M. *Tudor Puritanism.* Chicago: University of Chicago Press, 1939.

Knight, George Wilson. *The Imperial Theme: Further Interpretations of Shakespeare's Tragedies Including the Roman Plays.* London: Methuen, 1954.

———. *Shakespeare and Religion: Essays of Forty Years.* New York: Barnes & Noble, 1967.

———. *The Wheel of Fire.* New York: Barnes & Noble, 1966.

Knolles, Richard. *The Generall Historie of the Turkes.* London, 1603.

Kyd, Thomas. *The Spanish Tragedie.* 1592. Reprint. Leeds, England: Scolar Press, 1966.

———. *The Spanish Tragedy.* Edited by J. R. Mulryne. The New Mermaids Series. New York: Hill and Wang, 1970.

———. *The Spanish Tragedy.* Edited by Philip Edwards. The Revels Plays. London: Methuen, 1959.

———. *The Works of Thomas Kyd.* Edited by Frederick S. Boas. Oxford: Clarendon Press, 1962.

Law, Robert Adger. "The Roman Background of *Titus Andronicus.*" *Studies in Philology* 40 (1943): 145–53.

Levin, Richard. "On Fluellen's Figures, Christ Figures, and James Figures." *PMLA* 89 (1974): 302–311.

———. "The Indian/Iudean Crux In *Othello.*" *Shakespeare Quarterly* 33 (1982): 60–67.

———. "The Indian/Iudean Crux In *Othello*: An Addendum." *Shakespeare Quarterly* 34 (1983): 72.

———. *New Readings vs. Old Plays.* Chicago: University of Chicago Press, 1979.

———. "The Relation of External Evidence to the Allegorical and Thematic Interpretation of Shakespeare." *Shakespeare Studies* 13 (1980): 1–29.

Lewkenor, Lewes [Lewis], trans. *The Commonwealth and Gouernment of Venice. Written by the Cardinall Gaspar Contareno, and translated out of Italian into English, by Lewes Lewkenor Esquire.* London, 1599. Reprint. New York: Da Capo Press, 1969.

Lodge, Thomas. *Wits Miserie.* London, 1596. Reprint. Menston, England: Scolar Press, 1971.

Lucian. *Timon, or the Misanthrope.* In *Lucian: With an English Translation by A. M. Harmon.* Vol. 2. Loeb Classical Library. Cambridge, Mass.: Harvard University Press, 1953.

Lydgate, John. *The Hystorye Sege and Dystruccyon of Troye.* In *Lydgate's Troy Book.* 3 vols. Edited by Henry Bergen. Early English Text Society, Extra Series, nos. 97, 103, 106. London, 1906–1908.

MacCallum, M. W. *Shakespeare's Roman Plays and their Background.* London: Macmillan, 1935.

Maclure, Millar. *The Paul's Cross Sermons, 1534–1642.* Toronto: University of Toronto Press, 1958.

Mack, Maynard. *King Lear in Our Time.* Berkeley: University of California Press, 1965.

A Manual of the Writings in Middle English. 6 vols. Edited by J. Burke Severs and Albert E. Hartung. New Haven: The Connecticut Academy of Arts and Sciences, 1967–80.

Marlowe, Christopher. *The Plays of Christopher Marlowe.* London: Oxford University Press, 1959.

Marston, John. *Antonio's Revenge.* Edited by W. Reavley Gair. Baltimore: Johns Hopkins University Press, 1978.

————. *Antonio's Revenge.* Edited by G. K. Hunter. Lincoln: University of Nebraska Press, 1965.

————. *The Malcontent.* 1604. Reprint. Menston, England: Scolar Press, 1970.

————. *The Malcontent.* Edited by George K. Hunter. London: Methuen, 1975.

————. *The Malcontent* Edited by M. L. Wine. Lincoln: University of Nebraska Press, 1964.

McKerrow, Ronald B. *An Introduction to Bibliography.* Oxford: Clarendon Press, 1928.

Mendl, R. W. S. *Revelation in Shakespeare.* London: John Calder, 1964.

Milward, Peter. *Biblical Themes in Shakespeare: centring on King Lear.* Tokyo, Japan: The Renaissance Institute, 1975.

————. *Religious Controversies of the Elizabethan Age.* Lincoln: University of Nebraska Press, 1977.

————. *Shakespeare's Religious Background.* Bloomington: Indiana University Press, 1973.

The Mirror for Magistrates. Edited by Lily B. Campbell. Cambridge: Cambridge University Press, 1938.

Montaigne, Michel E. de. *The Essayes ... of Lo: Michaell de Montaigne, ... done into English by ... Iohn Florio.* 1603. Reprint. Menston, England: Scolar Press, 1969.

Morris, Ivor. *Shakespeare's God: The Role of Religion in the Tragedies.* London: Allen & Unwin, 1972.

Muir, Kenneth. "Samuel Harsnett and *King Lear.*" *The Review of English Studies,* New Series 2 (1951): 11–21.

————. *Shakespeare's Sources I: Comedies and Tragedies.* London: Methuen, 1957.

————. *The Sources of Shakespeare's Plays.* London: Methuen, 1977.

Mutschmann, H., and K. Wentersdorf. *Shakespeare and Catholicism.* 1952. Reprint. New York: AMS Press, 1969.

Nashe, Thomas. *Pierce Penilesse his Supplication to the Diuell.* 1592. Reprint. Menston, England: Scolar Press, 1969.

———. *Pierce Penilesse, His Svpplication to the Divell.* Edited by G. B. Harrison. New York: Barnes & Noble, 1966.

———. *The Works of Thomas Nashe.* Edited by Ronald B. McKerrow. 5 vols. Oxford: Basil Blackwell, 1958.

Neale, J. E. *Queen Elizabeth I.* 1934. Reprint. Garden City, N. Y.: Doubleday Anchor Books, 1957.

Nevo, Ruth. *Tragic Form in Shakespeare.* Princeton: Princeton University Press, 1972.

A New Companion to Shakespeare Studies. Edited by Kenneth Muir and Samuel Schoenbaum. Cambridge: Cambridge University Press, 1971.

Noble, Richmond. *Shakespeare's Biblical Knowledge and Use of the Book of Common Prayer.* London: Society for Promoting Christian Knowledge, 1935.

Ovid. *Ovid's Metamorphoses: The Arthur Golding Translation 1567.* Edited by John F. Nims. New York: Macmillan, 1965.

Painter, William. *The Palace of Pleasure.* 3 vols. Edited by Joseph Jacobs. London: David Nutt, 1890.

The Paradise of Dainty Devices 1576: With the Additional Poems from the Editions of 1578, 1580 and 1585. Menston, England: Scolar Press, 1972.

Patrick, Millar. *Four Centuries of Scottish Psalmody.* London: Oxford University Press, 1950.

Paul, Henry N. *The Royal Play of Macbeth.* New York: Macmillan, 1950.

Pearson, A. F. Scott. *Thomas Cartwright and Elizabethan Puritanism.* Cambridge: Cambridge University Press, 1925.

Perrett, Wilfrid. *The Story of King Lear from Geoffrey of Monmouth to Shakespeare.* Berlin, 1904. Reprint. New York: Johnston Reprint Corp., 1970.

Phillips, James E., Jr. *The State in Shakespeare's Greek and Roman Plays.* New York: Columbia University Press, 1940.

Plimpton, George A. *The Education of Shakespeare.* 1933. Reprint. Freeport, N. Y.: Books for Libraries Press, 1970.

Plutarch. *Les Vies Des Hommes Illustres Grecs & Romains.* Translated by Jacques Amyot. Paris, 1559.

———. *Les Vies Des Hommes Illustres.* 2 vols. Traduction de Jacques Amyot. Paris: Editions Gallimard, 1951.

———. *Plutarch's Lives: with an English Translation by Bernadotte Perrin.* 11 vols. Cambridge, Mass.: Harvard University Press, 1914–26.

Poisson, Rodney. "Othello's 'Base Indian': A Better Source for the Allusion." *Shakespeare Quarterly* 26 (1975): 462–66.

Pollard, A. F. *Henry VIII*. 1902. Reprint. New York: Harper & Row, 1966.
——, ed. *Records of the English Bible: The Documents Relating to the Translation and Publication of the Bible in English, 1525–1611*. 1911. Reprint. Folkestone, England: Wm. Dawson & Sons, 1974.
Pollen, John Hungerford. *The English Catholics in the Reign of Queen Elizabeth*. New York: Longmans, Green & Co., 1920.
Pope, Hugh. *English Versions of the Bible*. 1952. Reprint. Westport, Conn.: Greenwood Press, 1972.
Pory, John, trans. *A Geographical Historie of Africa, Written ... by Iohn Leo [Leo Africanus]*. London, 1600. Reprint. New York: Da Capo Press, 1969.
Procter, Francis, and Walter H. Frere. *A New History of the Book of Common Prayer*. London: Macmillan, 1907.
Rees, James. *Shakespeare and the Bible*. 1876. Reprint. New York: AMS Press, 1972.
Ribner, Irving. *Patterns in Shakespearen Tragedy*. New York: Barnes & Noble, 1960.
Rosenberg, Marvin. *The Masks of Macbeth*. Berkeley: University of California Press, 1978.
——. *The Masks of Othello*. Berkeley: University of California Press, 1961.
Rosinger, Lawrence. "Hamlet and the Homilies." *Shakespeare Quarterly* 26 (1975): 299–301.
Sargent, Ralph M. "The Source of *Titus Andronicus*." *Studies in Phiology* 46 (1949): 167–83.
Satin, Joseph. *Shakespeare and His Sources*. Boston: Houghton Mifflin, 1965.
Schanzer, Ernest. *The Problem Plays of Shakespeare*. New York: Schocken Books, 1965.
——. *Shakespeare's Appian*. Liverpool: Liverpool University Press, 1956.
Schoenbaum, Samuel. *Internal Evidence and Elizabethan Dramatic Authorship: An Essay in Literary History and Method*. Evanston, Ill.: Northwestern University Press, 1966.
——. *Shakespeare's Lives*. New York: Oxford University Press, 1970.
——. *William Shakespeare: A Documentary Life*. New York: Oxford University Press, 1975.
Scot, Reginald. *Discouerie of Witchcraft*. London, 1584. Reprint. New York: Da Capo Press, 1971.
The Scottish Metrical Psalter. Edited by Neil Livingston. Glasgow: Maclure & Macdonald, 1864.
Seaton, Ethel. "*Antony and Cleopatra* and the *Book of Revelation*." *The Review of English Studies* 22 (1946): 219–24.

Seaver, Paul S. *The Puritan Lectureships.* Stanford, Calif.: Stanford University Press, 1970.

Seneca. *His Tenne Tragedies.* London, 1581. Reprint. New York: Da Capo Press, 1969.

———. *Seneca's Tragedies.* Translated by Frank Justus Miller. 2 vols. Loeb Classical Library. Cambridge, Mass.: Harvard University Press, 1960–61.

Sewell, Arthur. *Character and Society in Shakespeare.* Oxford: Oxford University Press, 1951.

Shaheen, Naseeb. *Biblical References in "The Faerie Queene."* Memphis: Memphis State University Press, 1976.

———. "Echoes of *A Warning for Faire Women* in Shakespeare's Plays." *Philological Quarterly* 62 (1983): 521–25.

———. "Like the Base Judean." *Shakespeare Quarterly* 31 (1980): 93–95.

———. "Misconceptions about the Geneva Bible." *Studies in Bibliography* 37 (1984): 156–58.

———. "Shakespeare and the Geneva Bible: *Hamlet,* I.iii.54." *Studies in Bibliography* 38 (1985): 201–203.

———. "Shakespeare and the Rheims New Testament." *American Notes & Queries* 22 (1984): 70–72.

———. "'Trifles Light As Air': A Note on *Othello,* III.iii.313." *Notes and Queries* 225 (1980): 169–70.

———. "The Use of Scripture in Cymbeline." *Shakespeare Studies* 4 (1968): 294–315.

———. "*A Warning for Fair Women* and the *Ur-Hamlet.*" *Notes and Queries* 228 (1983): 126–27.

Shakespeare's England: An Account of the Life and Manners of his Age. 2 vols. Oxford: Clarendon Press, 1916.

A Short-Title Catalogue of Books Printed in England, Scotland, & Ireland … 1475–1640. Compiled by A. W. Pollard, G. R. Redgrave, et al. London: The Bibliographical Society, 1926.

A Short-Title Catalogue of Books Printed in England, Scotland, & Ireland … 1475–1640. 2d ed. Vol. 2, I–Z. Revised by W. A. Jackson, F. S. Ferguson, and K. F. Pantzer. London: The Bibliographical Society, 1976.

Sidney, Philip. *The Covntesse of Pembrokes Arcadia.* 1590. Reprint. Kent, Ohio: Kent State University Press, 1970.

Siegel, Paul N. "A New Source for *Othello?*" *PMLA* 75 (1960): 480.

———. *Shakespearean Tragedy and the Elizabethan Compromise.* New York: New York University Press, 1957.

Simon, Joan. *Education and Society in Tudor England.* Cambridge: Cambridge University Press, 1966.

Simpson, Richard. *The Religion of Shakespeare.* London: Burns & Oates, 1899.

————. *The School of Shakspere.* 2 vols. 1878. Reprint. New York: AMS Press, 1973.

Sims, James H. *Dramatic Use of Biblical Allusion in Marlowe and Shakespeare.* University of Florida Monographs. Humanities—no. 24. Gainesville: University of Florida Press, 1966.

Smith, John Harrington, et al. "*Hamlet, Antonio's Revenge* and the *Ur-Hamlet.*" *Shakespeare Quarterly* 9 (1958): 493–98.

Spenser, Edmund. *The Works of Edmund Spenser: A Variorum Edition.* Edited by E. Greenlaw, C. G. Osgood, and F. M. Padelford. 11 vols. Baltimore: Johns Hopkins University Press, 1932–57.

Spevack, Marvin. *The Harvard Concordance to Shakespeare.* Cambridge, Mass.: Harvard University Press, 1973.

Spurgeon, Caroline F. E. *Shakespeare's Imagery and What It Tells Us.* Cambridge: Cambridge University Press, 1935.

Stevenson, Robert. *Shakespeare's Religious Frontier.* The Hague: Martinus Nijhoff, 1958.

Stowe, A. Monroe. *English Grammar Schools in the Reign of Queen Elizabeth.* 1908. Reprint. Folcroft, Pa.: The Folcroft Press, 1969.

Swinburne, Charles Alfred. *Sacred and Shakespearian Affinities* 1890. Reprint. New York: Haskell House, 1971.

Taylor, George Coffin. *Shakespeare's Debt to Montaigne.* 1925. Reprint. New York: Phaeton Press, 1968.

Theobald, Lewis, ed. *The Works of Shakespeare.* 7 vols. London, 1733. Reprint. New York: AMS Press, 1968.

Thomas, R. George, ed. *Ten Miracle Plays.* Evanston, Ill.: Northwestern University Press, 1966.

Thompson, Craig R. *The Bible in English 1525–1611.* Charlottesville, Va.: Published for the Folger Shakespeare Library by The University Press of Virginia, 1958.

————. *Schools in Tudor England.* Charlottesville, Va.: Published for the Folger Shakespeare Library by The University Press of Virginia, 1973.

Tilley, Morris Palmer. *A Dictionary of the Proverbs in England in the Sixteenth and Seventeenth Centuries.* Ann Arbor: University of Michigan Press, 1950.

Timon, A Play. Edited by the Reverend Alexander Dyce. 1842. Reprint. New York: AMS Press, 1973.

The Troublesome Reign of King John. Edited by F. J. Furnivall and John Munro. 1913. Reprint. The Shakespeare Classics. Folcroft, Pa.: Folcroft Press, 1971.

The True Chronicle History of King Leir, and his three daughters, Gonorill, Ragan, and Cordella. London, 1605. Reprint. New York: AMS Press, 1970.

Veit, Richard S. "'Like the Base Judean': A Defense of an Oft-Rejected Reading in *Othello.*" *Shakespeare Quarterly* 26 (1975): 466–69.

Walker, Roy. *The Time Is Free: A Study of Macbeth.* 1949. Reprint. Folcroft, Pa.: Folcroft Press, 1969.

A Warning for Fair Women: A Critical Edition. Edited by Charles Dale Cannon. The Hague: Mouton, 1975.

A Warning for Faire Women. Edited by John S. Farmer. Tudor Facsimile Texts. 1912. Reprint. New York: AMS Press, 1970.

Watson, Foster. *The English Grammar Schools to 1660.* 1908. Reprint. London: Frank Cass & Co., 1968.

Webber, Frederick R. *A History of Preaching in Britain and America.* Part 1. Milwaukee: Northwestern Publishing House, 1952.

Weir, Richard Baird. "Thomas Sternhold and the Beginnings of English Metrical Psalmody." Ph.D. diss., New York University, 1974.

West, Robert H. *Shakespeare and the Outer Mystery.* Lexington, Ky.: University of Kentucky Press, 1968.

Westcott, Brooke Foss. *A General View of the History of The English Bible.* 2d ed. London: Macmillan, 1872.

Whitaker, Virgil K. *The Mirror up to Nature: The Technique of Shakespeare's Tragedies.* San Marino, Calif.: Huntington Library, 1965.

———. *Shakespeare's Use of Learning.* San Marino, Calif.: Huntington Library, 1953.

White, Helen C. *English Devotional Literature, 1600–1640.* 1931. Reprint. New York: Haskell House, 1966.

———. *The Tudor Books of Private Devotion.* Madison: University of Wisconsin Press, 1951.

Williams, George Walton. "Yet Another Early Use of *Iudean.*" *Shakespeare Quarterly* 34 (1983): 72.

Wilson, John Dover. *What Happens in Hamlet.* Cambridge: Cambridge University Press, 1951.

Wilson, Thomas. *A Christian Dictionary. Opening the signification of the chiefe Words dispersed generally through Holy Scriptures, ... tending to increase Christian Knowledge.* 2d ed. London, 1616.

Wordsworth, Charles. *Shakespeare's Knowledge and Use of the Bible.* 1880. Reprint. New York: AMS Press, 1973.

Wright, Louis B. "The Scriptures and the Elizabethan Stage." *Modern Philology* 26 (1928): 47–56.

Index

242